THE
RECOVERY OF
UNCONSCIOUS
MEMORIES

The John D. and Catherine T. MacArthur Foundation
Series on Mental Health and Development

THE
RECOVERY OF
UNCONSCIOUS
MEMORIES

Hypermnesia and Reminiscence

MATTHEW HUGH
ERDELYI

The University of Chicago Press / Chicago and London

Matthew Erdelyi is professor of psychology at Brooklyn College, and in the Graduate School of the City University of New York.

The University of Chicago Press, Chicago 60637
The University of Chicago Press, Ltd., London
© 1996 by The University of Chicago
All rights reserved. Published 1996
Printed in the United States of America
05 04 03 02 01 00 99 98 97 96   5 4 3 2 1

ISBN (cloth): 0-226-21660-8

The University of Chicago Press gratefully acknowledges
a subvention from the John D. and Catherine T. MacArthur
Foundation in partial support of the costs of production of this
volume.

Library of Congress Cataloging-in-Publication Data

Erdelyi, Matthew Hugh.
    The recovery of unconscious memories : hypermnesia and
reminiscence / Matthew Hugh Erdelyi.
        p.   cm. — (The John D. and Catherine T. MacArthur
Foundation series on mental health and development)
    Includes bibliographical references and index.
    ISBN 0-226-21660-8 (alk. paper)
    1. Memory.   2. Reminiscing.   3. Recovered memory.
4. Recollection (Psychology)   5. Psychology, Experimental.   I. Title. II. Series.
BF378.R44E73   1996
153.1'2—dc20   96-914
                                             CIP

To Mireya

Contents

Preface

A certain Frank Fitzpatrick, according to a recent article in the *New York Times,*

> had a successful business . . . a wonderful marriage, two well-adjusted children and a comfortable home. So why, he wondered, was he so depressed, feeling like crying every day.
>
> It was then, three years ago, that the memories began coming back, memories that he had repressed. Mr. Fitzpatrick, now 41 years old, says he recalled how he had been sexually assaulted by a priest 30 years earlier, when he was an altar boy. (Fox Butterfield, *New York Times,* 9 June 1992, A18)

Fitzpatrick wanted to find out whether other persons in and around his small community of North Attleboro, Massachusetts, might have similar recollections about the priest, the Reverend James R. Porter, and he placed an advertisement in the newspaper. As of the writing of the article, forty-eight men and women had come forward publicly and an unknown number privately. The former Reverend Porter had since left the priesthood and had moved to Oakdale, Minnesota, where he married and had four children of his own. The former priest acknowledged having abused some children as a clergyman: "There could have been quite a few. If it was 1, 10, or 100, whatever it was, it happened," he admitted on tape.

Many of the former victims had not forgotten the sexual incidents, but at least two had only recently recovered the memories. Thus John Robitaille, a businessman in Providence, Rhode Island, claimed that he had "repressed all memory of being assaulted by Father Porter until hearing the news on the radio [and] felt a sudden rush [and] the next thing he knew, he said, he was home telling his wife about events that he had forgotten for three decades" (A18).

Whether all the individuals to come forward with recovered or retained memories were actually accurate in their recollections is difficult to ascertain, but apparently some of the cases, if the former Reverend Porter's admission applied to any of them (and was true), were recalling real events.

Here is another newspaper excerpt about a priest, this one from the *New York Post*:

> Saying he could no longer trust his hypnotically induced memories, the man who charged Chicago's Joseph Cardinal Bernardin with sex abuse dropped his lawsuit yesterday.
>
> "Truth has prevailed," said the vindicated Bernardin, the highest-ranking Catholic priest ever to be charged with sex abuse in America.
>
> Steven Cook, 34, an AIDS patient in Philadelphia, said he had "remembered" the alleged abuse during psychoanalytic hypnosis but could no longer believe his own mind. (Kyle Smith, *New York Post,* 1 Mar. 1994, 8)

Presumably we have here an instance of what these days is often called false-memory syndrome (Freud called such confabulations false memories, false recollections, or paramnesias; also, by the way, he viewed hypnosis and psychoanalysis as antithetical). Yet, notwithstanding the recantation and denials, we cannot objectively ascertain the falsity of the recall, for the retraction itself could conceivably be false. This inability to escape uncertainty about objective events is the great problem of clinical data. One can surmise but one cannot prove beyond question, as can be done in the laboratory.

We have considered two recent newspaper accounts, one of a presumably correct set of recovered memories and another of a presumably false recovered memory. One more newspaper excerpt is now presented, this one involving an extremely long-term, presumably never forgotten memory, and an especially powerful type of memory at that, namely, recognition:

> "Ivan!" the witness cried, "I have no shadow of a hesitation of a doubt. It is Ivan from Treblinka, from the gas chambers—the man that I am looking at this very moment. I saw the eyes, the murderous eyes and the face." Another survivor testified: "There is Ivan the Terrible. I dream about him every night."
>
> On such compelling eyewitness testimony was John Demjanjuk, a retired auto worker from Cleveland, convicted in 1988 of executing tens of thousands of Jews in Poland during World War II. Sentenced

to hang by an Israeli court, he maintains they've got the wrong man—and he could be right.

Evidence from the archives of the former Soviet Union [which contradict the memories of numerous witnesses] now prompts Israel's Supreme Court to call on prosecutors for the clearest proof of Ivan's identity. (Editorial, "The Wrong Terrible Ivan?" *New York Times,* 9 June 1992, A26)

Because of growing doubts, Demjanjuk was finally let go, amidst much controversy. The archival records seemed to prove the eyewitness memories false. Many contend, however, that the records had been tampered with and that it was the archival material and not the eyewitness memories that were untrustworthy. Again, in rough-and-tumble real-life situations, including the clinic, one can never be sure. Confessions, mass witnessings, circumstantial evidence have all proved, in the past, capable of being false.

And so the courts and other interested parties turn to psychologists and psychiatrists and ask what science has to say about these matters. Are forgotten memories inevitably lost and are the claims of memory recoveries, whether malicious or innocent, fabrications? Or can one actually recover long lost memories? Does hypnosis help? What about free-associations? And what of "truth sera"?

The burgeoning public controversy, involving clinicians, police, the courts—but not, interestingly, experimental psychologists, who have by and large reached a consensus—is, as the newspaper quotes show, a riveting current issue, with, literally, life-and-death implications (such as for Demjanjuk).

Interestingly, the controversy recapitulates on a vast scale a crisis confronted almost a century ago by Sigmund Freud, in the solitary confines of his own clinical practice. And the emerging consensus, led by experimental psychology, confirms Freud's much maligned (and often misrepresented) conclusions: unconscious memories can be recovered; unfortunately, some of the recollections are false, even if some of them are true, and even recollections tending to be true are typically garbled and overlaid by distortions. (Freud did not deny, as is often thought, the reality of child sexual abuse; what he did was withdraw the hypothesis that childhood molestation was the cause of hysteria because *some* hysterics' recovered memories of abuse were deemed to be false recollections.) Also, Freud came to cast doubt, already in 1895, on the efficacy of hypnosis in recovering memories, something about which, as will be seen in chapter 7 of this book, laboratory scientists have achieved closure only in the last decade or so. Freud might have been a genius or a charlatan, or perhaps both, but on memory, Freud was extraordinarily astute.

But how can we know which claims about memory are true and which are false? The messy real world or the clinic (see chapter 2) can produce fascinating material but cannot settle these issues beyond doubt. The conclusions of all three newspaper excerpts above, chosen because of their persuasiveness, are in no instance conclusive, either in the direction of truth or falsity. Only experimental research, where the original, to-be-remembered event is recorded and is available for comparison with the memory of the event, can provide proof of the existence of the phenomena broached thus far.

This book, which began as an experimental project some two decades ago, before the upsurge of public interest in these issues, deals with the scientific foundations of the recovery of unconscious memories.

Science is beautiful but it is cruel. It kills its babies—when they are false. So it was with several of my hypotheses, which I sought to validate experimentally. Science is also generous. In the end, the truths it reprieves are far more interesting and satisfying than any false hypotheses.

The project, from which the present book evolved, began with the cruel side of science. It fell upon me in research for which Yale University awarded me my doctoral degree to demolish the research for which Yale had awarded me the master of science degree.

Although most of this book involves mainstream experimental psychology, the original project was an effort to verify one of the few laboratory phenomena of psychoanalysis. In 1917, Otto Pötzl, an influential Viennese psychiatrist, who, quite untypically for his time and place, took a fancy to psychoanalysis, published a fascinating if not altogether intelligible laboratory monograph, purporting to show that contents of subliminal stimuli, that is, stimuli that failed to become conscious but which presumably had been registered unconsciously, tended to emerge in the subject's dreams of the same night. Charles Fisher, a psychoanalyst with an experimental bent, translated Pötzl's work into English and published a programmatic series of experiments of his own in the 1950s in which he confirmed and extended Pötzl's findings. It became clear that stimuli, of which the subject claimed not to be aware, could emerge in the content of dreams, daydreams, free associations, and imagery.

The findings were readily replicable, but the methodology was weak. One problem was that in comparing direct efforts at recall with some alternate indicator of memory, like a daydream, one was in effect comparing apples and oranges. One indicator might reflect more information because it had different characteristics, not because the information was unconscious. Thus, just because my height in centimeters is a larger number than my height in inches, it does not mean I stand taller in metric worlds. It's a rough analogy, but it points to the underlying problem.

In order to resolve it (among others), I, in collaboration with my advisor, Ralph Haber, introduced a modification to the Pötzl design. Rather than search for differences between intentional recall and an indirect memory index (such as daydreams or free associations), why not compare prefantasy recall with postfantasy recall? At this time (in the mid-1960s) the expectation, grounded in the classic work of Hermann Ebbinghaus, was that recall would tend to decline over time. If an intervening period of free-associating (for example) had the power of making contact with unconscious traces, this contact with unconscious materials might carry over into a postfantasy second recall effort and produce a counterintuitive result: better recall later than earlier. This is exactly what we found (Haber and Erdelyi 1967). We showed also, with a control group, that without intervening free associations, recall of the original subliminal materials failed to improve. Thus we showed in apple-to-apple comparisons that recovery of subliminal information was in fact feasible. We additionally replicated the standard Pötzl effect by showing (in an apple-orange comparison) that the intervening free associations recovered subliminal items that had never been recalled by the subject, either in the first, prefantasy recall or the second, postfantasy effort. I took great pleasure in publishing this ostensibly psychoanalytic finding in the methodologically austere (if verbally prolix), *Journal of Verbal Learning and Verbal Behavior.* The fun was not to last for long.

Mathematical psychology, in the guise of signal detection theory, had introduced a paradigm of perception (later extended to memory) which called into question the theoretical reading of the findings, which incidentally are readily replicable. In very lay terms (in chapters 4, 5, and 8, and especially in the appendix, matters are pursued more technically), the question comes down to something like this: Is the subject really recovering unconscious traces (percepts, memories) or is the subject, after a period of loose cognition (free-associating), merely more indulgent about what he or she is willing to dignify as true recalls as opposed to fanciful hunches. In other words, maybe what subjects do after free-associating is not recover unconscious memories but merely report low-confidence percepts or memories.

To my shock—for my clinical intuition, in which until this point I had ironclad confidence, assured me that the signal-detection formalism was surely inapplicable to the type of robust data produced by subjects, often to their own astonishment—experiment after experiment converged on the dreadful conclusion that free associations merely loosen the subject's response criterion and cause the subject to produce more responses, some of which are true (and many of which are false). Thus if a group of control subjects who do not free-associate between the first and the second recall trial is forced, on the second recall trial, to produce as many responses as the free-association subjects, then the superiority in recall apparently conferred by the free associations disappears. I published this disheartening program of findings (Erdelyi 1970) and came close never to try again recovering, at least in an experiment, material from what had proved such niggardly unconscious.

Some years later, however, a "final" experiment was undertaken (for a scrupulous scientist worries about Type I and not just Type II errors) because of the gradual dawning of the obvious point that, however matters stood with the Pötzl phenomenon, the kinds of recoveries purportedly obtained by psychoanalytic clinicians were not of stimulus flashes but of complex, often painful events that had been lost to consciousness (presumably because of repression, but this is an ancillary issue). So the question became whether recovery of unconscious memories might be possible when "unconsciousness" resulted not from brief presentation of the stimuli but from forgetting (whatever the reason). This study, actually a pair of experiments, was published by Erdelyi and Becker in 1974.

The research, which is described in detail, along with its follow-ups, in chapter 5, was a defining experience for me. I became an experimental psychologist in heart as well as in mind. I recall warning my student, Joan Becker, that the experiment, given my past successes with this type of phenomenon, would in all likelihood yield nothing. (Several previous honor students, when given such cheery expectations, discovered a fascination for some other project.) I recall telling Joan Becker that the project was in effect a fishing expedition and, as such, it made sense to put more than one hook on our line, in case there were at least a few fish in this barren sea. For example, I decided to include more than one type of stimulus in the study, specifically, to add word items to the picture items on the memory list (pictures having been the stimulus of choice in my subliminal perception studies). The reasoning here was that, just possibly, words would be effective with free associations because of the cuing effects that free associations would likely engender, with one word leading to another and that one to still another until one of the stimulus items was triggered and recognized and thereby recovered in subsequent recall trials.

Also, on the chance that free associations were not, after all, memory enhancing, another treatment was interposed between recall trials, a silent thinking or concentration period. This procedure, which Freud called the concentration or pressure technique, had been briefly used by him (Breuer and Freud 1895) for recovering memories during his transition from hypnosis to free associations. The technique essentially involved hypnotic instructions without hypnotic induction: even if the patient insisted that he or she could not recall anything more, the patient was urged to think more, to concentrate, with the assurance, indeed the insistence, that the memories were there and would return with sufficient effort. We used a low-pressure variant of this concentration-pressure technique. Just in case incremental memory were obtained, we also included a group of subjects with no interpolated activity between recall trials, to evaluate which if any interpolated activity was effective. And finally, one more recall trial was added, so that now subjects had a chance to improve not only on a second trial but also on a third. There were a few additional nuances (all detailed in chapter 5).

When the data had been collected and Joan Becker brought in the group means in the $2 \times 3 \times 3$ table in which she had been instructed to organize the results (pictures, words $\times$ free associations, silent thinking, no-interval $\times$ recall 1, recall 2, recall 3) I, for the first time as a scientist, experienced the *mysterium tremendum* that is sometimes vouchsafed the seeker. The picture was clear, the table virtually spoke to us: no, my pessimism was not justified; yes, there were fish out there; yes, the stimulus was critical, only I had gotten it backwards, since it was the pictures and not the words that produced recall increments over trials; no, free associations helped not one whit and, if anything, they were a small drag on the effect; thinking, however, probably did enhance hypermnesia over trials.

It had finally become real and palpable that the experimental method, which I had dutifully learned but had secretly disdained (without fully realizing it), was no mere formalistic exercise: it could correct flawed clinical intuitions and logical expectations and, further, could uncover phenomena that had never occurred to the investigator.

Today these findings do not engender surprise; if anything, they are sometimes shrugged off as a trifle obvious. But at that time the results were met with skepticism by the handful of colleagues with whom I had shared them. Replication became an urgent priority. In our second experiment, we dropped the free associations (which showed no hint of promise) and in a methodologically tightened new experiment easily replicated our findings. Other laboratories, since then, have effortlessly succeeded as well. Thus the findings are no fish story.

When this became clear on the completion of the second study, I began to wonder if other literatures existed that complemented the findings. Until this time, the project had been seen as a psychoanalytic experiment. The free associations had failed, but the recovery of unconscious (or inaccessible) memory had been clearly achieved. I had a vague, hearsay knowledge of the reminiscence and the hypnotic hypermnesia literatures, but little direct familiarity. This perhaps reflects negatively on me, but in those days memory was a backwater topic in experimental psychology and no course on memory was even offered on the topic at Yale—where Claude Buxton, of all people (who figures in this story), had recently been chairman.

It turned out that some of these discoveries about memory had been made long ago—but they had been forgotten or badly garbled—and that the phenomenon of upward-trending memory, which had appeared exotic to most mainstream scholars of my era, had a long history and, if we include the clinical literatures, a vast scope. And so this book.

The book attempts to codify, in a scientifically stringent treatment, a century of research, both in the laboratory and the clinic, on the recovery of unconscious memories and to extract the rich vein of implications that bear significantly on psychology, both theoretical and applied.

Acknowledgments

For substantial and substantive help with this project, I thank the John D. and Catherine T. MacArthur Foundation.

Peter Nathan, formerly of the MacArthur Foundation and a past colleague at Rutgers University, who frequently did not share my theoretical proclivities, was scientist enough to support the undertaking. He has my gratitude and my respect.

Mardi Horowitz, of the Langley Porter Psychiatric Institute of the University of California in San Francisco and head of the MacArthur Program on Conscious and Unconscious Processes, incontestably a large-tent effort to bridge the experimental laboratory and the clinic, with which I had the honor to be associated, did some of the invisible work to make this more tangible work possible. As a man of many "states of mind"—and of many gifts—he touched me most with the Japanese ink-brush painting he made for me. Simplicity, I now see, is seamless invisibility.

I thank also T. David Brent, senior editor at the University of Chicago Press, for his help and his patience.

My thanks to Fred Frankel and the *International Journal of Clinical and Experimental Hypnosis* for permission to use in chapter 7 material on hypnotic hypermnesia that substantially overlaps with my 1994 article in a special issue of the *Journal* on "Hypnosis and Delayed Recall." My thanks also to Ken Bowers and Donald Meichenbaum, editors of *The Unconscious Reconsidered* (Wiley 1984), for permission to use two clinical excerpts from the chapter of John Nemiah, *Marie* (translated from Janet's *L'automatisme psychologique*) and Nemiah's own case of Alice V (see below, chap. 2).

I gratefully acknowledge the Department of Psychology of Brooklyn College, City University of New York, which has provided me with intellectual challenge and a home, and the Research Foundation, CUNY, for its financial support over the past two decades.

I owe deep debts of gratitude to my students, of all levels, and especially to my graduate students and undergraduate honor students (whose designation is most apt). Also, I thank the subjects who toiled as guinea pigs in many of the studies of memory described in the book.

Extra special were two little girls (then), Karina and Maya, who went long distances despite their short years in what turned out to be, although we did not suspect it at the time, a venture into a dreamlike, magical realm of memory. I am grateful to them and thank them for allowing me to use their creations in my own.

During the writing of this book, several great institutions of higher learning, notably Columbia University; New York University; the Medical Research Council at Cambridge, England; and the Langley Porter Psychiatric Institute at the University of California, San Francisco, were hospitable enough to welcome me as visiting professor, scientist, or scholar and share their space, facilities, libraries, staff, and faculty and students. I thank them all.

I was only six years old when I became a refugee from Hungary, and so I wonder, off and on, whether a coffee-shop gene is ensconced in descendants of the Austro-Hungarian Empire (Plato's "reminiscence" would be apposite here, but acknowledgments should have boundaries; the Greek connection does insinuate itself, however). For whatever reason, I work best at creative efforts in coffee shops, especially where one can stay as long as one wishes and get a bottomless cup of coffee. I therefore am particularly grateful to the Hungarian Pastry Shop, across from the Cathedral of Saint John the Divine and a short amble to Columbia University and its libraries, owned, this being New York City, not by Hungarians but, now, by two Greeks, Christos and Panagiotis Binoris, for giving me a place to get away and commune with the muse; and for the ambiance, especially the rich crop of regulars: prize-winning litterateurs, clergymen and women, chess masters, musicians, finicky physicists, future lawyers and physicians, psychologists and shrinks, and, yes, deep denizens of primary-process realms.

My special thanks to Christos Binoris for some scholarly assistance with the article of Boreas (see chapter 1), which is in Greek. Christos may have made a contribution to psychology with his translation of what apparently referred to nonsense syllables: "worthless materials" was Christos's rendition.

Also important in this firmament have been my generous friends Fred Kramer and Rachel Porter. *Grácias,* too, to Carmen, the gerente Dominicana, who behind the Greeks behind the former Hungarians, sort of ran the show; and *miau!* to China, the cat, the real genius and master of the place, who puts Garfield, that mere pussycat, to shame.

Finally, my thanks to the Creator for my dreadful memory, which left me no choice but to be creative and which inspired me to devote my research life (also) to the recovery of unconscious memories.

ONE

The Historical Background of Hypermnesia and Reminiscence in Experimental Psychology

Ebbinghaus and Forgetting

What is the course of memory over time?

For a hundred-odd years, experimental thinking on the question has focused on the fact of forgetting: retention tends to decline with time.

Hermann Ebbinghaus (1885) contributed both the basic laboratory approach and the basic finding. Using himself as his subject, Ebbinghaus memorized alternate series of nonsense syllables and relearned each series after intervals ranging from 20 minutes to 31 days, avoiding mental review of the materials during the period. His measure of retention, "the saving of work in relearning," was the time saved in relearning a series, as a percent of the time expended in the original learning. Thus if it took him 20 minutes to reach perfect mastery of a particular series, and 15 minutes to remaster it after 6 days, the savings would be 25%. If forgetting were total—if there were no retention—there would be, of course, no saving of work at all on the second learning trial and there would be no savings. If on the other hand retention were perfect, no forgetting having taken place, then no new learning trial would be necessary and savings would be 100%. The measure is a sensitive one and continues to be used to this day (Nelson 1978, 1985).

Ebbinghaus's results, which he summarized in tabular form (Ebbinghaus 1885, 76), are best presented as a graph showing extent of retention (in terms of percent savings) as a function of time (fig. 1.1).

The figure, sometimes known as the Ebbinghaus curve of forgetting, is a classic of experimental psychology. It depicts a quite obvious fact—that we forget over time—although, as Ebbinghaus pointed out, the actual shape of the function, especially its precipitous early decline, may not have been so obvious before the experimental results. Ebbinghaus also showed that the relationship between retention and elapsed time could be described by an inverse logarithmic function,

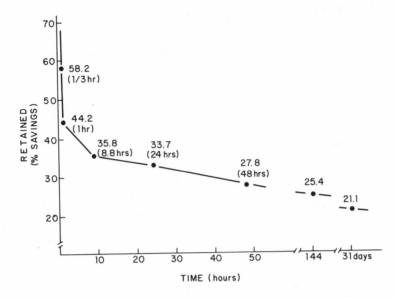

Figure 1.1 The Ebbinghaus Curve of Forgetting

$$R = \frac{100\,k}{(\log t)^c + k}$$

where R is retention, indexed by percent savings; t, the time elapsed; and c and k, two constants.

Since the results are based on a single subject and a particular method, the question arises—crucial for the present work—whether the outcome is reliable and, if so, how general it might be. Ebbinghaus, the careful scientist that he was, confronted the issue head on:

> Of course this statement and the formula upon which it rests have here no other value than that of a shorthand statement of the above results which have been found but once and under the circumstance described. Whether they possess a more general significance so that, under other circumstances or with other individuals, they might find expression in other constants I cannot at the present time say.

Experimental psychologists followed up Ebbinghaus's study and, on the whole, found impressive confirmation for it. Strong (1913), for example, using regular words rather than nonsense syllables, and a recognition measure of retention (in which subjects had to choose the stimulus items from a test set that included an equivalent number of distractors) pro-

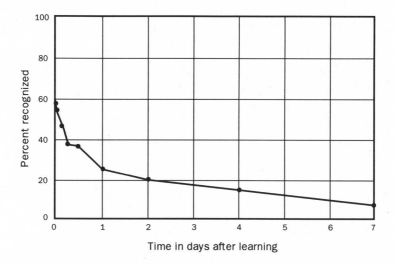

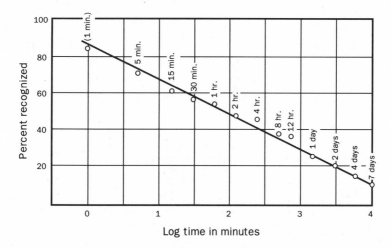

Figure 1.2 *Top:* Strong's (1913) retention curve for words with a recognition measure of memory. *Bottom:* Strong's retention data plotted against the logarithm of time. (Redrawn after Woodworth and Schlosberg 1954, 727)

duced a similar retention curve (fig. 1.2, top). When plotted against the logarithm of time, the function assumes a linear form (fig. 1.2, bottom) consistent with a logarithmic law of retention (albeit a simpler one than Ebbinghaus's, namely, the linear function, $R = A - B \log t$, where A and B are different parameters).

Woodworth and Schlosberg (1954, 727) juxtaposed several retention functions obtained by different investigators, including Ebbinghaus, which, when plotted on a logarithmic abscissa, again conform on the whole to a simple inverse logarithmic law (fig. 1.3).

Further underscoring the reliability and generality of the Ebbinghaus function is Luh's (1922) well-known plot of retention functions for different measures of retention (fig. 1.4).

Although the specific logarithmic formula and the constants may be in question, the basic Ebbinghaus curve of forgetting seems to be impressively corroborated.

Beyond the elementary questions of reliability and generalizability, issues of a more conceptual nature arise. Although at first blush it might seem commonplace to assert that retention decreases with time, some reflection shows the assertion to be substantially ambiguous. What, for example, do we really mean by *retention?* Suppose we adopted a distinction, currently taken for granted in psychology, between *available* and *accessible* memory (Tulving and Pearlstone 1967; also, *unconscious* vs. *conscious-preconscious* memories [Freud 1912, 1915, 1917]; *trace storage* vs. *trace utilization* [Melton 1963]; *unavailable* vs. *available* memories [Haber and Erdelyi 1967]), then to which type of memory is the Ebbinghaus function applicable? Available memory (in the Tulving and Pearlstone sense) refers to the total amount of information retained, regardless of whether the information is accessible to consciousness. What if all learned information is permanently retained but becomes progressively

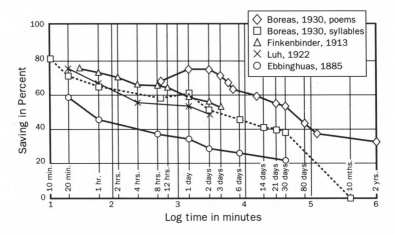

Figure 1.3 Woodworth and Schlosberg's (1954) juxtaposition of several retention functions, including Ebbinghaus's, plotted on a logarithmic abscissa.

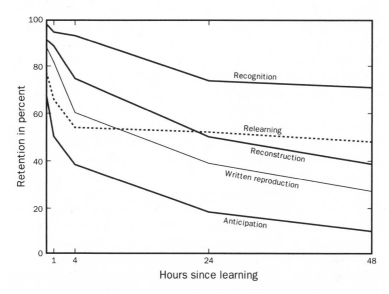

Figure 1.4 Forgetting of nonsense syllables over time as indexed by different measures of retention. (Luh 1922; redrawn after Woodworth and Schlosberg 1954, 724)

inaccessible to the rememberer, a possibility that Ebbinghaus himself briefly probed (62–63)? Then, would not a second retention function be called for, a perfectly flat function ($R = A$) for available memory? The problem, actually, may prove to be murkier than this, for neat dichotomies such as available vs. accessible could be hopelessly oversimple (Cermak 1982; Parkin 1987; Roediger and Craik 1989; Tulving 1983). Perhaps memory has a multiplicity of facets, each characterized by its own peculiar laws.

Not only the retention side but also the time side of the Ebbinghaus function poses problems. What does time have to do with memory and how, in any case, would we be in a position to tell from Ebbinghaus's curve? We could state with as much accuracy that retention (as measured by Ebbinghaus) is an inverse logarithmic function of the number of babies born in China since learning of the memory list. It is true, of course, that the number of babies born in China is highly correlated with time— indeed, it may be considered an unwieldy measure of time (whatever time is)—but the formulation has the advantage that no one would carelessly impute causal status to the variable. This type of concern did not fail to be raised by experimental psychologists. J. A. McGeoch (1932), for example, using another illustration, observed that rusting, although usually correlated with time, is not caused by time but by oxidation. Prevent oxidation and no amount of time will produce rusting.

To fill the theoretical breach, some investigators (J. A. McGeoch 1932) proposed that the causal mechanism of forgetting was the interfering effects of subsequently learned materials—that is, new memories—on the original memory. The more new learning, the more interference and therefore the more forgetting. This type of position is actually an ancient one, going back to the Greeks (for example, to Aristotle). Ebbinghaus himself discussed it briefly (62–63) and, at least on one occasion, gave implicit theoretical status to interference through the hedged wording of the question of forgetting: "How will the process of forgetting go on when left merely to the influence of time *or the daily events of life which fill it?*" (65; emphasis added).

The interference approach to the Ebbinghaus function is illustrated by the well-known study of Jenkins and Dallenbach (1924). Reasoning that during sleep little new learning would take place to interfere with memory acquired before sleep, they compared retention functions for equivalent time intervals following either sleep or wakefulness. As figure 1.5 shows, when awake, the subjects produced the regular Ebbinghaus function. But when they slept during the retention interval, they produced, after an initial transition period, a flat function. Time passes but retention fails to decline. The authors (see also Van Ormer 1932) concluded that "forgetting is not so much a matter of decay of old impressions and associations as it is a matter of the interference, inhibition, or obliteration of the old by the new" (61).

The use of sleep to evaluate the interference hypothesis has some interpretative problems (cf. Baddeley 1976; Crowder 1976; Ekstrand 1972). Taking a different tack—and enlisting rather unusual subjects—Minami and Dallenbach (1946) compared the retention functions of active and immobilized cockroaches. The results (fig. 1.6) were highly similar to those of Jenkins and Dallenbach and consistent with the interference hypothesis. The immobile cockroaches, presumably exempt from the interference "of the daily events of life which fill it," forgot little, producing a relatively flat retention function after the first hour.

If interference effects were as decisive as suggested by figures 1.5 and 1.6, it would make sense to substitute *interference* for the theoretically noncommittal variable *time* in the formulation of the forgetting function. Unfortunately, the picture is far too complicated (and confusing) to justify the switch. It turns out (cf. Baddeley 1976; Crowder 1976) that interference, though it can have powerful effects, is not the only variable; a host of other factors, including trace decay, failure of trace consolidation, motivational "set," variations in the ambient stimulus-cue field (external and internal), the similarity of the new material to the old, the type of memory

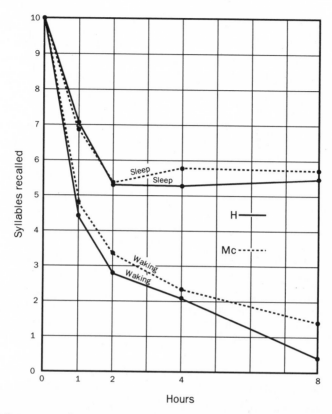

Figure 1.5 Retention of nonsense syllables by two subjects, H and Mc, as a function of time, when the subjects are either asleep or awake. (Redrawn after Jenkins and Dallenbach 1924, 610)

in question, all can have causal effects on retention. Moreover, interference is itself a complex factor: not just newly learned materials during the retention interval interfere with memory *(retroactive inhibition)* but old memories, extending back in time over the life of the subject, have disrupting effects on new memories as well *(proactive inhibition)*; and still further, interference, to the extent it affects memory traces, could do so by merely interfering with retrieval (J. A. McGeoch 1932, 1942) or by actually producing a weakening of the trace or "unlearning" (Melton and Irwin 1940), a position just now being debated again in the experimental literature in the context of eyewitness memory (Bekerian and Bowers 1983; Belli 1989; Erdelyi 1981; Loftus 1979; Loftus and Loftus 1980; Loftus, Miller, and Burns 1978; Loftus, Schooler, and Wagenaar 1985; Loftus and Hoffman 1989; McClosky and Zaragoza 1985; Tversky and Tuchin 1989; Zaragoza and McClosky 1989).

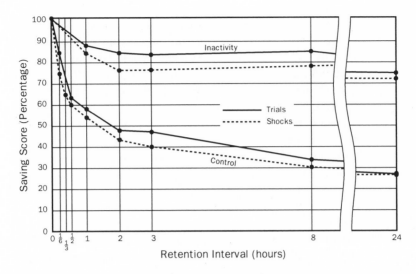

Figure 1.6 Minami and Dallenbach's (1946, 52) retention function for cockroaches who had been active or immobilized during the retention interval. Shocks were administered to cockroaches seeking to escape from a light compartment to a dark area, which they naturally prefer. A "correct" learned response was the cockroach's avoidance of the dark corner. "Trials" were an adjusted count of correct responses.

Fortunately, there is no need to resolve these imponderables here, though the issue of specifying the causal dimension over which retention is actually varying will come back to challenge us.

There is one critical point implicitly conveyed by these various conceptual preoccupations that should be underscored. However resolved, they do not really undermine the basic Ebbinghausian finding, whatever the precise shape of the decremental function might be. There may be no one curve of forgetting, and retention may decline more or less precipitously over time, depending on interference and other factors, but the course of retention seems to be fixed between the theoretical limits of 0 and 100%. Thus forgetting may be greater or not as great as suggested by the Ebbinghaus curve, but forgetting is nevertheless the basic trend of memory over time. This implication follows from both Ebbinghaus and simple interference theory.

In the case of Ebbinghaus, he made clear that internal review was avoided during the retention interval. Ebbinghaus did not explain why, probably because he thought the reason obvious: review would simply retard the decline of retention over time. Let us consider a rather trivial thought-experiment. Suppose that in the 20-minute condition, after mastering the series, Ebbinghaus had proceeded to do nothing but review the perfectly learned list until the relearning trial. It may be assumed that with continuous review, Ebbinghaus would still recall the list perfectly (or near perfectly) and that therefore savings would be 100%, or close to it. Thus, the limiting case is no or almost no forgetting. This is also so with a simple-minded interference approach. If somehow the situation could be contrived in which interference was completely (or almost completely) eliminated, then uninterfered-with memory should remain perfectly (or nearly perfectly) intact; hence, no or virtually no forgetting.

What is missing in all this—what seems not even to fit into the terms of the discussion—is the possibility that retention (whichever kind) might break out of the theoretical bounds implicitly set for it, between 0 and 100%, and actually *increase* with time, that is, exceed 100%. The very metaphors used militate against such a notion: *retention* or *savings* both imply conservative acts, acts of holding on to what the subject had before. Indeed, it may even appear illogical to consider the idea of retaining more than 100% of what was held earlier.

Upward-Trending Memory Functions

Let us turn to data. We have already looked at (and perhaps overlooked) some potentially significant evidence. Experimental psychologists, given the data with which they typically deal, are accustomed to substantial variability in their material. Even with clear-cut results, there is considerable overlap among conditions, and it is the overall pattern, verified by statistical tests (which take "error variance" as a premise) that defines "significant effects." The canvass of experimental reality is something like a pointillistic painting: one must draw back from the individual dots and dashes to discern the overall picture. Nevertheless, what for practical purposes is treated as error variance in experiments is often "ignorance variance," the effects of variables to which the experimenter is not yet wise. In hindsight, with the advance of the field, some of the ignored discrepancies may suddenly jell into a meaningful new pattern.

Thus it may be worth taking another look at Jenkins and Dallenbach's (1924) sleep-waking retention curves (fig. 1.5) and at those of Minami and Dallenbach's (1946) immobilized cockroaches (fig. 1.6). In both cases, after the initial decline of retention, the curves actually take a slight upward turn. The magnitudes are very small, and one is inclined to dismiss them as due to error variance. Still, even completely flat functions would be strange; mental activity, in the humans at least, is not likely to be completely eliminated in sleep, and so what one might more realistically have expected is a marked slowing of the decay of retention rather than its complete eliminations—and certainly not an upward trend of memory over time. It may yet turn out that the upticks in the retention functions are not all error after all. A recently published experimental article on humans, for example, testing the idea that dreams help consolidate memories of the previous day, showed memory levels significantly increasing over time with intervening dreaming (Karni et al. 1994).

Another subtle anomaly crops up in figure 1.3, which was presented as tending to confirm the retention function of Ebbinghaus. It is too easy automatically to "average" in one's mind—at least I did for many years— the individual functions and "see" a more or less declining linear function of the sort expected and therefore to ignore the peculiar upward-trending function of Boreas. Boreas's (1930) retention curve for poems is decidedly at odds with Ebbinghaus: retention *rises* with time for a period and only then begins its expected decline. Why should the function be different from the others? It could be an artifact (for example, Boreas was not as careful as Ebbinghaus about controlling for the time of day on which tests were administered), but more likely, given the literature that was to follow, the critical factor was the difference in stimuli used: poems in this study and nonsense syllables in the rest. Nonsense syllables, Ebbinghaus's creation, conform to Ebbinghaus, but poems go the other way, at least for a while. As will be seen, the stimulus factor turns out to be a crucial one, and it is clear that Ebbinghaus underestimated it:

> It is naturally not conceivable that by a mere caprice of nature the validity of the principles discovered should be limited exclusively to the character of the material in which they were obtained—*i.e.,* to series of nonsense syllables. They may be assumed to hold in an analogous way for every kind of idea-series and for the parts of any such series. (108)

Boreas's poetry data make clear, in any event, that it is not illogical to posit, as above, the idea of retaining more than 100% of what was held earlier. Obviously, retention at 2 days is more than 100% of retention at 8 hours. It is true, of course, that retention at 2 days is not better than initial perfect mastery, but then logic does preclude improvement over the perfect. Thus retention at 2 days may be greater than 100% relative to 8 hours, but not to initial perfect mastery (not included in the plot). What is revealed here is a hidden constraint in Ebbinghaus's specific measure of savings. The initial learning of the material to perfect mastery excludes, by definition, any possibility of improvement over initial memory and tends inadvertently to cast all retention levels in terms of greater or lesser degrees of *forgetting* vis-à-vis initial retention. Indeed, this is how Boreas construed his data: rather than noting an *increase* in retention over time, he merely observed that "forgetting according to our findings is less on the second day than that which is noted on the same day of learning" (Boreas 1930, 393). It will be seen presently that the Boreas type effect—retention increasing with time—can be readily obtained relative to the initial test as long as mastery is not perfect to start with.

It is commonplace in science that experimental "discoveries" are often not so much new findings as rediscoveries of old findings previously dismissed, ignored, or misunderstood, whose significance is finally appreciated—and successfully communicated to the scientific community. So it was with incremental trends in memory. From the time of Ebbinghaus, a wide smattering of investigators had noticed the phenomenon of upward-trending memory (among these are Binet 1904; Boldt 1905; Colvin and Myers 1909; Gates 1917; Gordon 1925; Guillet 1917; Henderson 1903; King and Homan 1918; Myers 1913, 1914, 1917; Norsworthy 1912; Pyle and Snyder 1911; Winch 1914, 1924). Already in 1904, Binet had asserted that "this type of improvement of memory over time, without being general, has been observed so frequently that it appears difficult to doubt it and attribute it to some error" (translated from the French quoted in G. O. McGeoch 1935, 65). Lobsien (1906) carried out a systematic study of the phenomenon. It was, however, Ballard (1913), in a massive research project, involving some 10,000 subjects, who finally forced experimental psychology to confront incremental memory. Ballard's is the reference work on hypermnesia and reminiscence.

Ballard's "Reminiscence" and "Improvement" (Hypermnesia)

Ballard's program began with a serendipitous finding. He wished to check the claim that children in a slum school had particularly poor memories. He had a class of boys (whose average age was 12 years and 10 months) memorize as much of a poem as they could in a 13-minute learning period. Only one of the 19 managed to learn the poem in full. Without warning (to the boys or the teacher), Ballard retested the boys after two days. "Much to the teacher's surprise, 8 of the boys wrote out the whole poem correctly" (1913, 2). On average the class improved by 10% over initial recall level. Ballard too was surprised: "This result seemed to be so remarkable that I set a similar test in several other types of schools, and always with the same result. After two days' interval more was remembered than immediately after learning" (2). From these findings, which posed "a crowd of questions" (2), Ballard's project was launched.

Figure 1.7 provides a typical set of results. Unlike Ebbinghaus, Ballard used recall as his measure of retention, usually counting the number of perfect lines rendered by the subject as his specific retention score.

After the initial recall test, R_1, which immediately followed a time-limited learning interval, subjects were retested (without expecting to be) for the original material after different retention intervals. The dependent measure was the number of items recalled on the later test, R_2, relative to the number of items recalled in the initial one, R_1, expressed as a percent; specifically, $R_2/R_1 \times 100$. If retention on the two trials were equivalent, that is, $R_1 = R_2$, the relative recall percent would be 100%, indicating neither improvement nor loss of memory. If on the other hand R_2 were greater than R_1, then the relative recall percent would be greater than 100%. If, finally, memory declined with time, and R_2 were less than R_1, then the relative recall would be less than 100%. For the three poems examined in figure 1.7 it is clear that, relative to initial recall, an *improvement* rather than decline occurred—for 6 days in the case of a section of "The Wreck of the Hesperus" and for only about 2 days, and to a lesser extent, for nonsense verses ("Inka rima rinka ro, / Banim bokew salib so, / Bick bock, Sec sim, / Thigger thogger donner dim. . . ." [7]).

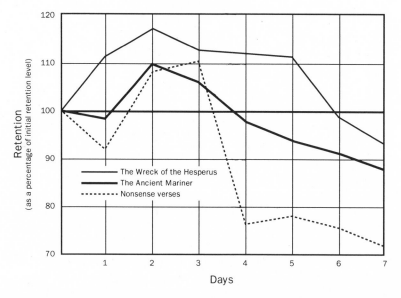

Figure 1.7 Ballard's retention functions for 12-year-olds for three poems, "The Wreck of the Hesperus" (A), "The Ancient Mariner" (B), and nonsense verses (C). The 100% line indicates no change in retention; above 100% indicates improvement in recall; and below 100% indicates decline in recall. (After Ballard 1913, 5)

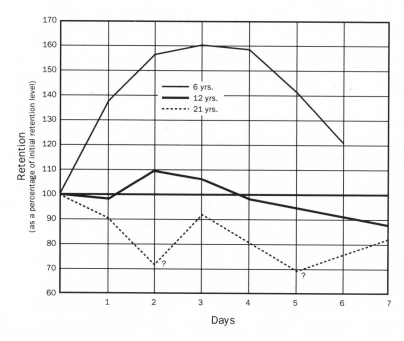

Figure 1.8 Retention functions for subjects of different ages: 6-, 12-, and 21-year-olds. (After Ballard 1913, 11)

One intriguing feature of Ballard's outcomes was that the improvement of memory over time appeared to be restricted to young children. Figure 1.8 shows this age effect. The 6-year-olds produced sizable improvement relative to initial recall for the full range of 6 days; the 12-year-olds improved, but slightly, and only for a period of about 2 days; the 21-year-olds evidenced only retention decrements. Ballard concluded that "as a rule a group of subjects over 20 years of age is incapable of improving upon its initial aggregate record" (15) and proposed the thesis that "improvement diminishes with increasing age of the subject" (13). Unfortunately, Ballard's data on age effects are contaminated by a number of potential artifacts, since not only age but other factors, such as the poem being remembered, the level of initial mastery, the specific mode of testing, were confounded with age. Although, as shown below, Williams (1926) was able to produce an age effect, other early efforts at replication (Brown 1923; Nicolai 1921) demonstrated clear improvement effects with adults—as did Boreas with poetry. G. O. McGeoch (1935) concluded that, on balance, the evidence did not support the relation between age and improvement. The modern literature, as will be seen, regularly shows improvement in adults, and in one contemporary developmental study (Paris 1978) a contrary pattern was obtained, with net improvement evidenced by 6th graders but not 2d graders. Ballard's age thesis, therefore, is not supported by the literature, though it remains something of a puzzle why he and Williams (who eliminated the potential confounds) obtained it. One factor to bear in mind, noted by Ballard (31), is the difference between "relative" and "absolute" improvement. Young children produce fewer initial recalls than adults, and so a small improvement in later recall results in a larger percent increase than the same improvement in adults.

At this point, a basic distinction, fatally garbled for several successive decades in the experimental literature, must be addressed. (Roediger and Thorpe [1978] deserve credit for the clarification of this issue; see also Erdelyi 1984; Erdelyi and Kleinbard 1978; Payne 1987.) Ballard's monograph was titled *Oblivescence and Reminiscence.* The former term, used also by Ebbinghaus, was just another word for forgetting. *Reminiscence,* however, was Ballard's technical term, conscripted by him into psychological service from Plato (who advanced the notion that all learning is actually the recovery of lost memories from past incarnations), to designate, without any of the metaphysical overlay, "the remembering again of the forgotten without relearning" (1, 17). Ballard noted that the tradition in memory research had been one-sided in positing that "traces gradually fade, and the curve of remembering has but one tendency—a downward tendency" (1). Ballard established that this was not the only propensity of memory: "oblivescence is at least partly counteracted by an opposing tendency toward reminiscence. We not only tend to forget what we have once remembered, but we also tend to remember what we have once forgotten" (1).

Thus retention at any point in time is the balance between two contradictory tendencies of memory. This simple and beautiful concept—retention as the dance between two opposite tendencies of memory, reminiscence and oblivescence—was largely lost on succeeding researchers, who were understandably drawn to the "paradoxical" retention functions (Huguenin 1914) that Ballard readily produced in his experiments. However, the incremental memory effects, which Ballard referred to as "improvement," and which is termed *hypermnesia* in the contemporary literature, is not what Ballard meant by reminiscence. Unfortunately, Ballard only got to making this unmistakably clear seventeen pages into his monograph:

> It will be observed that I have so far spoken mainly of the improvement in the capacity to reproduce lines of poetry memorised, and

have made but little reference to reminiscence proper. It might indeed be thought that since the improvement referred to is due to reminiscence, as according to my definition of the term it obviously is, the amount of improvement would indicate the amount of reminiscence. But this is not so. Suppose for instance a subject wrote correctly six lines at the primary test [R_1] and six lines at the secondary test [R_2]. One would naturally infer that the lines written at the two tests were identical. But a scrutiny of the actual papers reveals the fact that this is frequently not the case. What often happens is that the pupil loses one or more of the original six lines and remembers one or more that were not remembered at the primary test. In other words reminiscence has taken place. So it is when the pupil improves. The amount of reminiscence is frequently greater than the difference between the two measures. And not even when the pupil's record deteriorates does it follow that no reminiscence has taken place. . . . Indeed it always happens with a class of pupils, and nearly always happens with the individual pupil, that after the lapse of a few days there have been both a loss and a gain, and the final amount reproduced represents the balance. It will thus be seen that the amount of improvement by no means measures the amount of reminiscence. The latter is at least as great as the former, and is generally much greater. Among the large number of classes tested, although many have shown a loss at the secondary test, no instance has been found where no reminiscence has taken place. At the early stages of this investigation it was believed that the difference between improvement and reminiscence was too small to be significant, but as the investigation proceeded it became abundantly evident that the difference was far too great to be ignored. (Ballard 1913, 17–19)

Thus the distinction between hypermnesia (improvement) and reminiscence is this: *hypermnesia* is overall recall improvement from an earlier trial to a later trial; *reminiscence* is the recovery of stimulus items in a later trial that were inaccessible in an earlier trial, regardless of whether overall recall improves, declines, or stays the same from earlier to later trial (for a concrete example, see chapter 6, pp. 105–8). The distinction is well illustrated in figure 1.9, in which Ballard (27) summarizes some of his results with different stimuli. The top of each bar graph represents later recall level, R_2, relative to initial recall level, R_1, expressed as a percent. It will be seen that three stimuli (meaning of Latin nouns, nonsense poetry, and ballad poetry) produced improvement (hypermnesia), three (nonsense diagrams, nonsense syllables, and prose) produced recall

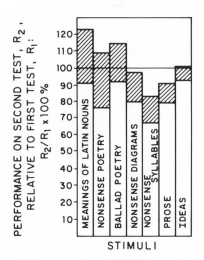

Figure 1.9 Ballard's recall data for different stimuli, partitioned into *reminiscence* (hatched sections), *oblivescence* (the sections from top of the white bars to the 100% line), and *recalled again* components (white part of bar graphs). *Hypermnesia* ("improvement") occurs to the extent that reminiscence exceeds oblivescence; it constitutes any portion of a bar graph that exceeds the 100% line. (After Ballard 1913, 29)

decrements (amnesia), and one (ideas) showed no change. What is theoretically groundbreaking, however, is Ballard's decomposition of each later recall performance, R_2, into its three components: the initially recalled items *recalled again* (repeated recall), the initially recalled items *forgotten (oblivesced),* and the initially unrecalled items *recovered (reminisced).*

The white section of each bar graph provides the percent of items *retained* from R_1 to R_2, that is, percent of R_1 items recalled again in R_2. Using a binary shorthand (Erdelyi et al. 1976), recalled-again items may be designated as "11" items (recalled on the first trial [1] and recalled on the second trial [1]). (Ballard's homologous convention was RR—right, right; Tulving's popular modern version, CC—correct, correct). The total number of R_1 items retained in R_2, in terms of the binary convention, is $\Sigma(11)$, which, expressed as a percent of R_1 ($\Sigma(11)/R_1 \times 100$), corresponds to the white segment of each bar graph. Note that for every recall bar graph this retention component is less than 100%. What does this mean? Obviously that in every case, forgetting of initial items occurred. Thus regardless of whether there was overall improvement or decline from R_1 to R_2, every recall pair features forgetting ("oblivescence") from R_1 to R_2, that is, "10" events (or RW [right, wrong]; CN [correct, not-correct]), this oblivescence component being rendered by the differences between the top of the white segment of the bar graph and the 100%-level line in the figure. For the Latin nouns, for example, the percent of R_1 items retained (recalled again) in R_2 is about 91% and the corresponding percent forgetting or oblivescence is 9%.

The final component of second-recall performance is the reminiscence component, the number of "01" items (or WR or NC items) as a percent of R_1, shown by the hatched segment of each bar graph. The reminiscence level for the Latin nouns, for example, is about 32% (123% − 91%).

The empirical yield of Ballard's analysis is that *both* oblivescence and reminiscence are basic to memory. The bar graphs show that for all stimuli probed, recall undergoes both reminiscence and oblivescence over time and that net recall depends on their balance. Thus, in absolute (rather than percent) terms, $R_2 = R_1 + \Sigma(01) - \Sigma(10)$, that is, second recall, R_2, is equal to the total number of items recalled initially, R_1, plus the number of items reminisced, $\Sigma(01)$, minus the number of items forgotten or oblivesced, $\Sigma(10)$. The difference between the initial and subsequent recall level is determined, as Ballard noted, by the balance of reminiscence and oblivescence: $R_2 - R_1 = \Sigma(01) - \Sigma(10)$. If reminiscence $\Sigma(01)$ exceeds oblivescence $\Sigma(10)$, improvement or hypermnesia results ($R_2 - R_1 > 0$), whereas if oblivescence exceeds reminiscence, a net decline or amnesia results ($R_2 - R_1 < 0$). In chapter 6, which gives concrete, numerical examples of reminiscence and hypermnesia, the definitions of reminiscence and oblivescence and of hypermnesia and amnesia, are generalized beyond the two-test situation considered by Ballard to multitrial recall involving any number of recall tests.

In view of the controversy that was to grow around Ballard's work (which will be examined in chapter 3), it is important to note that the unstable effect in figure 1.9 is improvement or hypermnesia, and not reminiscence. This should be borne in mind when considering later evaluations of Ballard's work, such as Buxton's (1943), who, acceding to the conflation of the reminiscence-improvement concepts that soon overtook Ballard's publication, was to conclude that reminiscence was a "now-you-see-it-now-you-don't" phenomenon (337). Reminiscence, however, as Ballard defined it, is clearly a bedrock feature of memory, on par with forgetting; it is improvement or hypermnesia, mislabeled "reminiscence" by Ballard's successors, that proved difficult to pin down experimentally.

It is also worth pondering that Ebbinghaus's percent savings measure is not amenable to the partitioning into components that recall invites, and so the reminiscence aspect of memory—regardless of whether net retention is decremental or incremental over time—is not reflected in the early Ebbinghaus tradition, even though Ebbinghaus himself several times alludes to the phenomenon on experiential grounds. For example:

in rare instances names, faces, bits of knowledge and experience that had seemed lost for years suddenly appear before the mind, especially in dreams, with every detail present and in great vividness; and it is hard to see whence they came and how they managed to keep hidden so well in the meantime. (Ebbinghaus 1885, 62)

The modern memory literature (cf. Nelson and MacLeod 1974; Shiffrin 1970; Tulving 1967) easily subsumes both reminiscence and oblivescence under "item variability" in multitrial recall, with the "intertest forgetting" component of item variability corresponding to oblivescence and "spontaneous recovery" to reminiscence. Earlier researchers may have blurred the concepts for lack of adequate schemas for assimilating Ballard's contribution. Perhaps, too, Ballard was a bit leisurely about getting to his distinction and its significance, and he did frequently use the term *reminiscence* in the misleading context of improvement effects. Still, the mode of analysis presented in figure 1.9, which makes the reminiscence-improvement distinction explicit, was Ballard's standard one, though he used curves rather than bar graphs as a rule (for example, fig. 1.10), with the shaded parts representing the reminiscence component. Figure 1.10 demonstrates the important fact that even after 33 days, there is an unmistakable reminiscence component to recall (segment E), though recall in this case had declined by about 30% from its original level. Ebbinghausian functions and reminiscence, clearly, are not incompatible.

A final figure from Ballard is presented (fig. 1.11) which shows (in absolute numbers rather than percentages) the three components of recall—repeated recall (11), reminiscence (01), and obliviscence (10)—as a function of serial position. Inspection of the figure suggests that reminiscence tends to be greatest in the middle section of the serial position curve, a finding also reported by later researchers (for example, Hovland 1938a), and attributed to the decay of *interference*, which is greatest in the middle of the serial position curve.

Early Replications of Ballard

Since, as detailed in chapter 3, Ballard's work was to be overtaken by doubts about its reliability, it is important to emphasize before concluding the present chapter that initial efforts at independent replication were quite successful (Brown 1923; Huguenin 1914; Nicolai 1921; Williams 1926).

The study of Williams (1926) is noteworthy in several respects, for it succeeded in producing Ballard effects as well as Ebbinghaus functions and, on the downside, contributed to the confusion of reminiscence with improvement.

In his first study, Williams used poetry as the stimulus and tested four age groups (the first three averaged 9.6 years, 12.7 years, and 16.2 years; the fourth was a group of "adults"—college students). As figure 1.12 shows, the two younger group of subjects produced memory improvement (the portion of the curves above 100%), the youngest generating by far the strongest effect. The older students, consistent with Ballard, were amnesic over time.

In a second study, four similar age groups (9.7, 12.8, 16.2 years old on the average, and college students) were tested for their recall of abstract words. These stimuli produced a quite different result (fig. 1.13). Regardless of age, retention declined over time, in conformity with the Ebbinghaus curve of forgetting. Obviously, the stimulus used is crucial for the outcomes.

Williams did not carry out a component analysis of recall and, unfortu-

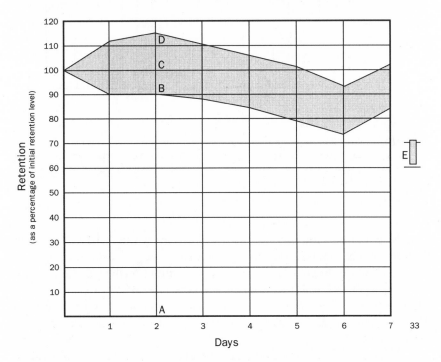

Figure 1.10 Retention (upper curve D), oblivescence (CB), and reminiscence (shaded area BD) over 33 days. Segment E, to the right of the graph, represents reminiscence manifested after 33 days. AB represents percent of initially recalled items recalled again on the second trial. (After Ballard 1913, 20)

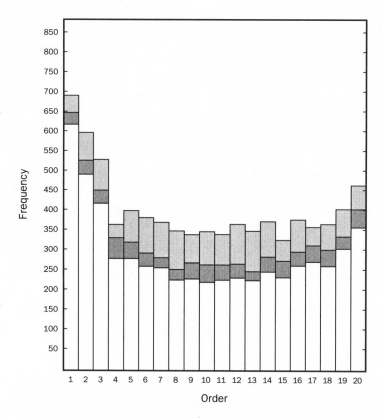

Figure 1.11 Serial position effects. The three components of recall—items recalled in both R_1 and R_2 (11 items, represented by the white bars), reminiscence (01, the combined shaded areas); and oblivescence (10, the darker-shaded segments)—as a function of serial position. (Redrawn after Ballard 1913, 67)

nately, confused reminiscence with improvement ("Ballard . . . secured certain curves different from the Ebbinghaus type. . . . Ballard called this phenomenon of improvement in memory without further learning 'reminiscence'" [1926, 368]). Although some later scholars (for example, G. O. McGeoch 1935) were aware of Ballard's distinction, they followed the lead of Williams and others in redefining reminiscence as net improvement in recall.

Brown (1923) replicated Ballard's effects with a different kind of stimulus. He maintained the component analysis introduced by Ballard, though he avoided, by and large, Ballard's terminology. In his first experiment, college students were asked to recall the names of as many of the states of the United States as they could. Then, without warning, they were asked again a half hour later to try to recall as many of the states as possible. The results are provided by the following summary of Brown's (p. 378):

Number of states remembered first test	36.31
Of these there appeared in the second test	34.37
And new items appeared in the second test	5.29
Making a total for the second test	39.66

Note that the subjects improved from 36.31 states on R_1 to 39.66 states in R_2, for a net increase of 3.35 states. As expected (from Ballard), reminiscence level ("new items"), is higher; $\Sigma(01) = 5.29$. Clearly, "oblivescence" occurred as well: $R_1 = 36.31$, $\Sigma(11) = 34.37$; hence $\Sigma(10) = 1.94$.

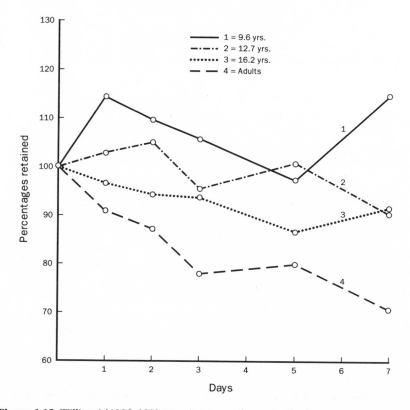

Figure 1.12 Williams' (1926, 323) retention curves for poetry for four age groups.

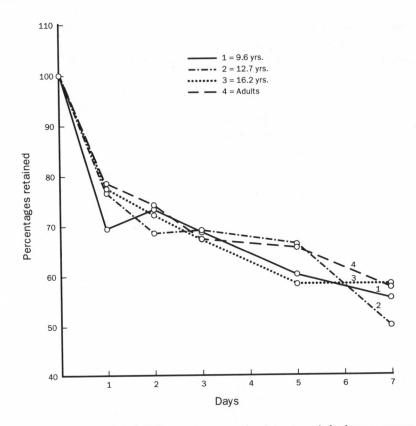

Figure 1.13 Williams' (1926, 374) retention curves for abstract words for four age groups.

The same subjects were used again two weeks later in an experiment involving a list of words. The results, summarized by Brown (p. 379), were as follows:

Number of words remembered first test	25.48
Of these there appeared in the second test	22.14
And new words appeared in the second test	4.33
Total words in the second test	26.77

Although reminiscence remained high—$\Sigma(01) = 4.33$ items—net gain was down to 1.29. Brown did not carry out a statistical test of his results so it is not clear whether the small numerical increment with words was reliable.

Brown's conceptual approach to incremental recall was framed somewhat differently from Ballard's. Brown's question was, "To what extent is memory measured by a single recall?" to which the answer is, obviously, not fully. Although Brown tended to avoid Ballard's terms, in a brief conclusion section he too appears to redefine reminiscence as improvement: "a second recall may contain more items than the first" (1923, 382).

Finally, Nicolai (1921) obtained recall improvement for real-life objects with adults, and Huguenin (1914) for poetry with children in multiple recall tests extending over two months.

With such promising results, obtained by four different investigators from four different countries, it is surprising that Ballard's work was to shipwreck on the issue of reliability. In part the problem was that experimenters turned largely to nonsense syllables in follow-up studies which, Ballard already had demonstrated, were not likely to yield hypermnesia. Another problem was that legitimate theoretical questions were miscast as methodological ones. Ironically, two genuine methodological problems in the early research, which could undermine the validity of improvement effects—of all early investigators—were never probed.

One of these, of no intrinsic theoretical interest, can be a fatal artifact in research done with large groups of school children, including college students. It is hard to believe that all students refrain from discussing their respective performance in the initial recall test, and, to the extent that such "cross-talk" occurs over the retention intervals (outside the classroom), a spurious increase in R_2 can be expected. In clinical contexts, to which we turn in the next chapter, the patient's discussions with family members may produce a similar spurious "recovery" of inaccessible memories. The later experimental literature, fortunately, resolves doubts on this score; hypermnesia can be obtained without the contamination of external information about the target stimuli.

The second problem is more conceptual and also is of relevance to recoveries reported in the clinic. Improvements may occur not because memory is augmented but because the subject produces more responses, some of which happen to be correct items. In signal detection theory terms (Green and Swets 1966; Swets 1964) response criteria may become more lax with successive recalls, resulting in more "hits"—as well as in more "false alarms." Early investigators of hypermnesia and reminiscence, such as Ballard, reported increases in correct recalls (hits) without reporting overall productivity in the recall trials. Hence it is not possible to assess this potential productivity artifact, which plays havoc with a number of hypermnesia literatures, including hypnotic hypermnesia (see chapter 7). Nevertheless, as will be seen, the basic hypermnesia effect—net improvement of recall over time with successive recall effort—does survive control over this factor as well.

TWO

Hypermnesia and Reminiscence in the Clinic

> When we leave the region of common experience and explore the
> realm of the abnormal we find abundant evidence of reminiscence
> taking place on an enormous scale. We find instances of whole systems
> of ideas passing for long periods quite beyond the possibility of recall.
> The study of hypnotism, trance-mediumship, double personality,
> and the various kinds of amnesia arising from hysteria, epilepsy and
> insanity reveals abundant examples of this kind. But with none of
> these do I propose to deal here: I limit my enquiry to normal condi-
> tions. (Ballard 1913, 52)

One of the peculiarities of psychology as a discipline is the extent
to which it abides dissociations among its subfields: for almost a century
the experimental laboratory and the clinic went their separate ways on
the issue of memory. Ballard was perhaps the only researcher in the
reminiscence-hypermnesia area even to allude to overlaps between
the amnesic and hypermnesic phenomena seen in the laboratory and the
clinic, although, as is clear from the quote beginning this chapter, he
avoided any efforts at integration. It is noteworthy that in the controversy
that was soon to envelop reminiscence and which led to serious doubts
about its very existence (see chapter 3), no contact was made with the
"abnormal" literature which, according to Ballard, yielded kindred effects
on an "enormous scale."

In some ways the clinic played hare to the experimental laboratory's
tortoise. In very short order, before the turn of the century, the clinic
uncovered some of the basic phenomena the experimental laboratory
so painfully unraveled over decades, and organized these in a dramatic
superstructure that linked memory to psychopathology and psychotherapy. Yet the clinic never quite managed to cross securely into the domain
of science, for its discoveries were never airtight methodologically and
one could not be sure whether the phenomena it turned up so brilliantly
were facts or figments. The experimental laboratory moved glacially—and

not always in the right direction—but it had a methodology for settling basic questions. Gradually, the laboratory has closed ground, though even today it tends to avoid the hurly-burly of real-world phenomena that the clinic willingly confronts in some of its messiest manifestations. Perhaps a partnership between the hare and the tortoise would be profitable. And, indeed, over the last decade there has been a flowering of collaboration between them.

Memory in Clinical Dynamic Psychology

From the beginning, the founders of modern dynamic psychology—the likes of Janet, Breuer, and Freud—considered memory the cornerstone of functional disorders such as hysteria and neurosis. Although they didn't, like Ballard, elegantly partition memory into its three constituents, all three tendencies of memory—the up-tendency, the down-tendency, and the inertial—were basic components of early clinical theories. Hysteria and neurosis were viewed basically as failures of forgetting, as excesses of retention or recovery of traumatic memories. According to Breuer and Freud's famous formula, "hysterics suffer mainly from reminiscences" (1895, 7, 221). Breuer and Freud's use of *reminiscence* is pre-Ballard, and signifies the notion of remembering in general. Janet's homologous concept was that hysterics suffered from *idées fixes,* ideas or memories that had become fixed and would not dissipate.

Forgetting in some sense was also fundamentally embodied in these theories, for the traumatic events that could not be forgotten in one sense, were often forgotten totally in another: recall could be pervasive but not conscious. Such memories persisted or reemerged, but they manifested themselves in recondite dialects—in body language, nightmares, inexplicable fears—that the patient (and others) failed to recognize as memories. The concept of "remembering without awareness" (Jacoby and Witherspoon 1982) has become a major theme in the experimental literature on memory of the past decade (for example, Cermak 1982; Graf, Squire, and Mandler 1984; Parkin 1987; Roediger and Craik 1989; Tulving, Schachter, and Stark 1982; Schachter 1987; Squire 1986; Bornstein and Pittman 1992). A classic clinical example of these various motifs is provided by Janet's case of Marie (in *L'Automatisme psychologique* [1889]):

> Marie was brought from the country to le Havre since they thought her insane and almost despaired of her ever being cured. . . . After a period of observation it was easy to determine that the illness consisted of recurrent symptoms regularly accompanying her menses. . . .

As her menses approached, Marie's character would change; she would become somber and passionate, which was unusual for her, and would suffer from pains and nervous twitchings in all her limbs. Despite this, everything would go fairly smoothly during the first day, but scarcely twenty hours after its appearance her menstrual flow would suddenly cease, and her whole body would be seized by a shaking chill followed by an acute pain starting in her stomach and rising to her throat, after which she would begin to have major hysterical crises. The convulsions, although very violent, did not last long and never manifested characteristic epileptiform movements, and were followed by an exceedingly long and intense delirium. . . . The delirium alternated with the convulsions for 48 hours, with only short movements of respite in between. The episode would end with copious vomiting of blood, following which everything returned pretty much to normal. After a day or two of rest Marie would calm down and would remember nothing that had transpired. During the interval between these major symptoms associated with her menses, she maintained . . . a variety of highly changeable anesthesias, and in particular a total and continuous blindness in her left eye. . . .

This illness, so obviously related to her menstrual periods, seemed entirely physical in nature and of little interest to the psychiatrist. I was thus initially not particularly concerned with this patient. At the most, I made a couple of attempts to hypnotize her, . . . but I avoided doing anything that might have disturbed her at the time of her periods, when her major symptoms appeared. Thus she remained in the hospital for seven months, during which time a variety of medications and hydrotherapy were employed without producing the slightest effect. Moreover, therapeutic suggestions, especially those directed at her menstrual difficulties, had only a bad effect and increased her delirium.

Toward the end of the eighth month she complained of her sad plight and said despairingly that she felt that everything was about to begin all over again. "See here," I said to her out of curiosity, "tell me what happens when you are going to be sick." "Why you know perfectly well—everything stops, I have a bad chill, and then remember nothing of what follows." I wished to have precise information concerning the manner in which her periods had begun and how they had been interrupted. She did not reply with any clarity since she appeared to have forgotten a large part of the details about which she was questioned. I thought then of putting her into a deep somnambulistic state, capable, as has been seen, of recovering apparently forgotten memories, and I was thus able to recall the exact memory of a scene that she had never been aware of before except in the most incomplete fashion. At the age of 13 she had had her first period, but, either as the result of some childish idea or of a conversation she had overheard and misunderstood, she got it into her head that there was something shameful about the process and tried to find a way of stopping her menstrual flow as quickly as possible. Approximately 20 hours after her period had started, she went out secretly and plunged herself into a large tub of cold water. Her action was completely successful, her period was suddenly arrested, and despite a severe shaking chill that followed, she was able to return home. She was ill for some time thereafter and for several days was delirious. Everything quieted down, however, and her periods did not recur for five years. When they did reappear, they were accompanied by the difficulties I have already described. Thus if one compares the sudden arrest of her menses, the shivering and the pains that she now recounts in her waking state, with the account she gave in somnambulism (which, moreover, was indirectly confirmed), one arrives at the following conclusion: Each month the scene of the cold bath is repeated, leading to the same arrest of the menses and to delirium. . . . In her normal state of consciousness, however, she knows nothing about that and is quite unaware that her shivering is brought on by a hallucination of cold. It is possible, therefore, that this scene occurs below consciousness and brings on all the rest of her difficulty in its train.

Finally, I wished to explore the blindness in her left eye, but Marie objected to it when she was awake, stating that she had been that way since birth. It was easy to demonstrate by means of hypnotic somnambulism that she was mistaken. If one changed her into a small child of 5 by the usual procedures, she recovered the sensation she had had at that age, and one could observe that she saw very well with both eyes. It was when she was 6 that the blindness had begun. What were the circumstances? Marie persisted in saying, when she was awake, that she had absolutely no idea. During hypnotic somnambulism, and by means of successive transformation in which I had her relive the principal scenes of her life at that age, I determined that the blindness had begun at a specific moment in connection with a trifling incident. She had been forced, despite her outcries, to sleep with a child of her own age *the left side of whose face was covered with scabs.* Marie herself, some time afterward, developed similar scabs, which appeared almost identical and had exactly the same distribution. These scabs reappeared for several years and then were completely cured, but it was noticed that from that point on *the left side of her face was anesthetic and she was blind in her left eye.* She has since always maintained this anesthesia, or rather, to stick within the realm of observation, to whatever past period in her life I regressed her by suggestion, she always had the same anesthesia. . . . I made the same attempt as before at curing her symptoms. I brought her back to the period of contact with the child of whom she had such horror. I caused her to believe that the child was very attractive and had no scabs, but she was only half convinced. After having her repeat the scene twice, I was successful, and she fearlessly caressed the imaginary child. The sensation in the left side of her face reappeared without difficulty, and when I woke her up, Marie saw clearly with her left eye.

It is now five months since these experiments were made. Marie no longer manifests the slightest sign of hysteria, she feels well and grows increasingly stronger. Her physical appearance has radically changed. I do not attach any greater importance to this cure than it merits, and I have no idea how long it will last, but I find this history interesting as demonstrating the importance of fixed unconscious ideas and the role they play in certain physical illnesses as well as in emotional disorders. (Quoted in Nemiah 1984, 49–51)

If we disregard for the moment a number of methodological issues and take as valid the events Marie recovered in hypnosis, we find in this single case excerpt dramatic variations on the memory themes of the experimental laboratory that were explored in chapter 1.

Most obviously, the phenomenon of hypermnesia—in this case, hypnotic hypermnesia—is illustrated by Marie's recovery of two pathogenic events: the circumstances surrounding her first menses and the incident of the disfigured child with whom she had been forced to sleep. Marie could not recall these events initially but recovered them following subsequent hypnotic recall efforts. Such recovery phenomena demonstrate, according to Janet, the "importance of fixed unconscious ideas." Ballard himself, with apparent reluctance, conceded that because of his laboratory findings, "we are . . . driven . . . to accept what virtually amounts to subconscious mental activity" (Ballard 1913: 55).

The case of Marie also underscores the remarkable permanence of certain emotional memories, though not necessarily in verbal or conscious recall. The persistence of the symptoms may be thought of as a pathogenic persistence of nonverbal memory. In a systematic modern study of the fate of early memories of documented childhood traumas, Lenore Terr remarks:

> The surprise comes when one looks at behavioral memories, at how early they appear, how long they continue, and how accurately they reflect what happened to the child. Behavioral memory appears to operate by different rules from those governing verbal remembrances. (1988, 103)

Elsewhere she concludes, as if in qualification of Ebbinghaus:

> The posttraumatic memory—a mental image which has the intensity of a current perception and does not decay with time—turns up again and again in repeated dreams, the hallmark symptom of the old "traumatic neurosis" or the more currently designated "posttraumatic stress disorder." (1985b, 497)

Actually, straightforward waking recall can itself be remarkably retentive in adults who have been exposed to traumas: "flashbacks," "intrusive images," "peremptory ideation," and so forth continue to trouble traumatized patients, possibly for the rest of their lives (Archibald and Tuddenham 1965; Horowitz 1986). Indeed, "recurrent and intrusive distressing recollections" of the traumatic event, in the form of flashbacks, dreams, behavioral reenactments, is one of the basic criteria of posttraumatic stress disorder in DSM-IV (American Psychiatric Association 1994, 428).

The complexity of real-life materials can make it difficult to align crisply some of the phenomena of the clinic with those of the experimental laboratory, as, for example, in distinguishing between retention of originally recalled materials (11) and recovery (01) effects. Marie's continuous blindness is presumably a permanent retention of the "11" type (any test 1 and later test 2 would be positive). Her monthly symptoms, however, are not so readily categorized. They might be conceived of as permanent remembrances (11) or as cyclic behavioral recoveries (01) and losses (10) of memories. Nevertheless, there is no question that behavioral or dream memories of trauma are often of the recovery (01) type. Indeed, so common are delayed effects of trauma that DSM-III (American Psychiatric Association 1980) included as a subclassification of posttraumatic stress disorder a "delayed" subtype. A simple example is provided by Horowitz in the stress reaction of a woman to the death of her boarder:

The old man . . . was a boarder in her home and had died there a
year previously. After his death, the patient was upset but did not
receive psychiatric treatment. Within a few weeks she felt better.
Then, almost a year later, the unbidden images of the old man returned and were associated with panic, confusion, and distorted thinking and behavior. The onset was a dream of the old man and afterward
he came to "haunt" her during the day. (1986, 142)

Although it might be a phenomenon different from the one produced
by Ebbinghaus, Marie also exhibited pervasive forgetting (10) effects: she
had apparently forgotten (as far as conscious recall is concerned) the two
critical incidents recovered through Janet's hypnotic intervention. There
has been little effort in the clinical or experimental literatures to relate
the forgetting produced by Ebbinghaus and the forgetting resulting from
repression or suppression—or, in Janet's preferred terminology, dissociation. I (Erdelyi 1990, 1993) have attempted to show that at the very
least there is considerable overlap between the two and that Ebbinghaus's
mental avoidance of the target material during the retention intervals
constituted a nondefensive repression (suppression, dissociation, and so
forth), a process that Freud variously conceptualized as "intentional
thought inhibition," "avoidance of the memory," "avoidance of thought,"
"conscious rejection," "splitting-off of a group of ideas," and so forth (see
Erdelyi 1990, 9–10).

Terr discusses "deletion" or "subtractions from verbal memory" by
traumatized children of key elements of the traumatic event through selective repression or suppression of the material:

William when he was 4 years, 5 months old, was stuck for 20 hours
on an elevator. . . . William lost part of his story through suppression
of the most painful part of his remembrance. What started out as
conscious eventually created a lost spot in William's memory. . . .
I reevaluated this boy at age 8 years. He was unable to remember
whether the elevator lights were on or off. He could recall everything
else from his ordeal, but the darkness now was lost. (1988, 101)

Also of relevance to the experimental literature on forgetting and
memory distortion is Janet's peculiar therapeutic tactic of replacing the
pathogenic bad memory with a benign counteracting false memory. This
paramnesic technique is a clinical application of the hotly debated effect
of postevent information on original memories, touched on in chapter 1,
and may be conceptualized as a special type of interference effect. Various

versions of retroactive "reframing" techniques continue to be used in modern-day therapies (Baker and Boaz 1983; Domangue 1985; Lamb 1985; A. Miller 1986; Rossi and Cheek 1988).

Breuer and Freud, who present numerous clinical examples of hypermnesias and amnesias of the sort reported by Janet, opted for a somewhat different therapeutic tack, one which laid stress on the recovery into consciousness of the pathogenic memories so that they could be properly "worked through" intellectually and emotionally. Breuer's *cathartic technique*, which Freud eventually modified into psychoanalysis, was essentially hypermnesic therapy:

> For we found, to our great surprise at first, that *each individual hysterical symptom immediately and permanently disappeared when we had succeeded in bringing clearly to light the memory of the event by which it was provoked and in arousing its accompanying affect, and when the patient had described that event in the greatest possible detail and had put the affect into words.* (1895, 6)

In the clinic, unlike in the early laboratory, the surprise was not in the phenomenon of hypermnesia, which was obvious to practitioners, but in its (putative) therapeutic effect. The goal for Janet and for Breuer and Freud, was permanent modification of the recovered pathogenic memory. On the whole, Breuer and Freud did not attempt a reconstruction of the original memory, though in their early experimentation with the cathartic technique they did tinker with the tactic of permanently ablating, through hypnotic suggestion, the recovered pathogenic memory: "my therapy consists in wiping away these [memory] pictures" (53); "in mitigating these memories" (55); "I extinguished her plastic memory" (58); "I wiped out all these memories" (59). In the main, however, hypermnesia itself was the key, as long as the traumatic affect associated with the recovered memories was *abreacted* (reacted out)—fully expressed and "extinguished."

There was substantial overlap between Janet's work and that of Breuer and Freud—so much so that bitter acrimony was eventually to break out between the Janet and Freud camps over priority and credit (Ellenberger 1970; Erdelyi 1986; Laurence and Perry 1984)—although Freud soon, and already in the *Studies on Hysteria*, introduced changes that increasingly demarcated his evolving psychoanalysis from Janet's "psychological analysis." One significant departure was Freud's abandonment of hypnosis in therapy. The impetus for this deviation was Freud's inability to hypnotize some of his patients. It was presumed initially—as most educated persons still do, and as Ballard obviously did—that hypnosis possessed unique hypermnesic properties, having the power to widen "the field of consciousness" (231). Since the cathartic technique required hypermnesia, hypnosis was assumed to constitute a crucial adjunct. Accordingly, Freud was faced with the quandary of rejecting his unhypnotizable patients, or, as he decided, of attempting to use the cathartic technique without hypnosis. Freud proceeded by using, essentially, hypnotic recall instructions without hypnosis, a procedure that he termed the "concentration" or "pressure" technique, in which he repeatedly probed for recall of events for which the patient claimed to have no memory. When the patient drew a blank, Freud would insist that the memory was nevertheless available and that the patient only needed to concentrate further for the material to be recovered. The procedure, as described in *Studies on Hysteria,* is a clinical variant of the modern laboratory's multitrial recall (Breuer and Freud 1895, 267–83).

Freud, of course, never carried out a proper experiment on the question of hypnosis and recall, with groups of subjects tested with or without hypnosis. Remarkably, such laboratory experiments were not to be attempted until the 1980s. Freud's clinical impression, however, in this case supported by the laboratory data of a century later (see chapter 7), was that hypnosis added nothing to hypermnesia. Concentration with repeated recall effort was as effective:

> But where I have carried out a cathartic treatment under hypnosis instead of under concentration, I did not find that this diminished the work I had to do. . . . I have become altogether skeptical about the value of hypnosis in facilitating cathartic treatments. (Breuer and Freud 1895, 284–85)

The import of this conclusion, if true, is that the substantial hypermnesias that are often taken for granted with hypnosis (as by Ballard) and the effect of repeated recall effort without hypnosis, which Ballard found "astonishing" in his initial study of poetry recall and which later came to be doubted in the laboratory, may be one and the same phenomenon. If hypnosis makes no contribution to hypermnesia and the distinction between "hypnotic" hypermnesia and regular ("waking") hypermnesia is spurious, then one effect could hardly be a legitimately established fact of "abnormal" psychology while the other a beleaguered hypothesis of the laboratory.

The modern clinical excerpt below, taken from a series of psychoanalytically oriented therapy interviews, demonstrates the growth of recall, without hypnosis, produced by repeated recall efforts over several "clinical trials," that is, successive therapy sessions. The excerpt from Nemiah's (1984) Alice V at once tends to corroborate Janet's clinical findings and to extend them to nonhypnotic recall—and also to introduce psychoanalytic nuances not met with in Janet's treatment of his data. The case of Alice V also touches on, in a clinical guise, the oblivescence-reminiscence distinction advanced by Ballard. In the psychoanalytic literature, too, there is an emphasis on the existence of opposite tendencies in memory—of an "inhibitory tendency" versus a "facilitating tendency" (Gorer 1965); a propensity for "extrusion" versus "intrusion" (Terr 1985, 518); of "oscillations" between "intrusions" and "omissions" (Horowitz 1986, 1988). In Alice V's case both extreme intrusions and omissions are in evidence, with the unbidden memory images—unwanted reminiscences—constituting the complaint of the patient.

At 25, Alice V was already the mother of five children. Her illness had started several months before her admission to the hospital. Although she was initially vague about the circumstances surrounding the onset of her symptoms, she described easily enough the sudden irruption into consciousness of "obscene thoughts" that distress her deeply. These consisted of mental images of herself and her father, naked, engaged in sexual activity. When they occurred, she would try desperately to push them out of her mind by shaking her head or thinking of other things. But to no avail, for the mental pictures invariably forced themselves back onto her attention with a power of their own. Asked for the details, she replied with hesitation that they were "just thoughts about sex. Sometimes I would ask him and sometimes he would ask me. I could see pictures of him in my mind—you know, with no clothes on." As the images persisted relentlessly day after day, the patient became increasingly anxious and depressed to a point where she was sufficiently disabled to require hospitalization.

The thoughts were not only deeply distressing, but Alice was surprised at their character for she had never liked her father and could not understand why they should portray such intimacy between them. In fact, she protested, she had always tried to avoid him, and found it difficult to talk to him when she was forced to be with him. He was, she said, "poison" to her. In the context of discussing this relationship, she recollected that her symptoms had started at the end of a period of a week during which her father had gone out of his way to be friendly and helpful to her in connection with a temporary financial difficulty that had overtaken her and her husband.

As Alice continued to talk about her father, a curious tone of ambivalence emerged. Initially she could say only harsh things about him—that he was always mean, sarcastic, and rejecting. Indeed, a quality of vehemence in her insistence on how unpleasant and hateful he was struck the listener as being a case of "protesting too much," and when the patient at length commented, "I sort of feel as though I missed something," she was asked to elaborate. "My mother," she replied, "said he was good to me when I was little, and he used to sing songs to me and take me on his lap, but I don't remember. I only remember when he was mean to me . . . I just am glad when he keeps on talking to me mean the way he always does. . . . I just wouldn't know what to do if he was nice to me. . . .

When the patient had regained her composure, she recalled a memory of an event she had not thought of since it had occurred some 15 years previously. When she was 11, she reported, while in the livingroom with her father, she had suddenly had the mental image of herself in a sexual embrace with him. Terrified, she had run into the kitchen to find her mother. There had been no subsequent recurrence of such imagery (until the onset of her current illness, that is), and the episode had remained forgotten until its recall during the interview. . . .

It had not been easy for the patient to tell the doctor of this recovered memory. She became increasingly agitated and tearful, hung her head to hide her face, and covered her ears with her hands. Between sobs and in an almost whisper, she confessed that she was then and there thinking of her father with his clothes off. Presently, after a pause and still agitated, she revealed a new bit of information— that as a child she had slept in a crib in her parents' bedroom. "I slept in their room till I was five," she said hesitantly and anxiously. "I was in a crib for a long time. I can't remember—I can't remember. I never thought about that before. I don't remember—," she broke off, overcome by convulsive sobs. Encouraged to continue, the patient became quieter and said, "When I was very young, my father used to take me to bed and tell me stories. I didn't even think about that. I was very little . . . I remember once my father being very mad and yelling at me real loud. He just yelled so loud at me when I was in the crib."

Nothing more was forthcoming during that interview, but the following day the patient added a new detail to the account of the onset of her illness that she had not remembered when initially giving her history. At the end of the period during which her father had been making the friendly overtures that had so troubled her, and the

night before the sudden outbreak of her symptoms, Alice had had a
nightmare. She was, she dreamed, at a zoo. It was nighttime, and she
heard strange noises in the darkness. She asked an animal keeper
standing next to her what these noises were. "Oh," he replied casually,
"that's only the animals mating." She then noticed a large gray ele-
phant lying on its right side in the grass in front of her. As she watched,
she saw the creature moving its left hind leg up and down as if it
were trying to get up onto its feet. At that point in the dream she
awoke with a sense of terror and during the morning experienced
the first episode of the frightening imagery of sexual activity with her
father.

In direct association to the dream, the patient recovered a long-
forgotten childhood memory of an episode that had occurred during
her fourth or fifth year. She had awoken one night while in her crib
in her parents' bedroom, to observe her parents naked, engaging in
sexual intercourse. They suddenly became aware of her watching
them and sprang quickly apart. The patient remembered seeing her
mother hastily pulling the bedclothes around her to hide her naked-
ness; her father, meanwhile, rolled over, half on his back, half on his
left side. The patient noticed his erection, and then saw him lift up
his left leg as he sat up and yelled at her crossly to go to sleep, at
which she hid her head under the covers and pretended to doze off.

It was not easy for the patient to communicate these memories.
She spoke haltingly, in a low voice, and was visibly ashamed and
anxious. Throughout the entire recital she discharged a great quantity
of affect, but after doing so appeared considerably relieved and emotionally composed. Following the interview, she became increasingly
relaxed, cheerful, and outgoing on the ward. Of particular note was
the complete disappearance of her central symptom—the sexual imagery involving her father and herself, which until that point in her
hospital stay had continued to plague her regularly. Her improvement
was sustained, and the patient was discharged within a week. When
she was examined again two months later in a clinic follow-up visit,
she reported that there had been no recurrence of her symptoms,
that she was feeling well, and that all was going smoothly at home
with her family. (Quoted in Nemiah 1984, 54–56)

Without hypnosis, repeated recall effort seems gradually to lead to
the recovery of a primal scene from Alice V's childhood. The hypermnesia
for the original event, as with Marie (without, however, reconstructive
memory work in this case) also produces a remission of symptoms. The

present clinical sample, reported more than a century after the appearance of Janet's Marie, serves to replicate and extend the original findings. Apparently, with or without hypnosis, critical hypermnesias can be obtained with persistent recall effort.

Methodological Issues in the Clinical Data

Up to this point, methodological scruples have been set aside and we have proceeded credulously, as if the observations in these cases constituted instantiation of valid memory phenomena. If they did, the issue of reminiscence-hypermnesia would be settled, and several decades of painful laboratory gropings could be circumvented. It is desirable, therefore, to confront the scientific bona fides of the evidence presented in the two prototype case histories.

There are some obvious methodological problems. Perhaps the most flagrant is the question of the veridicality of the recovered memories. A huge controversy in the clinical and forensic areas is currently swirling around this issue, which, interestingly, recapitulates Freud's struggle with the problem, roughly from 1895 to 1905, and which led Freud to the solution on which the modern scientific consensus is converging (Erdelyi 1995): Is "delayed recall" of childhood trauma, especially sexual abuse, veridical or part of a "false memory syndrome"? (See Banks and Pezdek 1994–95; Bass and Davis 1994; Ceci and Bruck 1993; Ceci, Huffman, Smith, and Loftus 1994; Erdelyi 1990, 1993, 1995; Erdelyi and Frame 1995; Frankel and Perry 1994; Harvey and Herman 1994; Herman 1992; Loftus 1993; Loftus and Ketcham 1994; Neisser and Harsch 1992; Terr 1994; Ofshe and Watters 1994; Wright 1994.) How could we possibly know whether these memories are true or false? The therapeutic effect of the hypermnesias are certainly not warrantors of veracity (Erdelyi 1986; Grünbaum 1984, 1986; Rossi and Cheek 1988). There is, simply, no way to establish, for example, that Marie had been forced to sleep with the disfigured child. Maybe Marie confabulated the memory to suit her symptoms. Now, clinicians are often not too worried about this question (Spence 1982; Rossi and Cheek 1988); if the recovery is therapeutic, it is clinically valid. For the present work on hypermnesia and reminiscence, however, the issue is make or break. Since patients have been known to recall confidently events from previous reincarnations (de Rochas 1896; Bernstein 1956) or even from the future (de Rochas, 1896; Kline 1958; Rubenstein and Newman 1954), it is not a forgone possibility that Marie's and Alice V's presumed hypermnesias were paramnesias (confabulations) instead.

Occasionally, independent verification is possible, as in the case of Terr's subject Sarah (Terr 1985a, 66–67), who, at the age of 15 to 18 months, had been sexually abused and photographed at the notorious Hillgard's Day Care Center. Interviewed at the age of 5 by Terr, Sarah stated, "Somebody scared me once with a finger part. I *can't* remember. *I'm afraid of a finger part on my stomach*" (67). Terr surmised that

> this child had feared penises (a finger-part) for many years as a result of her experiences with Leroy Hillgard, and . . . that she had displaced the original area of assault upwards from her genitals to her abdomen. Sarah's father showed me, however, that the second part of my hypothesis was wrong. I asked Sarah's father after Sarah's session exactly what the pornographic photograph the police had shown him of Sarah had depicted. "Hillgard's penis was touching the upper part of Sarah's abdomen," he said. "And Sarah was crying." (67)

Real-life situations, however, do not normally permit close scrutiny of the data, and even in Terr's documented case some distortions and interpretation are involved. For example, Sarah's recall is technically unsubstantiated, for no "finger-part" was shown to have been involved. Only through the interpretation finger-part = penis is the report verified. Terr assumes that the preverbal child does not have the vocabulary for accurately coding the events of the trauma. Another young victim, Brent, explained, "They're doing this! Pictures. They get excited! Then their penis unties—looses off—it comes off their bodies. . . . When the children stop playing, fussing, and taking pictures, their penis gets softer" (Terr 1988, 100). A stiltedly literal reading of Brent's statement would suggest that the child was confabulating, since the claim that "their penis unties . . . comes off their bodies" is not likely to have actually happened. So transparent is the meaning of the child's poetic expression, however, that most would dismiss the objection as a cavil. Nevertheless, the use of interpretation in the evaluation of clinical reports has been a pervasive criticism leveled against Freud and other clinicians, starting with Janet.

Without some interpretative leeway, however, virtually no memory could be credited historical reality (including those of Janet's Marie) since all narrative recall is substantially reconstructive and therefore subject to distortions (Bartlett 1932; Neisser 1967). This holds also for adults thought to possess exceptional powers of memory, as Neisser (1981) demonstrated in his comparison of the Watergate testimony of John Dean, whom some writers called "the human tape recorder," with the actual tape-recording of the events that were later discovered. The drift of Dean's recollections may have been substantially right but "no count of idea units or comparison of structure would produce a score much above zero" (Neisser 1981, 9–10). "Comparison of his testimony with the actual transcripts shows systematic distortion at one level of analysis combined with basic accuracy at another" (n.p.). The point, then, is that interpretation, even though it is often wrong (for example, Terr's displacement interpretation), cannot be sensibly discarded in evaluating recall of complex real-life events (Erdelyi, 1985). Distinguishing between a hit and a false-alarm is a murky business in the real world.

Even if the problems of interpretation and veridicality were somehow resolved, there remains another methodological question that clinicians have virtually ignored: the problem of *response bias* or *response criterion* (see chapters 4–8 and the appendix for experimental efforts to confront the issue). What passes for recoveries of memories may actually constitute enhanced willingness to *report* unpalatable or uncertain recollections. Nemiah emphasizes Alice V's difficulty in communicating some of her intensely disturbing memories. It is possible that the memories she gradually recovered were accessible initially but withheld from the therapist until sufficient rapport had developed. If so, we would have an increment in reporting and not in recall on the part of Alice V.

There are some additional methodological questions that could be raised about the clinical materials. Critical reading almost invariably shows case reports, despite their unwieldy bulk, to be insufficient to the conclusions drawn. Terr assumes, for example, that the photograph showing Leroy Hillgard's penis on Sarah's abdomen corroborates the penis interpretation but contradicts her displacement hypothesis. Strictly speaking, this is not so. The availability of any set of photographs is hardly exhaustive of the events that transpired. Perhaps genital contact with Sarah did take place but was not photographed; the second part of the hypothesis may be true after all. Also, it is possible that Hillgard frightened Sarah with his finger in some way but no finger incident was photographed. The "transparent" finger-part = penis interpretation may after all be wrong and Sarah may have simply forgotten the penis incident (just as William had forgotten that the elevator had been dark).

Typically, crucial details from the scientist's standpoint are insufficiently reported in clinical cases. Even aside from the response withholding problem, it is often not clear in the excerpted cases to what extent the recovered memories were truly inaccessible originally. The recall queries are often vague or implicit. The clinician, moreover, is not in a position to resolve many of these issues. To fuss unduly with such details in the therapy sessions would tend to interfere with the therapeutic intent of the interventions. And, besides, it is not clear that the clinical situation is capable in principle of providing clear answers, even if the patient were badgered for more details. The clinical hare may not be able to do without the experimental tortoise.

Physiologically Triggered Memory Recoveries

Before concluding this chapter on hypermnesia and reminiscence in the clinic, it is desirable to review, briefly, recovery phenomena arising from gross physical-biological factors such as electrical brain stimulation, hypnotic drugs ("truth" sera), and recovery of memory function from physical trauma.

In Ballard's quote at the beginning of the chapter, he mentions epilepsy as one of the abnormal conditions giving rise to striking reminiscence effects. He was, doubtless, alluding to the work of the great nineteenth-century British neurologist John Hughlings Jackson, who had collected extensive clinical observations on the "auras" or "dreamy states" associated with the onset of some epileptic attacks, during which patients report a range of mental experiences, often including vivid, coherent ideation that could be taken to constitute recoveries of past events.

A modern example of such a "dreamy state" experience is provided by Wilder Penfield. The patient, M. M., was a twenty-six-year-old woman whose reports of vivid mental experiences were recorded in the hospital during an epileptic attack:

She had the same flash-back several times. These had to do with her cousin's house on the trip there—a trip she has not made for ten to fifteen years but used to make often as a child. She is in a motor car which had stopped before a railway crossing. The details are vivid. She can see the swinging light at the crossing. The train is going by—it is pulled by a locomotive passing from the left to right and she sees coal smoke coming out of the engine and flowing back over the train. On her right there is a big chemical plant and she remembers smelling the odor of the chemical plant.

The windows of the automobile seem to be down and she seems to be sitting on the right side and in the back. She sees the chemical plant as a big building with a half-fence next to the road. There is a large flat parking space. The plant is a big rambling building—no definite shape to it. There are many windows.

Whether this is actually true or not she does not know but it looks like that in the flashes. (Penfield and Perot 1963, 649–51)

The images are vivid and detailed and could very well constitute "replays" of past experiences. But are they? Penfield suggests "that it looks like that," though that's only a surmise. As a descriptive term, *flashback* may not be altogether justified.

Electrical Recalls

Hughlings Jackson, who was a formative influence on Penfield, reported autopsies on several patients with histories of auras and noted that the temporal lobe was in each case involved. Jackson reasoned that brain "discharges" from this region were responsible for epileptic seizures. Penfield made medical use of this insight with severe chronic epileptics who had not responded to medication by performing unilateral excisions of portions of the temporal lobe that were epicenters of the attacks. Since the brain itself does not contain the usual pain receptors, it is possible to conduct such operations under local anesthesia and to probe electrically areas of interest prior to removal of the tissue. In a small number of his patients (2–8%), Penfield obtained coherent memorylike reports of past experiences.

So impressed was Penfield with these "electrical recalls" that he concluded that all memories, whether accessible or not, are permanent (an assumption more or less held in some guise by major figures in psychology such as William James, Ivan Pavlov, Clark Hull, and Sigmund Freud):

> Thus it would appear that the memory record continues intact even after the subject's ability to recall it disappears. . . . A provocative question is whether we could develop techniques which could elicit far more detail than heretofore. (Penfield 1951, 22–23; quoted in Adams 1967, 36)

Although Penfield did at times designate the experience of a stimulated patient "as not of a real event, but . . . a fantasy or a dream" (Penfield and Perot 1963, 616), he also lapsed into viewing many electrical recalls as "detailed reenactments" of past experiences (Penfield 1959; cited in Adams 1967, 35). The methodological question that was emphasized in connection with the psychological cases (Marie, Alice V, and so forth) is no less problematic in the neurosurgery context, however, and soon an influential group of critics took issue with the evidence—at least with its implications of a permanent brain record for all past events (Horowitz 1983; Mahl, Rothberg, Delgado, and Hamlin 1964; Loftus and Loftus 1980; Neisser 1967). Close scrutiny of the clinical materials reveals some quite implausible events: several patients, for example, saw themselves in their "memory" experiences; one woman actually saw herself being born. The electrical recalls obtained by Penfield, it is now clear, are similar to other records of narrative recall, involving, as they typically do, a variety of distortions and inventions (see chapter 8 for some detailed examples provided by two children recalling a story, "The War of the Ghosts," over a period of several months). Of course, this does not mean that electrical memories (epileptic or artificial) are not hypermnesic. The data, on the whole, are silent on the point. What is clear is that Penfield's data do not invoke a permanent tape-recorder model of human memory.

A careful study by Mahl et al. of a patient whom they interviewed during stimulation sessions indicated that the vivid imagery involved dreamlike mentation characterized by primary-process organization of past events, many of them immediately preceding stimulation. Some of the electrical images are in the Lewis Carroll mold: one young woman reported seeing "pigs walking upright like people" (Horowitz 1983, 225). Mahl et al. concluded:

> Electrical stimulation of the temporal lobe does not directly activate memory traces in the ganglionic record. Instead it induces a state of consciousness which makes it more probable that primary-process modes of functioning will prevail. If there is a background of subliminally excited memory traces in the ganglionic record at the time of stimulation, then all the conditions exist for the occurrence of hallucinatory experiences, and the content of these experiences would necessarily be related to the prestimulation mental events, for it would be determined partly by them. (Mahl et al. 1964, 361; cited in Horowitz 1986, 218)

This, essentially, is the received view in contemporary experimental psychology (although it tends to be expressed more in Bartlettian than in Freudian terminology). As interesting as the phenomenon of electrical recall may be, it seems to add little at this stage to the psychological literature on hypermnesia in the clinic.

Truth Sera

Another intriguing physiological approach to hypermnesia is "narcosynthesis," the intravenous administration of hypnotic drugs to produce recoveries (and abreactions) of presumably repressed traumatic memories. Grinker and Spiegel (1945) employed this biopsychological approach in

World War II to treat soldiers suffering from "war neurosis" (war-produced posttraumatic stress disorder), in the belief that barbiturates such as sodium pentothal produced more effective results than hypnosis, which had been used for the same purpose in World War I. Some of the clinical case reports can make a powerful impression. Unfortunately, but not surprisingly, the veridicality issue is no less germane to this approach than to the previous ones. Redlich, Ravits, and Dession (1951), for example, demonstrated that normal subjects could continue reporting lies during drug interrogation, and other investigators have shown that good-faith recall of past events in narcosynthesis is subject to "potential distortions" (Kolb 1988, 266). In a recent review, Kolb concludes:

> At this time, the relative merits of hypnosis versus narcosynthesis in eliciting repressed or suppressed memories cannot be stated with any clarity. All the clinical investigations undertaken to examine the validity of data obtained under states of altered consciousness brought about by barbiturate medication make it clear that fantasy may be reported as fact and may intrude upon and distort the factual material. . . . There does not exist sufficient scientific evidence to assume the validity in reality of information ascertained in altered states of consciousness induced by either hypnosis or drug administration. (272–73)

The veridicality issue seems to be a standard theme coursing through the clinical literature, psychological or physiological.

Brain Trauma

There is one broad class of biologically based memory recoveries about whose existence there is no uncertainty. These are the well-documented recoveries from amnesias caused by brain traumas such as concussion, brain hemorrhage, temporary reduction of blood supply to the brain (transient, cerebral ischemia), and electroconvulsive shock treatment (ECT). Since the observed hypermnesias do not involve enhancements over normal recall but recoveries from (often drastic) impairment of memory, these effects may not really belong in the same category as the hypermnesias examined heretofore. Nevertheless, these reversals of posttraumatic amnesias show unquestionably that vast strata of inaccessible memories can exist which may be subject to recovery.

Physical brain trauma can produce disruption of both past memories (retrograde amnesia) and the ability to lay down new memories (anterograde amnesia). The effects can be very short-term, for example, amnesia for events a few seconds preceding the trauma, or far-reaching, extending backward over periods of years or even decades (Crowder 1989; R. R. Miller and Marlin 1979; Parkin 1987; Squire and Cohen 1982). Typically, a time gradient is observed in retrograde amnesia, such that the closer the memories are to the occurrence of the trauma, the more likely they are to be inaccessible. It has been well established that, following posttraumatic amnesia, memory tends to return spontaneously with the passage of time. This holds for head injuries (Russell and Nathan 1964), ECT (Benson and Geschwind 1967), or episodes of transient global amnesia (TGA), which can be triggered in susceptible persons by mundane physical stress such as a sudden change in temperature, or even sexual intercourse. TGA typically involves memory impairment in the range of hours or days (Markowitsch 1983; Parkin 1967; Regard and Landis 1984). It has also been shown in animal studies of ECT (R. R. Miller and Springer 1973; R. R. Miller and Marlin, 1979) that at least some inaccessible memories in retrograde amnesia can be recovered with "reminders," that is, cues associated with or similar to the original learning experience.

The data on humans show nuanced patterns beyond mere temporal gradients. In some cases, for example, patients suffering from dense posttraumatic amnesia tend to recover first their personal identity, then their whereabouts, and finally their temporal orientation (Parkin 1987). Also, many dense retrograde amnesias involve "episodic" memories—that is, past events in the patient's life—but not "semantic" memories such as language skills. There is, however, no hard and fast rule, and a wide variation of patterns can be found in the brain trauma literature, with effects depending on many factors, including the nature, extent, and location of brain involvement.

The modern theoretical position on posttraumatic retrograde amnesia tends to emphasize the disruption of retrieval functions (R. R. Miller and Marlin 1979) and less, as the classical view did (Müller and Pilzecker 1900), the disruption of trace consolidation. Just why posttraumatic amnesia recedes with time is not well understood. Insights into the mechanisms involved may or may not ultimately shed light on the operation of hypermnesia and reminiscence observed in the psychological clinic and laboratory.

THREE

*The Shipwreck of Hypermnesia and Reminiscence in the
Laboratory: The Midcentury Period*

Reminiscence is demonstrated when recall following a short interval
of rest is greater than if no rest occurred. As is well known, this is
one of the most elusive phenomena extant in the whole area of verbal
learning. Many investigators have been unable to produce the effect.
Its magnitude, when found, is very small. (Underwood 1961, 242)

With Ballard's programmatic demonstrations of reminiscence and improvement, the successful replication of his improvement effect by early
experimental investigators, and the vast if not always conclusive clinical
evidence, it might have been expected that the reminiscence and hypermnesia phenomena had been securely established. This did not prove to be
the case. Experimental psychologists began to tinker with Ballard's approach and, as if struggling in quicksand, became progressively mired in
confusion and doubt. As has been already noted, Buxton felt obliged to
conclude in his influential review of 1943 that "reminiscence" (that
is, improvement) was a "now-you-see-it-now-you-don't" phenomenon
(337). Keppel and Underwood echoed the sentiment two decades later
in stating that "reminiscence . . . is found to occur sometimes (and sometimes not)" (1967, 375). Reminiscence was an "ephemeral" phenomenon,
according to Underwood (1961, 243). Research activity rapidly declined
following Buxton's review, to the point that Keppel and Underwood, as a
result of a few experimental successes, felt obligated to relegitimize the
phenomenon by asserting "that reminiscence is no longer a pre-war phenomenon" (1967, 382).

Negative, Mixed, and Unsatisfying Results

The frustrating aspect of the literature was not the failure to find memory
improvement but the inconstancy of the data (Underwood 1966). One
could feel comfortable neither in espousing the phenomenon nor in re-

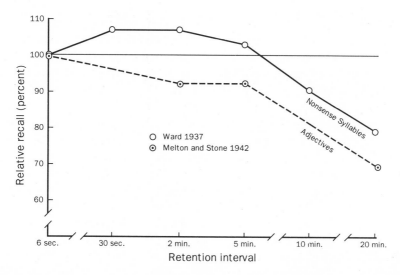

Figure 3.1 Juxtaposition of recall functions obtained by Ward (1937) and Melton and Stone (1942).

jecting it. Figure 3.1 juxtaposes the outcomes of two very similar experiments (one having been modeled on the other). Ward (1937), using nonsense syllables, produced a "reminiscence" effect (as improvement or hypermnesia came to be known in this era), with maximum hypermnesia occurring in a retention interval of between 30 seconds and 2 minutes. Ward noted that research on forgetting since Ebbinghaus had failed to probe the initial minutes following learning (Ebbinghaus's shortest retention interval, it will be recalled, had been 20 minutes) and now demonstrated that the initial minutes after learning were hypermnesic rather than amnesic. He showed also that at 20 minutes his own data meshed nicely with Luh's replication of the forgetting curve, the implication being that Ebbinghaus and his followers had missed a memory upswing that occurs before the precipitous decline of memory. Yet Melton and Stone (1942), using a list of adjectives as their stimuli, found no evidence of an early improvement in recall (Fig. 3.1). Mindful of other laboratory failures to produce memory increments (specifically Hovland 1938b, 1939a; Shipley 1939), Melton and Stone concluded that a "non committal position" was "justified" on the phenomenon (1937, 306).

Despite the cautious stance on memory improvement taken by Buxton, Underwood, Melton, and others, it is not that easy to find pure failures of incremental memory in the literature. Melton and Stone's results are among the few, and some of the failures they cite actually involved mixed outcomes. The Hovland data referred to were a subset of a program of studies (Hovland 1938a, 1938b, 1939a, 1939b) that, on the whole, were positive (and so treated by Hovland). Thus in the first of this series (Hovland 1938a), statistically significant recall improvements were found after a 2-minute retention interval following massed practice, but not (reliably) following distributed practice. In the next Hovland (1938b) study, no improvement was found with nonsense syllables presented at a 4-second per item rate (a failure more or less predicted by Hovland), but significant improvements were obtained (as predicted) with a 2-second rate. Hovland (1939a) then obtained a significant improvement effect for serially learned nonsense syllables after a 2-minute interval, though he did fail to obtain a parallel hypermnesia effect ("reminiscence," in Hovland's parlance) for nonsense syllables acquired through paired-associate learning.

The Shipley study was unambiguously negative: "The general effect of the pause was to impair retention" (1939, 116). Shipley wondered whether the 2.3-second per item rate he used, as against Hovland's successful 2.0-second rate, might have been responsible.

There were some other negative or mixed findings. McClelland (1942) reported two experiments involving serial verbal discrimination learning which resulted in failures of "recall" to improve after a retention interval of 2 minutes. Interestingly, in one of the two studies, memory as measured by the savings method did improve. (The two clear failures of Shipley's actually involved recognition and not, as he termed it, "recall," a fact that will gain in significance in the discussion of recognition hypermnesia in chapter 7.)

Perhaps the most impressive experimental failures were those of Brown (1924), Whitley and J. A. McGeoch (1928), and Gray (1940). Brown's is particularly noteworthy in view of his well-known positive findings of the preceding year (Brown 1923). The 1924 study was more elaborate than the previous one: recall for a list of words (the same as those used in the second experiment of 1923) was evaluated for a large number of subjects on three different occasions, over a wide range of retention intervals. All subjects attempted an immediate recall (R_1), then a second recall (R_2) after either 8 minutes or 16 minutes, and a third recall (R_3) after an interval of 3, 4, 5, 6, or 7 days. Figure 3.2 provides a graph summary of Brown's (1924) results.

The only difference between the two curves in figure 3.2 is that for one, R_2 occurred 8 minutes after R_1, whereas for the other, R_2 occurred 16 minutes after. Despite some variability, both functions are decremental over time. In this study, Brown omitted the component analysis for 01, 10, and 11 items, and therefore did not check on reminiscence proper,

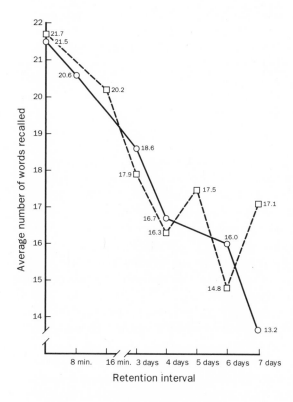

Figure 3.2 Average number of words recalled as a function of retention interval for two groups. The 8-minute group received the second test, R_2, after an interval of 8 minutes, whereas the 16-minute group received the second test after 16 minutes. (After Brown 1924, 470, table 1). Note that no recall data were provided by Brown for the 8-minute group at the 5-day retention interval.

focusing instead on the failure of the subjects to evidence recall improvement over time. Of special interest to Brown (1924) was the fate of retention over the 8- and 16-minute intervals, since he had obtained an upward trend ($R_2 - R_1 = 1.3$) with the same words after a 30-minute interval in the 1923 study (see chapter 1, 22). The slight numerical increment, as noted before, was not evaluated statistically. In the present case, both the 8-minute and the 16-minute intervals produced *decremental* trends instead: $R_2 - R_1 = -1.0$ and $R_2 - R_1 = -1.5$, respectively. These contrary trends, which were tested statistically, proved not to be reliable. Thus retention of words over intervals of 8 to 16 minutes showed no hint of being hypermnesic. These outcomes, of course, are not inconsistent with those of 1923: in all three cases, multiple recall tests for words over retention intervals ranging from 8 to 30 minutes failed to produce statistically documented changes in recall level. It was only in study 1 of Brown (1923), involving what these days would be termed "semantic memory," that a large (though statistically untested) hypermnesia effect

Table 3.1 The course of retention for poetry over intervals of 15 days to 120 days

R$_1$	t$_i$	R$_2$
21.20 ——	(15 days)	—— 13.56
22.86 ——	(30 days)	—— 10.13
22.33 ——	(60 days)	—— 10.58
22.46 ——	(90 days)	—— 9.31
20.97 ——	(120 days)	—— 6.00

Source: Whitley and McGeoch 1928, 472.

was observed. Moreover, reminiscence—in Ballard's sense—would almost surely have been obtained, had Brown checked for it, as no experiment I know of that looked for reminiscence proper has failed to find it.

Whitley and J. A. McGeoch's study (1928) is also noteworthy for producing a clear-cut failure to obtain improvement in recall over an impressive range of retention intervals: 15, 30, 60, 90, and 120 days. The stimuli, moreover, comprised poetry, one of the effective stimuli of Ballard. Table 3.1 summarizes the basic outcome. The pattern is clearly decremental. The authors concluded:

> The curve of retention for poetry over long intervals of time, falls quite abruptly from immediate recall to recall after thirty days and very gradually from thirty days to over one hundred twenty days. . . . The form of the curve of retention for poetry approximates more closely the Ebbinghaus curve of retention. (Whitley and J. A. McGeoch 1928, 479)

Does the Whitley and McGeoch study constitute a failure to replicate Ballard? Hardly. Outside of intervals of 1–6 days, Ballard's own retention functions were also decremental. After 33 days, for example (see fig. 1.10), retention had substantially declined, even though reminiscence continued to be manifest. J. A. McGeoch, McKinney, and Peters (1937) were later to report memory improvement effects over a 10-minute retention interval in two studies involving paired associates consisting of Chinese-English words.

Finally, Gray (1940) reported a set of clearly decremental retention functions with three types of stimuli (none of Ballard's successful ones, however): a set of words, a set of brief sentences, and a paragraph of prose. For all three types of materials, recall declined over a 24-hour retention interval (for words, R$_1$ = 13.50 and R$_2$ = 9.62; for sentences, R$_1$ = 5.43 and R$_2$ = 3.93; and for the prose paragraph, R$_1$ = 12.38 and R$_2$ = 12.14).

Despite some of these negative results, it must be emphasized that the literature was positive on the whole. Any box score of outcomes would show a substantial majority of studies producing incremental memory; the pure negative findings are atypical. What seemed to undermine confidence in the phenomenon was less the difficulty of finding hypermnesia than of finding it in a ruleful, predictable way. It was more confusion than failure that cast a pall over the phenomenon.

Consider the following three relatively recent studies on "short-term" hypermnesia. Keppel and Underwood (1967) examined retention for a 5-item paired associate list presented once at 4 seconds per pair, over filled intervals of 4, 19, 64, 184, and 304 seconds. The outcome was relatively straightforward: for three different levels of (bigram) meaningfulness, retention first increased up to 19 seconds and then decreased till 64 seconds; thereafter retention decreased further or stayed level, depending on meaningfulness.

Scheirer and Voss (1969) conducted six different studies on hypermnesia ("reminiscence") over filled intervals of 0, 2, 8, 32, and 128 seconds. In experiment 1, five different stimulus exposures were probed: 0.5, 1, 2, 4, and 6 seconds, over the four retention intervals. Whereas Keppel and Underwood's data (1967)—and also, it might be recalled, Ward's (1937)—showed retention first increasing and then decreasing, the Scheirer and Voss experiment produced an impressive but contrary pattern: for the different exposure durations, retention declined first (usually from 0 to 8 seconds) and then increased (from 32 to 128 seconds). With a slight design modification in experiment 2, however, no memory increments were found. In experiment 3, again no increments were obtained. In experiment 4, however, the pretty pattern of experiment 1 reappeared. Experiments 5 and 6 were also, on the whole, positive.

Peterson also conducted a study on "reminiscence [hypermnesia] in short term retention" (1966, 115). The stimuli were 5 word pairs presented at a rate of 4 seconds per pair (the same as Keppel and Underwood's, but also the rate at which Hovland found no improvement for lists of single items) over filled intervals of 0, 8, 16, and 24 seconds. Peterson's data, like Scheirer and Voss's, but unlike Ward's and Keppel and Underwood's, showed retention first decreasing and then increasing. Inspection of the outcomes as a function of the serial position of the stimulus pairs shows a scatter of patterns. The first position items increased from 0 to 24 seconds; the fifth position items first decreased, then increased; the third position items increased from 8 to 16 seconds and then decreased from 16 to 24 seconds.

In sum, in the three experiments, improvement occurred sometimes

(Scheirer and Voss, experiments 1 and 4) and sometimes not (experiments 2 and 3); when improvement was observed, the pattern was first a retention decrement followed by retention increment (Scheirer and Voss 1967; Peterson 1966)—or the reverse, first a retention increment followed by retention decrement (Keppel and Underwood 1967; Ward 1937). Moreover, the number and the serial position of the items in the memory list also seem to interact with the effect: the pattern for the first and third position is not necessarily the same as that for the fifth and last position; moreover, the improvement found with a five-pair list is not observed with a two-pair list, which yields decreasing memory over time (Peterson and Peterson 1962).

A box score for the above three articles would be 100% positive, since all three reported memory improvement effects. Reckoned on experiments, 75% (six out of eight) studies were positive. The phenomenon is hardly ephemeral. It is, however, perplexing. Efforts at explaining the patterning of the data did not readily generalize beyond local contexts. It was this failure to fathom an underlying coherence in the results that probably led to the decline of the phenomenon. Earlier systematic efforts (Buxton 1943; G. O. McGeoch 1935) to discern a relation between improvement effects and a variety of potentially effective factors such as intelligence, initial level of mastery, the nature of the material, sex differences, age, retention interval, amount of material to be learned, never quite succeeded. Demoralized, researchers moved on to other problems.

Redefinitions of "Reminiscence"

Yet there was something unaccountably perverse about the literature. The quote from Underwood at the beginning of this chapter captures some of the peculiarities. First, the definition of reminiscence, which was the one universally adopted in this era, was not what was originally meant by it; aside from the recasting of the terminology, the change discarded a distinction that is probably crucial theoretically. Further, the quote asserts that memory improvement is "one of the most elusive phenomena" in all verbal learning, when, as already noted, a substantial majority of published studies obtain improvement. Also, it seems to link gratuitously the retention interval to "rest"—actually, to "a short interval" of rest.

There are other puzzles in the literature. If a serious question existed about the reliability of Ballard's improvement effect, would it not have been reasonable to attempt a straightforward replication? Not a single true replication was undertaken using equivalent materials and time intervals (the one near exception, that of Ammons and Irion [1954], will be examined presently). This was not worrisome with the early replications of Ballard with different stimuli since the findings were positive. But with doubts about the phenomenon mushrooming later, would it not have made sense to return to the original experiments and determine if the results were replicable, and only then change conditions to reconnoiter the perimeters of the phenomenon? Most of the studies examined in the previous section did not probe the effective intervals of Ballard (somewhere between 1 and 6 days). A majority focused on intervals of seconds or minutes; the few long-term studies typically tested longer intervals than Ballard's without including those that had worked for Ballard. The only clear exception was Brown's 1924 study. But in this experiment Brown used stimulus material (a list of disconnected words) for which there existed little evidence of positive results. As noted earlier, Williams (1926) showed this type of material, in contrast to poetry, to produce uniformly decremental functions. Further, Ballard's least effective stimuli had been nonsense syllables, which produced pronounced amnesia rather than hypermnesia over time, yet it was this worst stimulus material, along with disconnected word lists, that became the stimulus of choice in the laboratory literature.

So baffling, in retrospect, was the experimental strategy pursued in this period that it might occur to one to wonder whether a conspiracy existed to discredit memory improvement. There is, however, no hint of bias in the literature, and the treatment of the phenomenon was typically sympathetic, if critical.

With the exception of Hovland's series of studies, moreover, there was a failure to undertake programmatic research in which variables were varied one at a time. None of the separate publications, with the exception of Hovland's, can be sensibly compared. For example, Ward (see fig. 3.1) used the reading of jokes as filler activity between recall trials, but Melton and Stone used fast-paced color naming instead. Hovland, on the other hand (but consistently), used a less pressured color-naming procedure. Can the discrepancies in the results be explained by these differences? Quite possibly (for example, demanding filler tasks but not easier ones knock out the effect), but there is no scientific way of deciding on the basis of the extant data.

It is as if researchers in the field felt exempt from the obligation to take into account the pattern of conditions of earlier investigations. With a mechanical rather than a conceptual approach, even the founding studies could be parlayed into having produced a sometimes-and-sometimes-not phenomenon. After all, in Ballard's summary figure (fig. 1.9), three studies showed improvement, three showed impairment, and one produced no change over time. In the case of Williams's 1926 study (figs. 1.12 and 1.13), one study produced improvement but the other, decline over time. The box score is less than 50% positive, lower than that of the later literature.

Nomenclature and Operations

Ballard's distinction between "reminiscence" and "improvement" has already been detailed in chapter 1. It is not clear why the distinction was abandoned. Perhaps it was carelessness. Or, possibly, reminiscence in Ballard's sense was too obvious to invite further investigation, although this is neither likely nor justifiable. Since improvement represents the positive balance between two contradictory tendencies of memory, a tendency to recover items and a tendency to lose items, a conceptual rather than rote understanding of the balance phenomenon requires a consideration of the many factors that differentially affect reminiscence and oblivescence. Indeed, by focusing on just one of the components of improvement, the researcher is bound to be surprised (and confused) by the action of the other, ignored component. So the real problem was not so much terminological inconsistency, to which one could adjust easily enough, but the effective loss of the concept itself.

In retrospect, one perceives a pervasive tendency to redefine improvement and reminiscence. At the most obvious level, this occurred in the offhand redefinition of the technical term *reminiscence* and the disregard of the reminiscence-improvement distinction; at a less explicit level, this took place operationally, in the failure to implement the operations that had successfully produced the effect. Related to the last point was the foisting of methodological strictures which, though universally espoused in this period, do not follow, or, at most, follow arguably from Ballard's concept.

"Practice" as Artifact

A widely held insistence developed, starting with Bunch (1934; and Bunch and Magsdick 1938) and fostered by G. O. McGeoch (1935) and Ward (1937), to exclude the effects of formal "practice" (and later of covert practice or "review") from the memory improvement effect.

The argument on formal practice went as follows: it is inappropriate to compare, as Ballard (1913), Williams (1926), and others did, R_2 performance against R_1, since R_1 provides "practice" that could account for improved performance on R_2. The solution was to hold recall trials constant while varying the retention interval. This could be achieved by introducing a control condition in which the recall trial of interest, R_i, is not preceded by a retention interval, t_i (or is preceded by a shorter interval than t_j). The control R_i thus becomes the standard against which the experimental R_i is evaluated.

The basic design may be schematized as follows:

Control condition: $\quad\quad — t_j \rightarrow R_i$
Experimental condition: $\quad —————— t_i —————\rightarrow R_i$

Instead of comparing a later recall trial against an earlier one (for example, R_2 versus R_1), the crucial comparison becomes that between experimental R_i (R_i preceded by t_i) versus control R_i (R_i preceded by a shorter interval, t_j).

A number of variations on this design are possible. The simplest (Ammons and Irion 1954; Gray 1940) is to compare a single recall performance, R_1, that was preceded by a retention interval, t_i, with one that wasn't preceded by an interval. Thus:

Control condition: $\quad\quad R_1$
Experimental condition: $\quad —————— t_i —————\rightarrow R_1$

It should be noted, as Ballard did (1913, 36), that reminiscence proper (01 events) cannot be evaluated with a single test.

With two successive recall trials, R_1 and R_2, several variations are possible. For example:

Control condition: $\quad\quad R_1, R_2$
Experimental condition: $\quad R_1 ———— t_i ————\rightarrow R_2$

or (also used by Ammons and Irion 1954),

Control condition: $\quad\quad R_1 — t_j ————\rightarrow R_2$
Experimental condition: $\quad R_1 —————— t_i ——————\rightarrow R_2$

where $t_i > t_j$. With two or more tests, reminiscence proper can be evaluated along with improvement effects. The comparison in this version of the design is either experimental R_2 versus control R_2 or experimental $R_2 - R_1$ versus control $R_2 - R_1$.

Because of the widespread interest during this period in the question of massed versus distributed practice, a popular variation on the basic between-condition design was to introduce the retention interval t_i at some point in the learning sequence and evaluate recall following a "rest" period (experimental R_i) against the corresponding recall without the rest interval (control R_i). The learning trials would be continued after R_i

until some predesignated criterion of mastery was reached. Two separate issues could be simultaneously addressed with this design variation: the effect of a rest interval on recall (memory improvement over time) and the effect of a rest interval on subsequent learning (the distributed versus massed practice effect). To the extent that the rest interval reduces the number of trials needed to reach criterion, it is a type of savings measure, and can be viewed as another index of incremental memory. Ward (1937), Hovland (1938a, 1938b, 1939a, 1939b) Melton and Stone (1942), among others, made use of this particular between-condition design.

Although the convention was somewhat arbitrary, it might be mentioned as a historical footnote that the between-condition tactic was occasionally designated the "Ward-Hovland design" (Ammons and Irion 1954; Hovland 1951; Woodworth 1938) and contrasted with the within-condition, the "Ballard-Williams design," in which later recall is compared against earlier recall.

Also, it should be made explicit that whereas relative recall in the within-condition (test-retest) design is R_2/R_1, relative recall in the between-condition design is experimental R_f/control R_f. The relative recall percents of Ward (1937) and Melton and Stone (1942) plotted in figure 3.1 are based on the latter; Ballard's, of course, on the former (fig. 1.9).

There is little question that the between-condition design effectively partials out the effects of the previous test. Methodologically, the tactic is sound. What is not so clear is its theoretical rationale. It may be interesting to evaluate the contribution of an earlier test on performance on a later test (which Ballard did, as shown below), but why is it mandatory to exclude the effects of the earlier test for reminiscence/improvement to be valid? Ballard did not.

Certainly, "practice" on R_1 does not guarantee memory improvement. With repeated recall tests, as we have seen, decremental functions are often obtained. Ballard showed this (fig. 1.9), as did Williams (1926) in his second study (fig. 1.13) and in two of his four age groups in the first study (fig. 1.12); Brown (1924) obtained substantial memory decrements over a 1-week interval with three successive tests (fig. 3.2); Whitley and J. A. McGeoch (1928) obtained such recall decrements with the test-retest procedure with poetry from 15 to 120 days (table 3.1). Obviously, "practice" on R_1 does not provide a simple accounting of the data. Either "practice" effects are not so straightforward or they are easily overwhelmed by more powerful effects.

Still, why not control for practice, even if it is not always a decisive variable? The nub of the issue is the meaning of *practice,* which was not carefully probed in the literature.

One point that was often made and about which there can be little question is that an initial recall test can have a beneficial effect on subsequent recall performance (usually by mitigating forgetting, not by producing net improvements of memory). Test or "recitation" effects on memory have been consistently demonstrated throughout the history of memory research (J. C. Bartlett 1977; Bjork 1975; McDaniel and Masson 1985; Darley and Murdock 1971; Gates 1917; Gray 1940; Izawa 1968, 1969; Raffel 1934; Spitzer 1939; Thompson and Barnett 1985). Gates (1917), in one of the classic studies, showed that active learning (involving substantial recitation) led to better learning and retention than passive learning (consisting mostly of reading the material, with little or no recitation). Spitzer (1939) showed that recitation, even with no feedback (further exposure to the stimulus) was a powerful counter to forgetting. Similarly, Raffel demonstrated that the effect of previous recall effort was "to retard forgetting" (1934, 837). More recently, Izawa (1968, 1969) showed that unreinforced test trials in paired-associate learning had "forgetting preventing effects" (1969, 600) and generally potentiated learning.

Gray (1940) and Ammons and Irion (1954) sought specifically to evaluate the extent to which reminiscence/improvement was explainable in terms of the effect of repeated testing. Interestingly, Ballard himself had carried out two studies "to assess the importance of the primary test" (1913, 36), though this was not widely recognized. The tactic used by these investigators (including Ballard) was to compare the magnitude of reminiscence/improvement obtained with the test-retest (within-condition) procedure with that obtained with a single test. The approach, in effect, is a hybrid of the two designs, involving both the within- and the between-condition comparison. Ballard's specific variation was:

$$R_1 \xrightarrow{\quad t_i = 2 \text{ days} \quad} R_2$$
$$\xrightarrow{\quad t_i = 2 \text{ days} \quad} R_1$$

Ballard's two studies, done on different poetry segments, were somewhat informal (in each study, the same two groups were used, A and B, in a counterbalance fashion, but subjects were not randomly assigned and the groups may have differed in recall ability). Table 3.2 presents, for each poem segment, the total number of correct lines generated by each group in each recall trial. For both poetry segments, there was a substantial memory increment over 2 days with the test-retest procedure. For poem segment 2, moreover, there was also a substantial increase of mem-

Table 3.2 Ballard's group recall data over a 2-day interval with and without retesting, with two different poetry segments from "John Gilpin"

	Poem Segment 1		
Group			
A	$R_1 = 114$ ——————— 2 days ————————→		$R_2 = 140$
B	——————— 2 days ————————→		$R_1 = 118$
	Poem Segment 2		
Group			
A	——————— 2 days ————————→		$R_1 = 194$
B	$R_1 = 149$ ——————— 2 days ————————→		$R_2 = 174$

ory over the 2-day interval with the between-condition comparison (from group B $R_1 = 149$ to group A $R_1 = 194$). For poetry segment 1, however, this between-condition effect virtually disappeared (group A $R_1 = 114$; group B $R_1 = 118$). No statistical tests were done on these data and Ballard treated the latter trend as a null effect and attributed the inconsistency of the two studies on the between-group comparison to differential recall ability in the two groups. If such group differences in recall ability actually existed, the interpretation of observed between-group differences becomes problematic. Ballard's overall conclusion was that the initial test has an effect "but only a slight one" (1913, 37).

Gray (1940), as has been already noted, failed to get any memory improvement with either the within- or the between-procedure, possibly because all three of the stimulus classes she used (words, sentences, and prose paragraphs) were ineffective materials. She could report only that the test-retest design resulted in less drastic memory decrements.

Ammons and Irion (1954), by shifting to one of Ballard's successful stimulus materials (poetry)—and also, it should be mentioned, testing children only slightly older than Ballard's effective age group—reported more striking results: upward trending memory with the test-retest design for one of two retention intervals but consistent decremental memory with the between-condition technique. Table 3.3 summarizes their results. Conditions 1, 2, and 3, all involved a single memory test administered after no delay (1), after 2 days (2), or after 7 days (3). This between-condition comparison shows memory declining over the 1-week period and very much in the negatively accelerated Ebbinghaus mode. Conditions 4 and 5, however, involved the within-condition design: after an immediate recall test, R_1, the groups were administered a second recall test, R_2, 2 days later (4) or 7 days later (5). What is satisfying about this study is that in the condition where Ballard had typically obtained hypermnesia—after a 2-day retest—an upswing in recall was observed, whereas in the over-long retention interval, in which Ballard no longer got improvement, Ammons and Irion similarly failed to get it. The Ammons and Irion study, clearly, is a more satisfactory experiment than many of the parametric assays of the previous decades. By reconstituting the effective conditions while simultaneously introducing a single variation, they were able to extract a conceptual conclusion: Ballard's improvement effect is replicable but his effect is due to repeated testing.

Although it does not alter the basic question about "practice," we should note that Ammons and Irion's improvement effect after 2 days, their only positive outcome, was not statistically reliable. The authors overcame this inconvenient point by juxtaposing relative recall percents obtained by Ballard at the two intervals tested that were close to Ammons and Irion's own figures. Since, however, Ammons and Irion did not use the same poetry material as had Ballard, and since Ballard, as we have seen, reported a wide range of results with different materials, the choice of Ammons and Irion was somewhat arbitrary. For example, after a 2-day interval Ballard did get 108% relative recall for "The Ancient Mariner" but 117% for "The Wreck of the Hesperus." Moreover, relative recall for Ammons and Irion's condition 4 was actually 103% and not 107%. The latter value was obtained by comparing R_2 of condition 4 against the *mean* R_1 of conditions 1, 4, and 5.

Strictly speaking, then, Ammons and Irion did not get much beyond Gray's demonstration of the well-known fact that a first test tends indeed

Table 3.3 Ammons and Irion's recall data over a 2- and a 7-day interval with and without retesting

Condition	Immediate	At 2 Days	At 7 Days
		Time of Test	
1	$R_1 = 9.23$	—	—
2	—	$R_1 = 6.81$ (73%)	—
3	—	—	$R_1 = 6.13$ (65%)
4	$R_1 = 9.73$	$R_2 = 10.05$ (107%)[a]	—
5	$R_1 = 9.00$	—	$R_2 = 7.96$ (85%)[b]
	$\bar{R}_1 = 9.33$		

Source: Ammon and Irion 1954, 185, 186.
[a]Ballard = 108%.   [b]Ballard = 87%.

to reduce forgetting in the second. But supposing, for the sake of the argument, that the positive numerical trend in recall was a true increment or that the pattern found by Ammons and Irion could be statistically clinched by using a different poem, younger subjects, or whatever, what follows conceptually? According to Ammons and Irion, the implication of their results was that Ballard's improvement effect ("reminiscence") and all other such findings based on the test-retest technique "are spurious," constituting "an artifact of the experimental method employed" (1954, 186).

But granting that R_1 has a beneficial effect on R_2, why should such a test effect be an "artifact"? Retesting, obviously, does not ensure improvement; despite retesting in condition 5, a memory decrement was obtained at 7 days (although a smaller one than that found without an earlier test). We seem to be back where we started. Ammons and Irion did not address the question of why the same practice effect that ostensibly produced improvement at 2 days failed to do so at 7 days. Perhaps the explanation was too obvious: the positive practice effect of R_1 was insufficient to overcome the extensive forgetting that took place after a long interval such as 7 days. This tack might explain why no forgetting was obtained when retesting after only 2 days.

Although "practice" on R_1 would seem to explain the mitigation or, even, the elimination of forgetting, it is not clear how it explains a memory increment such as Ammons and Irion claimed to have demonstrated. How can the subject "practice" what he or she cannot remember? Memory improvement was a puzzle for the practice hypothesis, as was acknowledged by several investigators (for example, Buxton 1943; Raffel 1934), notwithstanding their espousal of the notion that formal practice constituted an "artifact."

Earlier, Brown (1923) had invoked a test-effect notion to explain memory improvement, although, contrary to later readings of his proposal, it was offered as an explanatory hypothesis and not as a criticism of the improvement effect (or, even, of Ballard's alternative hypotheses of the phenomenon involving neural consolidation). Brown's was a simple idea with two points: "a second recall may contain more items than the first because repetition tends to fix the items of the first recall while chance tends to introduce new items into the second" (382).

The first part of the hypothesis, that the initial test helps to "fix" the items in memory, is a test-effect notion; it is commonsensical and, as we have seen, well supported empirically. Note, however, that this part only accounts for the untroublesome idea that "practice" retards forgetting. The second component of the hypothesis, however, which attempts to explain the puzzle of actual memory increments, is both ambiguous and problematic. If Brown is suggesting that more responses are added in the second test, some of which are liable to be correct by chance, he is proposing a productivity or response-criterion explanation of improvement (see chaps. 1, 4, 5), which *ought* to be treated as an artifact, since it is not a memory effect. The modern literature (see chap. 5), which controls for productivity effects, clearly rules out such an accounting of hypermnesia and reminiscence. With the response number held constant across trials, memory improvement occurs. Why should "chance," if that's all there is to it, favor R_2 over R_1?

Consider the following thought experiment. A subject is given a recall protocol with 60 spaces. The first 30 spaces are already filled out for him with the first 30 items of a 60-item stimulus list (which he never sees). The subject's instruction for R_1 is to fill in the remaining 30 spaces with guesses. Although the subject never saw the stimulus list, some of these guesses are bound to be correct by chance. Now, after collecting his first "recall" effort, R_1, we hand the subject a fresh recall protocol with the same 30 (indelibly "fixed") stimulus items and request another try at producing 30 guesses. This is R_2. Let us repeat the exercise once more, for an R_3 (since, deceitfully, the author has gone beyond the thought phase and actually carried out versions of this study for the purpose of gathering base rates; see chap. 4). What is the sensible expectation? Is there any reason to assume that "chance" should favor later recall trials? Obviously, no. The expected value of R_1, R_2, and R_3 should be the same. "Practice" without feedback should produce no increments in correct recalls.

It might be noted how differently matters would stand if Ballard's reminiscence-improvement distinction had not been discarded: initially correct items, in line with Brown, would tend to be fixed by an initial recall, increasing the probability of "11" events and decreasing the probability of "10" events in R_2. Moreover, on R_2, reminiscent items (01 items) would appear—since they always appear—and now in conjunction with the higher 11s and lower 10s (thanks to the fixing effects of R_1) would tend to produce improvement in overall recall level. Thus in this scenario, practice helps by fixing the original items, but the actual improvement is due not to chance but to reminiscence. Improvement due to reminiscence, obviously, is no artifact.

A common if offhanded explanation in the literature of this period of why test effects constituted artifacts is that the initial test in the test-retest design is effectively a learning trial:

a written reproduction of material immediately after learning might function as an extension of the learning period. (Gray 1940, 37)

Improvement obtained . . . at several subsequent successive tests of retention after various intervals is not reminiscence, but is instead, continued learning under conditions of distributed practice, in which practice-periods consist of recitation without knowledge of the accuracy of the performance. . . . The immediate recall is tantamount to a practice period. (G. O. McGeoch 1935, 82)

This position, however, either recasts the usual meaning of *practice* in the learning literature or begs the question. Memory improvement is interesting precisely because learning-type curves are obtained over retention intervals instead of Ebbinghaus functions. Indeed, some investigators define improvement ("reminiscence") "in terms of increments of learning which occur during a rest period" (Eysenck 1965, 163).

In the learning literature, *practice* usually refers to learning trials in which the subject not only produces responses (for example, recitation) but also gets feedback on the responses. Thus the term *practice* in massed versus distributed practice referred to response-feedback cycles in verbal or motor learning in which some rest was or was not interpolated between cycles. In verbal learning, for example, the subject was reexposed to the stimulus set after each recall effort. Not surprisingly, the subject improved. In motor tasks (for example, learning to type) the feedback is inherent in the results (for example, I note that I am transposing *g* and *h*; or that I have a tendency to type *r* when I want *t*). Thus *practice*, as typically used, is not just the production of responses but also the feedback attendant on them. It usually is, in short, another term for learning trials:

Learning is a relatively permanent change in behavior resulting from conditions of practice. (Kling 1971, 551)

The term "condition of practice" ordinarily implies controlled exposure to specific experiences . . . a defining characteristic [of which] is presentation of knowledge of results, feedback of information, or presentation of reinforcing or punishing stimuli. (Kling 1971, 553)

For this reason it can be misleading to designate the initial recall effort in the Ballard design a "practice" trial since no feedback is given to the subject. This precisely is what makes the phenomenon intriguing or "paradoxical": the subject behaves as if he or she were learning, even though no formal learning trials are being administered. Ballard had defined reminiscence as "the remembering again of the forgotten without re-learning" (1913, 1, 17)—or without "outside help" (47). Only if practice involved "re-learning" in the sense of "outside help" would the practice in question be artifactual.

If *practice,* on the other hand, were used in the less typical sense of mere response production, then practice effects should lead to performance decrements and not increments: "Practice *alone* does not produce learning, but only fatigue or extinction. In order to insure the occurrence of learning, it is necessary to employ, in addition, the operation of reinforcement" (Kimble 1961, 5).

The concern over practice effects probably arose from the theoretical ethos of the period. In some sense learning is undoubtedly taking place in improvement effects; however, this learning involves internal feedback, that is, feedback from *memory,* a notion that did not have wide currency in this period. The test-effects that tended to be viewed as inadmissible "learning" artifacts in precognitive psychology transmuted unnoticed into memory effects in the modern era. Thus McDaniel and Masson examine "five explanations of how tasks involving retrieval of target information may influence the original memory representation of that information" (1985, 371). All five of these are memory theories of one sort or another. As a memory phenomenon, a test-effect is, of course, no artifact. "Practice" is only an artifact if external feedback or formal learning is implicated in reminiscence/improvement effects.

True practice artifacts can intrude into reminiscence/improvement studies when the memory indicator employed involves a response system that is not well mastered by the subject and the improved performance results not from an improvement in memory but from an improvement in *response proficiency.* For example, let us imagine an experiment in which the subject is required to type the words he recalls from a stimulus list. He is given 2 minutes to produce his recalls. Let us assume that this subject has a good memory but poor typing skills. He recalls 50 items from the list but is able to type only 20 words in the time provided. He may even complain that he recalled much more but could not type fast enough. We tell him not to worry, as he will be given extra opportunities to produce the items. Over several successive 2-minute trials the subject manages to type more and more correct items per trial. Is he producing evidence of memory improvement? In this case we would rightly have our doubts since practice—at typing—may have enabled him to improve his typing proficiency and therefore to produce more of the items he could recall than he was able to do at the beginning. Such a performance improvement might well be a legitimate artifact: a purported memory improvement that is not a memory improvement.

True practice artifacts are likely to arise when stringent time limits are imposed on the subject. Interestingly, many of the early experiments on short-term hypermnesia featured such time pressures. Thus, using the method of serial anticipation, Ward (1937) required his subjects to produce each response within a 2-second period, beyond which no credit was given for the response. It might well be expected that with practice at the task (involving feedback on the acceptable response interval), subjects would substantially improve on their performance, independent of their memory for the items. Ward, not surprisingly, obtained impressive practice functions in which subjects progressively improved in their performance on *different* lists as a function of extent of experience with earlier lists. Thus practice can be an artifact. It is an artifact when the subject is actually learning a production skill through external feedback about his or her performance and performance improvement results from increased response proficiency rather than from increased memory.

"Review" (Covert Practice) as Artifact

"Recitation" need not be conceptualized narrowly as overt verbal repetition of what is remembered. The subject may recite or "practice" covertly by mentally reviewing the remembered material. Such silent recitation (review, rehearsal, revival, and so forth) produces hefty "test-effects," for silent rehearsal retards or eliminates forgetting. Not surprisingly, such covert "practice" was also excluded by investigators of this era from the purview of memory improvement and reminiscence. Thus:

> Reminiscence is defined in this paper as the improvement of incompletely learned material after an interval of time without intervenient formal relearning or review. (G. O. McGeoch 1935, 65)

> reminiscence is defined conventionally as improvement in recall after an interval of time in which there had been no overt practice or rehearsal of the material. (Gray 1940, 37)

> many investigators have been reluctant to ascribe much importance to improvements in retention after formal practice has ceased because of the possibility that the Ss had casually or intentionally revived the learning material between cessation of practice and the retention test or tests. (Buxton 1943, 315)

It is noteworthy that in this midcentury period the idea of *retrieval* processes during the retention interval was not broached. The activity in the retention interval was invariably conceived of in terms of rehash processes: revival, review, rehearsal, and so forth. What failed to be recognized, however, was that a review explanation cannot account for memory improvement. The subject cannot rehearse (just as the subject cannot overtly recite) what he or she cannot remember. Therefore, as in the case of overt test-effects, review can only explain the retardation of forgetting. Only with the recovery of initially inaccessible items in the retention interval, that is, with reminiscence, can improvement occur.

The exclusion of review from the improvement effect represents one more redefinition of Ballard's concepts. Ballard had specifically addressed the review issue both empirically and conceptually, though he, unlike the midcentury investigators, did not treat review as a mere rehash phenomenon. Indeed, he usually used the term *recall* or *effort of recall* to refer to *both* overt (test) and covert activity to retrieve the target material. Ballard is to be faulted for implying early in his monograph that internal review might be undesirable, as when he states, "In dealing with the children in the senior school it was necessary to take precautions so that the subjects did not suspect a second test" (1913, 9). But, as in the case of the reminiscence-improvement distinction, his explicit treatment of the question later on cast matters in a different light, and he made clear that internal "recall" was a legitimate aspect of reminiscence.

In his initial evaluations of the effect of review, in which he queried subjects at the end of the experiment whether they had "thought of the poetry at home . . . or repeated it to their mothers" (33), or, in one case, actually urged subjects to recall the material during the retention interval, the results suggested that review played a negligible role. In some of his probes, Ballard actually found hints that informal review (unsystematic review initiated by the subject) might produce some diminution of recall (33). This curious finding, which in Ballard's case was probably unreliable, was obtained more clearly by Ward, who found more improvement occurring after a retention period filled with what he considered a more effective rehearsal prevention activity (color association) than a less exacting one (silent reading): "Engaging in the task of color association during the 2-minute interval was shown to produce almost 3 times as much reminiscence [improvement] as was found when the subjects merely read to themselves during the interval" (1937, 61). Ward concluded "that rehearsal of the items is not in any way an explanation of reminiscence" (42).

G. O. McGeoch also found that subjects' self-reports on review during the retention interval were not significantly related to improvement and that, actually, to the extent that there was a trend, "a greater degree of reminiscence [was obtained] with the No-Review Group" (1935, 69). She concluded that the "data justify the conclusion that there is no consistent relationship between reminiscence [improvement] and rehearsal" (71).

Bunch and Magsdick tested the covert review hypothesis by using white rats as subjects, on the assumption that these subjects did not "employ symbolic processes" (1933, 39) and could not therefore covertly "practice" their memories. Bunch and Magsdick's results were positive (even though their premise may have been flawed): rats showed unambiguous improvement effects in maze learning, especially at a 1-hour retention interval.

In general, when "review" is systematic and overt, that is, when it is a formal recall trial, strong hypermnesias can be obtained. Ballard found, for example, that the interpolation of a second overt recall trial between an initial and a third recall trial administered 4 days later, produced hefty memory increments, R_3 being 120% of R_1 recall level. (R_2, after 2 days, was only 1% above R_1.) Ballard's overall conclusion was that with *informal* review (when recall is left up to the subject) "reminiscence is influenced, though to no very great extent, by repeated efforts to recall" (1913, 31). However, "when a *systematic* effort is made to recall the test-piece it always has a marked influence upon the reminiscence that follows" (34).

It is very clear that Ballard did not view covert or overt recall before the final test as artifacts. Indeed, he specifically introduced the term *simple reminiscence* to refer to the case when no review occurs except for the initial formal test, and distinguished it from *compound reminiscence,* in which "there was a repetition or series of repetitions" of recall effort between the first and the last test (1913, 33). The initial test, R_1, far from being an artifact, was an intrinsic component of the reminiscence concept, for, as already noted, a reminiscent event, 01, is *by definition* one which was forgotten on trial 1 and remembered on trial 2. In Ballard's words, "in all the experiments I have so far described there have been two tests, the primary [R_1] and the secondary [R_2]. Neither of the tests can be dispensed with if reminiscence is to be measured or even detected" (36).

It is clear in retrospect that the failure of researchers to maintain the reminiscence-improvement distinction caused a multitude of problems. What scholars of the midcentury period designated as "artifacts" were actually something quite different: they were variables that these investigators happened not to consider interesting but which seemed important for the improvement effect. The question of what is "interesting," however, is a tricky problem in science, often reflecting as much on the researcher as on the phenomenon.

The process of repeated recall effort, especially internal retrieval effort, is of great significance to the psychodynamic approach to memory. As discussed in chapter 2, the "work of recollection" (Freud 1914)—so similar to Ballard's "effort of recall"—is actually the key to early psychoanalytic therapy (Breuer and Freud 1895; Erdelyi 1985, 1990). Moreover, the process of *repression,* around which so many gratuitous complexities are strewn (Erdelyi 1990, 1993; Erdelyi and Goldberg 1979), may turn out to be nothing other than the opposite process, the selective inhibition of recall of certain classes of materials, resulting, in line with Ebbinghaus, in relative amnesia for these materials (Erdelyi 1990, 1993).

In order to remove any ambiguity caused by the semantic drift that had overtaken the reminiscence-improvement concepts, I introduced the term *hypermnesia* into the mainstream experimental literature (from the hypnosis and clinical literatures) to designate memory improvement effects *regardless of whether intervening review/retrieval was or was not involved* (Erdelyi and Becker 1974; Erdelyi and Kleinbard 1978). *Hypermnesia* is simply another term for Ballard's memory *improvement,* without the methodological or conceptual restrictions imposed by the midcentury literature. Moreover, *amnesia,* as used here, is the negative counterpart of *hypermnesia:* when the balance between reminiscence (in Ballard's sense) and oblivescence (forgetting) is positive, hypermnesia results; when the balance is negative, amnesia. Just as hypermnesia is not reminiscence, amnesia is not oblivescence or forgetting. Reminiscence is the converse of oblivescence; hypermnesia, of amnesia.

Spontaneous Recovery and Motor Reminiscence/Hypermnesia

Before concluding this overview of the midcentury period, which took such a dim view of incremental memory effects, we should touch on two hypermnesic phenomena about which no skepticism arose. The first, one of the basic phenomena of classical conditioning, is *spontaneous recovery* from extinction. According to Pavlov, "Left to themselves, extinguished conditioned reflexes recover their full strength after a longer or shorter interval of time" (Pavlov 1927, 58; cited in Kling 1971, 570).

Although Pavlov is overstating the phenomenon, since spontaneously recovered responses rarely if ever reach the magnitude of the original conditioned response, the fact that "a response which has been extinguished recovers some of its strength with rest" (Kimble 1961, 82) is undisputed. Pavlov's phrasing of spontaneous recovery is strikingly similar to Ebbinghaus's statement of forgetting, except that, of course, Pavlov is proposing an opposite effect over time. The relationship between spontaneous recovery and Ballard's memory improvement was not usually addressed explicitly, but Pavlov's theoretical notions about conditioning and extinction played a central role in mainstream theorizing about "reminiscence" (improvement) in this period (Hovland 1938a, 1951; Kimble 1961).

Pavlov had proposed that each conditioning trial, involving the pairing of an unconditioned stimulus (US) and conditioned stimulus (CS) resulted in an increase in the *excitation* of the conditioned response (CR). A nonpairing (extinction) event, on the other hand, was thought by Pavlov to produce an active *inhibition* of the CR. Thus extinction resulted not from the dissipation of excitation alone but from the buildup of active inhibition. When inhibition exceeded excitation, extinction was observed. It was Pavlov's theory that both excitation and inhibition spontaneously decayed over time, except that inhibition decays faster than excitation. For this reason, after a period of rest, residual inhibition falls below residual excitation for a net positive balance in favor of excitation, hence spontaneous recovery of the response. This dialectical position certainly brings to mind Ballard's own opponent-process conception of reminiscence and oblivescence. What is somewhat novel, and more in the Freudian mold, is the whimsical notion that forgetting (in effect) produces remembering. Indeed, not just the temporal dissipation of inhibition but also any external or internal phenomenon that inhibits the inhibition— Pavlov referred to all of these as *disinhibition*—results in spontaneous recovery.

This Pavlovian thinking was transposed by learning theorists (for example, Eysenck 1965; Hovland 1938a; Hull 1938; Kimble 1949; Lepley 1932) into an inhibition hypothesis of memory improvement. The dissipation of inhibition should result in a recovery of memory level. Consequently, any learning condition that tends to build up high levels of temporary inhibition (massed practice, fast list presentations, and so forth) should result in an initially depressed memory level that increases as inhibition dissipates over time. The tendency for the middle part of the serial position curve to produce greatest memory increments (already suggested by Ballard's work, as shown in fig. 1.11), could be explained in these terms (Hovland 1938a). Because the middle items of the list are interfered with by both the earlier and the later items of the list, most inhibition builds up around the center. For this reason, the middle region of the list tends, according to the explanation, to produce the poorest retention levels, but also the most recoveries of memory.

The second hypermnesic phenomenon that was not overtaken by doubt in the midcentury period was the "improvement of skill" (Ballard 1913, 50) that follows a period of rest. Such net increments in motor performance over time, in line with this period's tradition, were universally designated "reminiscence." Since it is possible to recover a *component* of a skill without improving in the overall skill (for example, one's typing might deteriorate even though *g-h* transposition errors decrease) the improvement-reminiscence distinction remains a valid one in the motor skill domain and will be maintained.

Authorities in the field who expressed misgivings about verbal hypermnesia were quite clear in their acceptance of its motor counterpart. In the year before his critical review of the verbal literature, Buxton published a paper on "reminiscence in the acquisition of skill," which was straightforwardly positive. Instead of a now-you-see-it-now-you-don't phenomenon, he found "wide-spread occurrence of reminiscence" (1942, 195). In a discussion of short-term improvement effects, Woodworth and Schlosberg underscored the verbal-motor distinction:

> short-time reminiscence in *verbal learning* is a rather slight effect, varying from experiment to experiment, and often absent. . . . When we turn to motor *learning,* we find a very different state of affairs. Reminiscence, defined as improved performance after a short rest, is a large effect and very dependable. (1954, 797–98)

Eysenck, in a major theoretical article, did not even deign to address verbal improvement effects: "Verbal learning and nonsense-syllable learning are excluded from our discussion because of the great difficulties which seem to attend the very demonstration of reminiscence in their field" (1965, 164).

Actually, hypermnesia for skills—today it might be called hypermnesia for procedural memories—was known and apparently well accepted by the turn of the century. Ballard reviewed some of this literature toward the end of his monograph (under the heading "kindred phenomena") and concluded that the improvement in skills such as swimming, skating, dancing, typing, piano playing, and the like "has been abundantly demonstrated" (1913, 70). Some of the increments reported, moreover, occur over very long time intervals (calling into question the adequacy of "rest" as the description of the interval). He cites work by Swift (1903) suggesting that the skill of throwing and catching a ball improves over 30 days "when no practice at all took place" (1913, 50). One subject was reported to have improved after an "intermission" of 463 days and another after 633 days. Book found typing skill to improve, in one subject, "after a rest interval of a year and a half, during which time a typewriter was not even seen" (1910, 185). Cleveland (1907) reported improvements in chess play over periods varying from weeks to months.

Such long intervals bring to mind the clinical literature discussed in chapter 2 in which highly charged real-world memories increase after prolonged intervals of time. As suggested already, crisp dichotomies of memory such as verbal versus skill, verbal versus behavioral, declarative versus procedural, and so forth should not be espoused uncritically, even if they can be helpful shorthand descriptions. Freud (Breuer and Freud 1895, 297) proposed an interesting alternative: that memory representations ought to be considered to lie on a continuum ranging from highly abstract (verbal) to somewhat concrete (imagery) to very concrete (bodily or behavioral symptoms). Bruner (1964) was later to use the terms, *symbolic, iconic,* and *enactive.* The skill/motor/enactive memory literature might thus have great bearing on clinical phenomena, since many psychopathologies involve sensory-motor symptoms or maladaptive "skills" (sick skills).

This whole area calls for theoretical development (Erdelyi 1985, 1990). For example, how should emotions such as anxiety be handled in the context of memory? Do we remember and forget emotions as we forget words—or skills? How should dream contents be conceptualized? Freud placed them toward the concrete end of the memory-code contin- uum: concretistic ("plastic word") representations of ideas and emotions, or hallucinatory enactments ("dramatizations"). Should oneiric materials be conceived of as procedural memories? Or maybe as a witches' brew of skills, images, affects, words, declarative and procedural memories? To the extent that dreams tap into the domain of so-called skill, sensory- motor, behavioral-procedural memory, it might be expected that they would yield characteristic memory effects. It might not be surprising, therefore (if true), that "dreams are hypermnesic (Freud 1900, 11–21, 589).

The motor "reminiscence" paradigm can be viewed as a positive vari- ant of Pavlovian spontaneous recovery: the subject is exposed to a period of skill learning (instead of a period of "unlearning" or extinction trials) followed by a "rest" period. On retesting after this rest period, the subject exhibits enhanced performance, relative to his prerest level. Two exam- ples of motor hypermnesia are provided in figure 3.3. In both cases, after

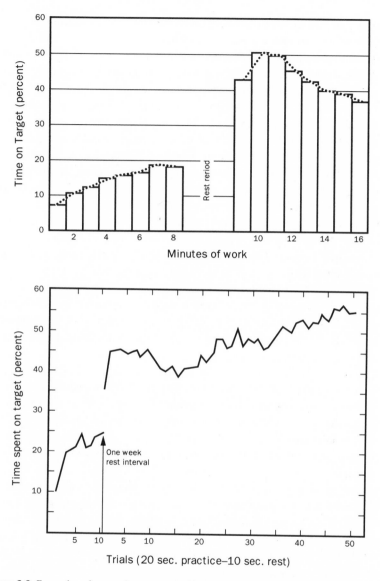

Figure 3.3 Examples of motor hypermnesia. *Top panel* is a plot by Woodworth and Schlosberg (1954, 531) of rotary pursuit performance data from Ammons (1947b, 398) for short rest intervals. The *bottom panel* is a plot by Ammons (1947a, 398) of rotary pursuit data from Pomeroy (1941) for a 1-week interval.

a retention interval of minutes (Ammons 1947a) or a whole week (Pomeroy 1941), performance level starts higher than it left off before the interval.

Others have reported improvement effects with the pursuit motor task (Doré and Hilgard 1937, 1938; Eysenck 1965; Travis 1936), and similar results are readily obtained with other sensory-motor activities such as mirror tracing (Snoddy 1935), letter substitution (Gentry 1940; cited in Buxton 1942), ladder climbing (Stelmach 1968), and (as already noted) maze learning (Bunch and Magsdick 1933).

Thus in the context of sensory-motor skills, the verdict of the midcentury literature on hypermnesia stands in sharp contrast to that on verbal hypermnesia. According to Hovland, "there is . . . no doubt about the *fact* of reminiscence [improvement]" (1951, 653). Yet, as Hovland notes, the interpretation of the effect is not settled: "Truly crucial experiments have still to be performed to demonstrate that reminiscence is a genuine phenomenon of learning, rather than merely of performance" (654–55). In raising the classic learning-performance question, Hovland is in effect raising the issue of whether improvement in skill after a time interval constitutes an artifact: are subjects truly more skillful or are they only producing superior responding? In modern terms, the issue transposes to the distinction between a bona fide memory effect versus a response effect of some sort (for example, response bias). One obvious concern in these studies (which Hovland mentions) is that fatigue sets in after too many learning trials, depressing response performance. The rest period might merely enhance the subjects' capacity or willingness to respond proficiently. We have here a negative test effect. Instead of worrying about the positive effects of previous testing, the negative consequences become the concern.

As with positive test effects, negative effects need not be artifacts. Some performance improvements—as in the "gross motor-task" of "ladder climbing" (Stelmach 1968)—may be nothing but recoveries in the response production system. However, to the extent that "fatigue" or any other disdained variable affects *retrieval efficiency*, hence memory proper, it should not be discarded as artifactual. It may not be surprising—or interesting to many—that fatigue interferes with recall efficiency. Yet this does not mean that the effect (and the recovery from it) is artifactual. Indeed such "obvious" variables may account, unsuspectingly, for quite interesting phenomena in other contexts, as, for example, the possible role of anxiety or depression in perception and memory. Many phenomena that are construed as defensive in nature by psychoanalytically inclined theorists (for example, perceptual defense, repression effects) may result from retrieval disruption brought about not by efforts at defense but by selective disruption by anxiety (Erdelyi 1985, 1990, 1993; Erdelyi and Appelbaum 1973; Erdelyi and Goldberg 1979; Holmes 1974).

To the extent that recovery from fatigue, anxiety, depression, or any other internal state leads to the enhancement of memory, the effect is not artifactual (even if such an effect may not be uniformly interesting to all concerned). Test effects are artifactual only when performance improvements due to more proficient *responding* are confused with more proficient *remembering*. Since, however, motor/skill memories are so entwined in the response system, the separation between learning and performance (or memory and response) effects may prove far more intractable methodologically in the procedural context than in the declarative one. For this reason, perhaps, motor reminiscence/hypermnesia, though it is uncontroversial, has produced little theoretical excitement or elaboration.

FOUR

The Recovery of Information from Complex Subliminal Stimuli

Although it continues to be controversial (for example, Holender 1986), the notion that subliminal stimuli can exert influence on the unaware observer is rapidly evolving into the consensus view in experimental psychology (Bargh 1984; Bornstein, Leone, and Galley 1987; Bornstein and Pittman 1992; Dixon 1981; Greenwald 1992; Kihlstrom 1987; Marcel 1983a, 1983b; Schachter 1987; Reingold 1990; Weiskrantz 1986).

If true, do such "subception" effects imply that the stimulus is registered and stored unconsciously, as has often been assumed (Pötzl 1917; Fisher 1956, 1960a, 1960b, 1988; Shevrin and Dickman 1980); and if so, might it be possible to go beyond indirect stimulus effects—for example, influences on free associations, social judgment, semantic disambiguation, fantasy—and demonstrate the existence of unconsciously registered stimulus contents by recovering them directly into consciousness? It is this last question, on the direct retrievability into consciousness of subliminal inputs, that the present chapter examines.

The Pötzl Phenomenon

Uncharacteristically, this experimental literature arose in a clinical context, that of clinical neuropathology, and evolved in the framework of psychoanalytic theory. It comprises one of the few experimental traditions of psychoanalysis and has, until recently, unfolded in isolation from mainstream laboratory psychology.

The reference study is that of Otto Pötzl (1917), a professor of psychiatry and neurology at the University of Vienna. The background of Pötzl's work was his clinical involvement with a number of patients suffering gunshot wounds in the occipital cortex. What intrigued Pötzl about these patients was that in addition to suffering from a variety of expectable perceptual deficits, some of these patients also evidenced paradoxical enhancements of perceptual sensitivity.

For example, many of these patients were described by Pötzl as having abnormally sensitive peripheral vision—although, at the same time, they also had little or no central vision left. They did, however, often exhibit one form of enhanced central vision: they could perceive their blind spot in perimetry. Another common feature of these patients' visual world was that they often saw in double images ("physiological diplopia"). Finally, and most intriguing to Pötzl, was a phenomenon he termed "delayed piecemeal delivery" into consciousness. The patient would fixate on a stimulus and generally see little (because of the loss of central vision). A short time later, however, coherent fragments of the unseen stimulus would emerge in consciousness, often merged with ongoing (peripheral) percepts. (The phenomenon, as described by Pötzl, makes one think of a reverse Pritchard stabilized-image effect.) Here are two examples reported by Pötzl from a patient named Obszut:

> A military decoration—a gold cross on a white field—is shown to the patient against a dark background. He sees only the white field. When all this is removed and replaced by a dark surface, the patient makes the labored focusing movements which he uses to bring an object into his residual peripheral visual field, and says, "A cross, yellow," indicating the shape by pantomime.
>
> He is shown a bouquet of flowers, from which a conspicuously long, thin stalk of asparagus is sticking out. He sees only the red rose, in keeping with his predilection for red. Now the bouquet is removed and the patient is asked to identify the regimental color on the collar of an officer who is present. By his forced focusing movements he manages to bring the neck of the subject into his residual visual field, and says, "A green tiepin." (Pötzl 1917, 44)

Pötzl notes that "these delayed developments, just like dream images, undergo all sorts of condensations" (44).

Since these types of perceptual "enhancements" resulted from destruction rather than from any addition to the perceptual hardware, Pötzl reasoned that such heightened perceptual sensitivities had to result from the destruction of inhibitory mechanisms that normally blocked maladaptive hypersensitivities. In other words, all of us, in principle, can perceive our blind spot or see the world in double images, but some merciful inhibitory system (Pötzl called it the "abstracting process") intervenes to spare us from such embarrassment of perceptual riches. The clear implication is that much more of the input is registered and processed than is normally accessible to conscious perception.

It occurred to Pötzl to wonder whether it might be possible to demonstrate such disinhibition effects in normal, that is, neurologically intact, subjects.

It will be recalled from chapter 3 that Pavlov in the context of his research on classical conditioning, had also used the notion of disinhibition to account for the phenomenon of *spontaneous recovery* of extinguished conditioned reflexes. Pötzl's inspiration, however, was not Pavlov but Freud. Actually, Pötzl was one of the few established academicians in Vienna of this period to take an active interest in psychoanalysis—indeed, he was a member of the Vienna Psychoanalytic Society for many years.

Thus it may not be surprising that Pötzl settled upon dreams as the special disinhibited state in normal people that might produce the effects seen in his neurological patients. He carried out an experiment upon a dozen subjects (Pötzl 1917), involving the following steps: (1) a *complex pictorial stimulus* (a landscape scene, for example) was flashed for 10 milliseconds by means of a tachistoscope; (2) the subject was required to produce an exhaustive *reproduction,* in the form of a drawing, of what he had seen—which was generally little (in mimicry of the visual agnosics); and (3) the subject was requested to have a *dream* that night and to return next day and report the dream and draw elements of it.

Pötzl's finding was that many initially inaccessible stimulus elements emerged in the content of the subjects' dreams.

Freud was impressed with Pötzl's experiment, which Pötzl presented to the Vienna Psychoanalytic Society in 1917, and in his 1919 revision of the *Interpretation of Dreams,* Freud added the following footnote regarding this work:

> An important contribution to the part played by recent material in the construction of dreams has been made by Pötzl (1917) in a paper that carries a wealth of implications. . . . The material that was taken over by the dream-work was modified by it for the purposes of dream-construction in its familiar "arbitrary" manner. [Here Freud is referring to primary-process operations such as condensations, displacements, primitive symbolizations, and the like.] The questions raised by Pötzl's experiment go far beyond the sphere of dream interpretation as dealt with in the present volume. (1990, 181–82)

Freud is not too specific about the "wealth of implications" he had in mind, but the following might be interpolated: (1) the reality of the unconscious (in this case, unconscious percepts and memory); (2) the possibility of rendering the unconscious conscious; and (3) the power of dreams ("the royal road to the . . . unconscious") to effect such recoveries ("dreams are hypermnesic" [Freud 1900, 11–21, 589]).

Despite Freud's enthusiastic footnote, only a few follow-up studies appeared in the next several decades (Allers and Teler 1924; Malamud and Linder 1931; Malamud 1934) until Charles Fisher revived the area in the 1950s, at the height of the New Look movement (Fisher 1954, 1956, 1960a, 1960b, Fisher and Paul 1959).

Allers and Teler made some important contributions at both the conceptual and procedural levels. They argued that Pötzl's findings did not need to be interpreted in terms of disinhibition, nor linked to dreams as such. Adopting an early dual-code approach (Paivio 1971), Allers and Teler argued that perceptual information was coded in both *word-near* (verbal) and *word-distant* (imagistic) formats, with both formats encoding some nonoverlapping stimulus information. Intentional recall by and large tapped information in the verbal system, missing some of the nonoverlapping information in the imagistic system. Imagery production of various sorts (including but not limited to dreams) would tend to access some of the residual stimulus information.

Allers and Teler sought to corroborate this claim by showing that subjects producing free-associative imagery after trying to reproduce the contents of a complex 40-msec stimulus recovered stimulus information in the imagery that was absent in the preceding intentional perceptual report. The "belatedly emerging elements" (1924, 141) were recovered, according to Allers and Teler, not because of disinhibition but because of the tapping of dissociated information in the nonverbal system. Whether *active inhibition* (as in Freud) or *passive dissociation* (Janet) explains certain types of inaccessibility has reemerged lately as a lively topic in clinical and personality psychology (Bowers and Meichenbaum 1984; Erdelyi 1990). Regardless of this theoretical issue, the Allers and Teler technique of producing the Pötzl phenomenon in waking imagery streamlined the demands of the experiment by circumventing the cumbersome overnight dream requirement and made for a far simpler laboratory demonstration; not surprisingly, most of the modern literature has adopted some variant of the Allers and Teler approach.

Malamud and Linder (1931) also foreshadowed modern developments by showing that Pötzl effects could be obtained with nontachistoscopic stimuli. They showed, with psychotherapy patients as subjects, that unreported elements of a complex stimulus (for example, a picture of the Madonna and child), presented for 30 seconds, emerged in the content of dreams. These recoveries often involved omitted elements associated with the patients' psychological conflicts which, Malamud and Linder as-

Figure 4.1 Fisher's (1956, 24) stimulus of a parakeet perched between two cats.

sumed, had been repressed in the immediate recall. Malamud (1934) extended the procedure to connected verbal materials, showing that omissions or distortions in recall of a passage containing sexual symbolism tended to emerge in dreams. In chapter 8 of the present book, which deals with hypermnesia for prose passages and the issue of Bartlett effects (innocent and Freudian), some of the issues raised by Malamud and Linder are examined further.

Thought provoking as much of this early research might have been, it drifted into obscurity until its revival by Fisher, who was able to replicate Pötzl's effect with dreams and also to show, after Allers and Teler, similar effects with free associations and imagery. A study published in 1956 gives the flavor of the endeavor and illustrates the types of effects that are readily obtained in the laboratory.

Subjects were presented the stimulus in figure 4.1 for a $1/100$ of a second duration and then asked to describe and draw what they had just seen. No subject ever reported awareness of the parakeet at this brief tachistoscopic exposure. The subjects were then asked to produce a word associate to each of a series of stimulus words and to draw the image that came to mind between the stimulus word and the word association.

One subject, for example, in reproducing what she had just seen in the stimulus flash, reported that the stimulus contained "two white and black animals which resembled dogs or pigs" (Fisher 1956, 22). Yet in her reproduction of the two mammals (fig. 4.2), obvious birdlike features appeared. Such fusion of mammal and bird features illustrates the types of *condensations* that Pötzl reported and which are readily obtained in reproductions of tachistoscopic stimuli. To the stimulus word *dog,* the subject in question produced the association *house.* The subject reported that she had "imagined a watchdog standing in front of a house." Her drawing of this image is shown in figure 4.3.

The "dog," clearly, resembles a bird. According to Fisher, "The subject became very confused, wanted to know what was wrong, could not understand why she continued to draw a bird, stating that she knew very well how to draw a dog and had done so many times" (23–24).

Figure 4.2 Subject's drawing of the "two white and black animals which resembled dogs or pigs." (Fisher 1956, 23)

Figure 4.3 Subject's drawing of her free-associative image of "a watchdog standing in front of a house." (Fisher 1956, 25)

Another subject, after the ¹/₁₀₀ second stimulus presentation, produced the drawing in figure 4.4. No bird characteristics are in evidence. However, her subsequent imagery drawings were replete with birdlike figures. Thus to the stimulus word *feathers* she responded, *pillow.* Her image was of a pillow with feathers pouring out at one end. Her drawing of the image is shown in figure 4.5. One bird (or two) are in evidence. The subject suggested that the spilling "feathers" resembled the body and face of a cat.

To the stimulus word *sick* this subject responded, *patient* and drew her image of a sick person in bed (fig. 4.6). Her drawing shows a number of concealed birds in the folds of the blanket. Fisher notes that "reduplication or multiplication" of unconscious percepts is a characteristic feature of these Pötzl effects.

Could these drawings of birdlike figures be the result of chance? Pötzl and also Allers and Teler had raised the question of chance correspondences between the items drawn and the stimulus content but had dismissed it on common-sense grounds. Fisher took a more empirical tack

Figure 4.4 Another subject's reproduction of what she saw in the tachistoscopic stimulus. (Fisher 1956, 27)

Figure 4.5 Drawing of the image of a pillow with feathers spilling out at the right end. (Fisher 1956, 29)

Figure 4.6 Drawing of the image of a patient in bed. (Fisher 1956, 30)

and incorporated a handful of control subjects (6 in all) into the study. These control subjects were presented with a blank stimulus and were then asked to associate to the stimulus words and to draw images, just as the experimental subjects had done. None of the control subjects, according to Fisher, produced any birdlike drawings.

No formal (or blind) scoring scheme was employed by Fisher, however, and so the possibility of a chance base-rate artifact cannot be discounted. Although this early experimental approach was on the impressionistic side, more modern research, based on objective, quantified scoring procedures (Haber and Erdelyi 1967; Shevrin and Luborsky 1958) shows clearly that chance base rates cannot account for these types of outcomes (see below).

There are additional methodological issues, however. One pervasive problem, which will be taken up later in this chapter, is the possibility that differential *reporting criteria*—differential willingness to report out uncertain memories or percepts, irrespective of sensitivity—might account for Pötzl-type effects. Subjects may adopt a laxer response criterion when generating free-associative imagery and dream reports (producing more correct as well as incorrect responses) than when producing an intentional recall. Thus the stimulus recoveries in dreams or fantasy drawings may reflect not the recovery of unconscious materials but only the recovery of unreported materials.

Also, *response number* and *chance base rates* may differ for intentional reports and fantasy. For example (Johnson and Eriksen 1961), more animal images may be produced in fantasy on a chance basis than in intentional recall guessing. If so, blind subjects exposed to stimuli with animals will produce a Pötzl subliminal effect that is entirely spurious.

Moreover, contextual elaboration in fantasy of *part cues* (for example, a subject barely sees a cowboy but embellishes his fantasy report with likely details such as a hat, boots with spurs, a horse) may yield compelling "recoveries" of stimulus content in fantasy (Erdelyi 1970, 1972, 1985; Eriksen 1960; Hilgard 1962; Johnson and Eriksen 1961). Although these various methodological nuances complicate the interpretation of Pötzl effects, control procedures for dealing with them have been introduced in the more modern literature (Giddan 1967; Haber and Erdelyi 1967; Hilgard 1962; Shevrin and Luborsky 1958).

A fundamental problem exists, however, that may prove methodologically refractory (but see Reingold 1990; Merikle and Reingold 1991; Reingold and Merikle 1988). It arises from the fact that Pötzl-type effects are based on the contrast of two different indicators of perception, some kind of *intentional recall* versus some *fantasy* indicator (Erdelyi 1985, 1986; Eriksen 1958; Goldiamond 1958).

Indicators of perception must be relied upon because there is no direct way of assessing what is perceived, consciously or unconsciously. Although it is not typically spelled out, the implicit assumption underlying these types of studies is that one indicator (for example, intentional recall) indexes conscious perception whereas the other indicator (for example, fantasy) reflects unconscious (or conscious plus unconscious) perception. When the indicator of conscious perception, let us designate it α, shows less information than the other, more inclusive indicator of availability, ϵ, the researcher infers the existence of available information that is not accessible to awareness, hence unconscious perception. Thus the discrepancy or dissociation between the output of the two indicators ($\alpha < \epsilon$) is taken to imply a corresponding dissociation between the psychological subsystems indicated, that is, the conscious and unconscious subsystems. For this reason, the general class of designs based on the contrast of two different indicators, α and ϵ, is termed the *dissociation paradigm of the unconscious* (Erdelyi 1985, 1986; Holender 1986; Reingold 1990; Reingold and Merikle 1988).

The problem with the dissociation paradigm is that the face validity of the chosen indicators may not translate into construct validity (Erdelyi 1986). The indicators α and ϵ may not indicate what they are supposed to indicate or they may not be *exhaustive* or *exclusive* (pure) indicators (Reingold 1990; Reingold and Merikle 1988). Further, even if the indicator validity could be assumed, the indicators may not be *comparable* (Reingold 1990; Merikle and Reingold 1991); the indicators may intrinsically differ in a variety of ways, including difficulty, sensitivity, and criterion setting, and so the observed indicator dissociations may not reflect corresponding psychological dissociations.

Hypermnesia for Complex Subliminal Stimuli

In an effort to bypass what they concluded was an unresolvable problem, Haber and Erdelyi (1967) introduced a basic design modification to the standard Pötzl study. In Pötzl-type experiments, a stimulus, S, is presented, followed by an intentional recall, R (for example, a drawing of the stimulus), which is then followed by a fantasy report, F (drawing of dream contents). Thus S–R–F. As noted, the Pötzl phenomenon consists of an interindicator discrepancy F > R, the interpretation of which is complicated by the fact that F and R are two different indicators. Haber and Erdelyi's solution was to transpose the design into an intraindicator comparison. They added an extra step to the Pötzl design, a second, postfantasy recall trial, R_2. Thus $S–R_1–F–R_2$. They reasoned that if fantasy production makes contact with unconscious traces, it is possible that the accessed traces might be carried over into a postfantasy intentional recall and that a postfantasy intentional recall would therefore reflect more stimulus content than a prefantasy intentional recall.

Whereas the traditional Pötzl phenomenon rested on the dissociation paradigm, the between-indicator inequality F > R, the new design type, termed the direct *recovery* or *hypermnesia paradigm* (Erdelyi 1985, 1986), involved the within-indicator inequality $R_2 > R_1$. The *same indicator* is assessed—at two different times. In effect, the Haber and Erdelyi study addressed the question whether stimulus information that was initially inaccessible (unconscious) on R_1 might become accessible (conscious) on a later recall effort, R_2, after a period of free-associative fantasy. The design was seen as a test of the psychoanalytic claim that free associations help recover unconscious memories.

Experimental subjects were presented the stimulus shown in figure 4.7 for a 100 msec exposure. They were then asked to draw everything they had seen in the flash and to label the details in their drawings. This constituted the first intentional recall trial, R_1. Once completed, the recall drawing was collected and never again shown to the subject. The free-associative fantasy task, which lasted some 35 minutes, followed. First the subject was asked to stare at the blank screen for a while and to keep thinking of the previously flashed stimulus. Upon a signal, he was to generate words as they occurred to him. The experimenter stopped the subject once 12 words had been produced. The words thus generated served as

Figure 4.7 The stimulus presented for 100 msec. (Haber and Erdelyi 1967, 624)

cues for further, more extensive free associations involving storylike fantasy productions as well as further word associations (10 per stimulus word). The word associations were later analyzed for semantic relatedness to the stimulus content, whether reported or not. At the conclusion of the free-associative fantasy task the subject was handed a blank sheet of paper and asked to try, once more, to draw as much of the stimulus as he had seen in the original flash. As in the first drawing, he was urged to include all he had seen, even highly uncertain items, short of outright guessing.

To ensure that any memory increments that might be obtained could be ascribed to the free-association activity, a control group was employed that was treated identically except for the free-association task. A sensory-motor task, *dart* throwing, was substituted for the free associations. (A sensory-motor task was used because verbal filler activity was shown by pilot subjects to produce significant interference effects on R_2.)

An additional control group, the *yoked* subjects, was included. These subjects never saw the stimulus but instead copied the R_1 drawing of an experimental counterpart. Thereafter these yoked subjects were treated like experimental subjects, producing free-associative fantasy and a "second" recall, R_2, in which they were encouraged to supplement the contents in their R_1 drawing. The purpose of the yoked group was twofold. First, it provided a control for possible part-cue elaborations, for example, smart guessing based on R_1 content. The second function of the yoked group was to provide free-association base rates against which the experimental subjects' free associations could be evaluated.

The recall drawings were scored by blind judges in a number of ways, all of which lead to essentially the same results: the experimental subjects' postfantasy recall, R_2, contained significantly more stimulus content than the prefantasy recall, R_1. The two control subjects either failed to produce a recall increment or produced significantly less improvement than the experimental subjects. For example, a blind evaluation of R_1-R_2 recall pairs produced a perfect hypermnesic outcome for the 20 experimental subjects: all 20 R_2 drawings of the experimental group were judged to contain more stimulus information than the R_1 drawings ($p = \frac{1}{2}^{20}$). Corresponding evaluations of the recall pairs of the two control groups failed to yield a significant R_2 superiority. Haber and Erdelyi concluded that free-associative fantasy leads to the recovery of unconscious percepts. Figure 4.8 provides two examples of pre- and postfantasy recall drawings by experimental subjects.

An analysis of the free associations was also undertaken with the Pötzl effect in mind. A blind judge subjectively scored each association for semantic relatedness to the stimulus contents. The aggregated scores for all the free associations of a subject was the stimulus emergence measure for the subject. (Interjudge reliabilities for these aggregate subjective scores are surprisingly high, in the region of $r = 0.85$.) The resultant scores showed that stimulus content that was never reported (either in R_1 or R_2) nevertheless emerged significantly in the content of the experimental subjects' free associations compared to the yoked subjects' free associations. Thus $F > R_1$ and R_2. Both the hypermnesia and the dissociation paradigms seemed to document unconscious perception and its recovery into consciousness.

Signal detection theory (Green and Swets 1966; Swets 1964; Swets, Tanner, and Birdsall 1961) was entering the mainstream of experimental psychology around this period, and the question of response-bias effects stood out as a salient issue. Positive as the Haber and Erdelyi study had been on all counts, the results were also open to a response-criterion interpretation. Thus postfantasy recall might be better than prefantasy recall because response criteria were relaxed in R_2 relative to R_1, resulting in more hits—and also more false alarms. Similarly, free associations might

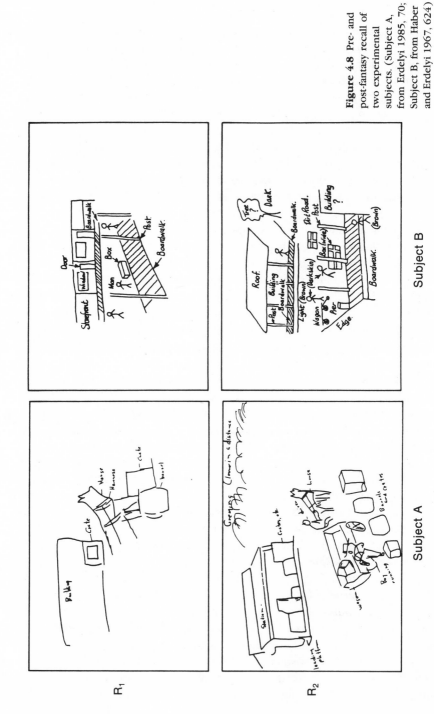

Figure 4.8 Pre- and post-fantasy recall of two experimental subjects. (Subject A, from Erdelyi 1985, 70; Subject B, from Haber and Erdelyi 1967, 624)

Subject B

Subject A

R_1

R_2

reflect low-criterion information that was hazarded in neither R_1 nor R_2. Since the criterion interpretation posed a major stumbling block to the Haber and Erdelyi conclusion, I undertook a series of studies to address the issue (Erdelyi, 1968, 1970, 1972).

Two basic strategies were pursued. One was to determine whether the recovery effect would survive the control of response number in R_2. The basic Haber and Erdelyi design was used with one important extension. After subjects had completed their posttask free recall (free in the sense that the subject was free to produce as many responses as he felt appropriate), the subject was instructed to generate best guesses of remaining items until a preset response number was reached. The *free recall* R_2 responses plus the *guessed* responses constituted the R_2 *forced-recall* performance (forced in the sense that the subject was forced to produce a predesignated number of responses).

When response number was not controlled, the Haber and Erdelyi recovery effect was replicated (Erdelyi 1968, 1970). As table 4.1 shows, the experimental free-recall scores (a composite measure) increased reliably from an initial 3.43 to 4.48, for a difference of 1.05. This increase, moreover, was significantly greater than the corresponding R_1 to R_2 increments of both the dart and yoked control groups (0.34 and 0.42), which were not reliable. However, as table 4.1 shows, when *forced* R_2 (R_2^*) was compared to R_1, the experimental group's change score (4.02) was no longer greater than the dart control group's (4.37). Clearly, free-associative fantasy does not improve memory, even if it does induce, when not controlled, enhanced responding and therefore more hits and false alarms. The two groups that actually saw the stimulus, the experimental and dart subjects, did exceed the forced-recall performance of the yoked subjects, who had not seen the stimulus. This difference is entirely consistent with signal detection theory: The yoked subjects were only guessing, whereas the experimental and dart subjects were, in addition, producing subcriterion recalls.

Table 4.1 The recovery effect with and without control over posttask response productivity: Experimental, dart, and yoked group's average R_1 and R_2 free-recall and R_2 forced-recall (R_2^*) scores

	R_1	R_2	R_2^*	$R_2 - R_1$	$R_2^* - R_1$
Group					
Experimental	3.43	4.48	7.45	1.05	4.02
Dart	3.82	4.16	8.19	0.34	4.37
Yoked	3.38	3.80	5.92	0.42	2.54

Source: Erdelyi 1970, 104.

The second approach to the criterion question was to transpose from a recall to a recognition test of memory and actually measure rather than merely control *sensitivity* and *criteria.* Signal detection theory procedures were employed (Swets 1964) to generate receiver operating characteristic (ROC) curves, which depict hit rate as a function of false alarm rate, and from which the sensitivity parameter (d', p(A), or another homologue) and the criterion (β, and so on) can be calculated. As the top panel of figure 4.9 shows, the experimental group's postfantasy ROC curve (R_2) did not exceed prefantasy (R_1) sensitivity, even if the criterion points (obtained from confidence ratings and represented by the points on the ROC curves) did shift following fantasy, with strict criteria becoming laxer and lax criteria, stricter.

The bottom panel of figure 4.9 shows the corresponding results for the dart subjects. No sensitivity change occurred after dart throwing, nor were there any criterion shifts in evidence. The distinct criterion-shift pattern after fantasy without a concomitant shift after dart throwing was obtained in another study (Erdelyi 1968), and so it should not be laid to a regression to the mean effect. Rather, the ROC functions suggest that, at least in recognition, fantasy does not have a homogeneous effect on response criteria but, rather, a buffering effect such that following fantasy, strict criterion settings are relaxed and lax criteria are made stricter. (This unexpected result, as noted in Erdelyi 1988, may apply to hypnosis effects on memory, which heretofore have been viewed as yielding overall relaxation of response criteria; see chap. 7.)

Both the recall and recognition measures thus converged on the disappointing conclusion that free associations do not yield the recovery of information in a complex subliminal stimulus; rather, free associations relax response criteria (in the strict criterion region, anyway), yielding both more correct and incorrect recalls. In a study bearing on the Pötzl phenomenon, Erdelyi (1972) assessed the emergence of undetected stimuli in free associations as compared to their emergence in (an equivalent number of) guesses. Although in both cases performance was better than chance, the guesses were actually superior to the free associations in reflecting undetected stimulus content. (For a similar finding of a direct indicator yielding superior performance to an indirect one, see Merikle and Reingold 1991; Reingold 1990, study 1.) These results raise the question whether the classic Pötzl phenomenon along with derivative followups, such as those of Allers and Teler (1924) and Fisher (1954, 1956, 1960a, 1960b; Fisher and Paul 1959), constitute nothing but a criterion effect in which—not surprisingly—subjects adopt laxer response criteria in fantasy than in intentional recall.

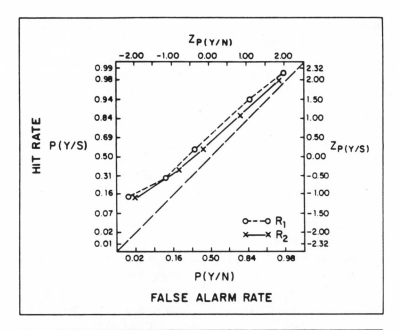

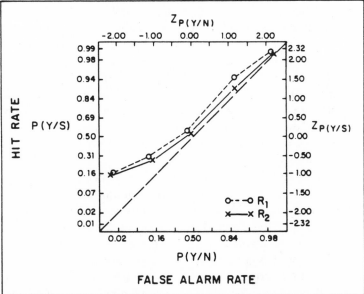

Figure 4.9 R_1 and R_2 ROC functions for the experimental (top panel) and dart control (bottom panel) groups, plotted on normal-normal coordinates. (Erdelyi 1970, 108)

In an effort to overturn the disappointing recovery findings of Erdelyi (1968, 1970), Ionescu (1993; Ionescu and Erdelyi 1992) set out to correct a flaw in the design of the earlier recall studies. The use in these studies of forced recall in R_2 had ensured that any possible group differences in recovery would not be artifacts of differential response criteria. Since the free association and dart control subjects did not, in fact, differ in posttask forced recall (R_2^*), no hypermnesic property could be ascribed to free-associative fantasy. What the design failed to address, however, was the possibility—not seriously considered at the time because of a lack of familiarity with the Ballard tradition—that subliminal stimuli could be recovered in the second recall trial *irrespective of the preceding task.* That is, both groups exposed to the stimulus, the free association and the dart subjects, might be hypermnesic, and to an equivalent extent. The recognition data, with overlapping R_1 and R_2 ROC functions, seemed to argue against any such general hypermnesic trend. What was not known at the time, however, was that multitrial recognition performance is decidedly not parallel to multitrial recall performance (Erdelyi 1985, 1988; Erdelyi and Stein 1981; Payne and Roediger 1987) and so cannot be used as a basis for generalizing to recall. (Recognition hypermnesia, hypnotic and nonhypnotic, will be taken up in some detail in chap. 7.)

In order to evaluate recall hypermnesia for subliminal stimuli, it is necessary to use forced recall not only in R_2 but also in the initial recall trial, R_1 (or, in multitrial recall exceeding two trials, in all recall trials). Ionescu (1993; Ionescu and Erdelyi 1992), implementing the necessary adjustment of using forced recall in both earlier and later trials, evaluated hypermnesia for the tachistoscopic stimulus that had been used by Erdelyi (1968, 1970). Testing subjects at three different exposure durations—10 msec, 50 msec, and 500 msec—Ionescu found no hypermnesia at any of the exposure levels.

As far as the recovery of information from tachistoscopically flashed stimuli is concerned, the results have been unremittingly negative up to this point. A reasonable conclusion is that direct recovery of subliminal inputs, beyond criterion effects, does not occur. This surmise might not turn out to be the final word on the topic, however. Chapter 7 takes up some subliminal studies growing from the modern experimental literature on hypermnesia (described in the next two chapters) and suggests that recognition hypermnesia for subliminal stimuli might be obtained for *lists* of simple stimuli (in contrast to a single complex stimulus).

FIVE

Rehabilitation of Hypermnesia and Reminiscence in Modern Experimental Psychology

What could be legitimately concluded from the negative results reported in the previous chapter on the retrievability of subliminal stimuli? Were clinicians mistaken in their belief that unconscious materials could be reactivated, confusing confabulation or response-bias effects with true memory recoveries? Are past events of which we are not conscious irretrievably lost?

Not only clinical experience but also common sense militates against such sweeping rejection of recovery phenomena. Do not, for example, "tip-of-the-tongue" effects (Ballard 1913, 36; R. Brown and McNeill 1966) or bouts of "momentary forgetting" (Luborsky, Sackeim, and Christoph 1979) offer compelling everyday examples of the retrievability of inaccessible materials? Or are they also only unsuspected criterion artifacts? That this was not the case was readily apparent to me from a number of annoying tests I performed upon myself for a few weeks in the early 1970s. On the occasions I could not remember a name, I would force myself to write down some dozen guesses. Not once did these guesses lead to the target name. Failure to recover the information was, apparently, no criterion artifact. Moreover, consistent with common experience, the fugitive name would often reappear spontaneously a little while later, with no sense of doubt attached to it.

Perhaps a distinction was in order between *subliminal inputs*—stimuli that were never conscious to the subject—and *subliminal memories*—stimuli that may have been conscious but subsequently became inaccessible (see Erdelyi 1984, 1992). Possibly, subliminal tachistoscopic inputs are not registered or processed sufficiently to be amenable to subsequent recovery; subliminal memories, on the other hand, might behave quite differently and be subject to recovery. The types of memory recoveries that clinicians report are, after all, not the contents of stimulus flashes but information that was conscious at one time but subsequently forgotten.

Thus it could be the case that recovery effects that refuse to materialize with subliminal percepts manifest themselves with subliminal memories. With this perception-memory distinction in mind, and with no familiarity with the Ballard tradition, my student Joan Becker and I attempted, in the early 1970s, a last experiment (last because I was ready to give up on the research area, barring some positive results) in which the study was transposed from one on subliminal perception to one on subliminal memory. Instead of a single stimulus flash, the "stimulus" became a memory list of 80 items, *each individually exposed* for the incontrovertibly supraliminal duration of *5 seconds.* Unless subjects close their eyes at these exposure durations, they operate at a 100% perception level, as can be established by having them call out each stimulus item as it is being shown.

Despite perfect initial perception, memory for the stimulus list is limited. Immediate tests after the presentation of the list typically yield about 50 items forgotten out of the 80 presented. The question becomes whether the 50 forgotten items are lost for good or are retained unconsciously; and, if so, whether they are potentially recoverable. It was this question, the retrievability of subliminal memories, that Erdelyi and Becker (1974) sought to address.

Effects Over Short Time Intervals (Minutes)

Of the 80 stimuli used by Erdelyi and Becker, 40 were simple pictures and 40 were words. Each picture was a sketch of an object (for example, a watch, a fish, a boomerang, a feather); each of the 40 words was a printed verbal label for an item selected from the same set as the pictures. The stimuli were copied to slides and randomly mixed so that the word and picture slides occurred in an unpredictable order. Word stimuli were used along with the pictures on the chance that recall of verbal as opposed to pictorial material would be sensitive to free-associative activity, the idea being that free associations, wandering unrestricted across the semantic landscape, would from time to time cue verbal items (Tulving 1983) and result in verbal recoveries.

Each of the 80 slides was successively presented for 5 seconds, for a total presentation duration of approximately 7 minutes. After some brief instructions (to eliminate recency effects), subjects were administered their first recall, R_1.

Subjects were instructed to enter their recalls into blanks in a recall protocol, in the order in which the items occurred to them. Further, all recalled items, whether they had been pictures or words, were to be rendered in written form; thus when recalling a picture, the subject was to enter the name of the picture rather than attempting to draw it. (This procedure avoided the problem of individual differences in the ability to draw and the high variability in time taken to draw pictures.) When the subject could recall no more, she (all subjects were female) was asked to draw a line under the last bona fide recall and then to produce unrepeating "smart guesses" in the remaining recall blanks. If, as often happened, an item from the stimulus returned in the course of guessing, the subject was to place a check next to the response to indicate that it was a true recall and not just a guess. Thus the above-the-line responses plus the checked items below the line constituted the free recalls of the subject. These free-recalls plus the guesses (the unchecked, below-the-line guesses) comprised the forced recalls. The analyses, unless otherwise indicated, were based on the forced-recall measure, that is, the total number of test responses, 60 in this case.

This first recall test, which was collected from the subject upon completion, was followed by 7 minutes of fantasy activity which, because the subjects were tested in groups, was in written form (that is, "automatic writing"). Subjects were handed booklets and instructed to write whatever occurred to them, with minimal conscious direction or censorship. The automatic writing was collected after 7 minutes and then a second recall test, R_2, administered. Because of the shortened fantasy activity between R_1 and R_2, a second 7-minute fantasy period was administered, followed by a third and final forced-recall test, R_3.

Since by this time I had developed doubts about the hypermnesic nature of free-associative fantasy, a second experimental group was tested which engaged in *silent thinking* between recall trials rather than free associating. This group was suggested by a similar technique used by Freud in the *Studies on Hysteria* (1895), which he called the *concentration* or *pressure* procedure, after he gave up hypnosis but before he took up free associations. At this early stage, the consciousness-raising goal of cathartic therapy and psychoanalysis was essentially hypermnesia (for facts and affects) rather than "insight," the emphasis to which the therapy shifted with the ascendancy of free associations.

Freud's concentration-pressure technique essentially comprised hypnotic motivational instructions without formal hypnotic induction. When the patient could recall no more, Freud would assert that the information was in fact available and it was only a question of the patient trying harder to recover the material. Basically, Freud refused to take no for an answer. He put "pressure" on the subject to concentrate more (often placing his hand on the patient's forehead) and admonished the patient not to give up until the recalcitrant memory returned. The silent-think procedure of

Table 5.1 Recall over three successive trials for the three groups (free-association, think, and no-interval)

	Average Recall Scores					
	Pictures			Words		
Group	R_1	R_2	R_3	R_1	R_2	R_3
Free association	16.65	18.30	18.59	14.00	14.17	14.23
Think	15.76	17.76	18.94	16.35	16.82	17.00
No interval	15.82	17.11	18.05	13.41	12.47	13.00

Source: Erdelyi and Becker 1974, 163.

Erdelyi and Becker was essentially a soft-sell version of Freud's badgering concentration technique. The lights were dimmed and the subject was told to sit quietly, closing her eyes if she wanted, and to think back to the stimulus list that had been presented earlier and which she had just tried to recall. (The subject was not touched by the experimenter.) In every other respect this think-concentrate group was treated identically to the free-association group.

A third group of subjects, who engaged in no interpolated activity between recall trials but immediately proceeded from one trial to the next, served as a control group to assess whether either of the interpolated activities, free association or thinking, affected hypermnesia, if any were found. Although I was not aware of it at the time, the adopted design, excluding the interpolated activity, was a recapitulation of Ballard's repeated testing procedure, except that three trials were elicited instead of the usual two in Ballard's case. The results of this experiment are summarized in table 5.1.

The most striking (and unexpected) finding was the difference in recall trends for pictures and words. Whereas words, regardless of intervening activity, were not hypermnesic (so much for my hunch about free associations augmenting verbal recall), picture recall was significantly incremental for all three groups. Free associations produced the numerically lowest recall increments, the think group the highest, although this interaction (group × recall-trial) was not reliable. Thus although no evidence was garnered for free-associative fantasy as a hypermnesic agent, significant hypermnesias were obtained—but only for picture recall.

The handful of psychologists to whom the unpublished results were shown were also surprised by them. Contemporary research on multitrial recall of word lists (Darley and Murdock 1971; Donaldson 1971; Hogan and Kintsch 1971; Nelson and MacLeod 1974; Rosner 1970; Tulving 1967) usually showed retention functions to be flat or slightly amnesic. The pattern obtained by Erdelyi and Becker with word lists was the typical outcome; it was the incremental picture recall functions that were aberrant. Replication of the findings became a high priority. Moreover, it was important to check the effect with a pure rather than a mixed-stimulus list since there was a possibility that a subtle response-bias artifact might account for the picture-word differences in hypermnesia. This could happen if subjects relaxed their criteria for reporting pictures over successive trials and concomitantly adopted stricter criteria for words over trials. The forced-recall procedure only controlled for criterion shifts for the list as a whole and not for any subset, for example, the picture items. Consequently, in the replication study a pure-list design was adopted in which subjects were presented either just pictures (60 of them) or verbal labels corresponding to the pictures.

Since the interpolated free-association activity had shown no hint of augmenting the hypermnesia effect (numerically it produced the lowest picture recall increment), this group was dropped from the replication, which became a 2 × 2 independent group design with two stimulus conditions (pictures vs. words) crossed with two interpolation conditions (silent thinking vs. no interpolated activity). In this study, either 60 pictures or 60 words (the names of the pictures) were presented to subjects. The procedures were otherwise the same as in the initial study. Subjects were required to produce 60 written forced recalls in each of the successive recall trials. The results of this follow-up study are shown in figure 5.1.

The outcomes were fully consistent with the earlier study. Word recall failed to improve over time and recall trials whereas pictures improved significantly. This time, the statistical analysis suggested that the interpolated think intervals enhanced hypermnesia.

No mysterious properties were attributed to the think intervals. They were viewed, simply, as covert counterparts of overt recall. The more recall effort, overt or covert, the more hypermnesia. This can be garnered from figure 5.2, which plots recall as a function of retrieval time, both overt and covert, in study 2 of Erdelyi and Becker (1974).

Clearly, it makes no difference, at least in this study, whether retrieval is in the form of official recall trials or covert recall trials in the form of silent thinking; recall of pictures (but not of words) increases with retrieval time, overt or covert (Erdelyi and Kleinbard 1978; Roediger and Thorpe 1978; Shapiro and Erdelyi 1974). From this vantage point, free-associative fantasy may be viewed as inefficient retrieval effort.

The Erdelyi and Becker studies experimentally corroborated the exis-

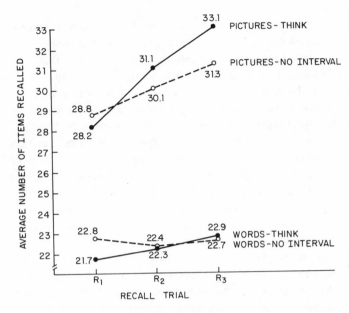

Figure 5.1 Picture and word recall over successive recall trials with and without interpolated think intervals. (Erdelyi and Becker 1974, 165)

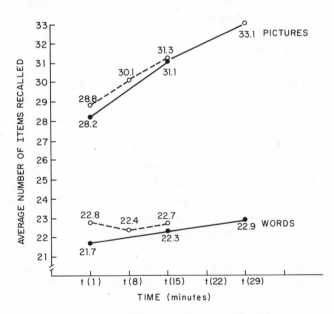

Figure 5.2 Recall of pictures and words as a function of retrieval time, overt or covert, in study 2 of Erdelyi and Becker 1974. (Erdelyi 1977)

tence of hypermnesia for "subliminal stimuli"—in a manner of speaking. After failing to obtain hypermnesia for inaccessible (subliminal) perceptual inputs, hypermnesia was obtained for inaccessible (subliminal) memories.

Also, this work, along with that of Erdelyi (1972) on the superiority of direct guessing over free associations, suggested that free-association activity had no effective role in hypermnesia, except insofar as it functioned as retrieval effort.

Aside from surface details, my experimental program had unwittingly merged with the Ballard tradition. Whether two or three recall trials were used, the basic phenomenon was that recall for certain classes of stimuli increased rather than decreased over time. Some of the issues that had bedeviled the Ballard literature began to be addressed.

Various arguments were advanced, for example, against overt recall practice (whether artifact or not) providing an explanation for the obtained hypermnesia effects (Ballard's "improvement"). To begin with, it seemed unlikely that "practice" effects would be involved in the writing of words onto a recall protocol. Further, if a practice effect was subtly operating, the same "practice" that produced picture hypermnesia was not producing word hypermnesia. And still further, the subjects who engaged in silent thinking produced heftier hypermnesias than those who didn't, even though the number of "practice trials" were constant throughout.

That hypermnesia could not possibly be a simple function of previous overt practice was demonstrated directly by Shapiro and Erdelyi (1974). They showed (using a standard between-condition design; see chap. 3) that subjects tested *only once* after a 5-minute interval of silent thinking recalled reliably more pictures than subjects tested after only half a minute of thinking: R_1 (0.5 min) = 29.61; R_1 (5 min) = 33.06. With word lists, however, recall tended (though not significantly) to be amnesic: R_1 (0.5 min) = 24.33; R_1 (5 min) = 22.78.

The subjects in the Shapiro and Erdelyi study were urged to think of the stimuli during the retention interval. Thus "covert practice" was explicitly encouraged. Unlike the post-Ballard literature, retrieval effort, overt or covert, was conceived of as a critical variable and not as an artifact. Indeed, it was in order to underscore the inclusion of covert practice in the phenomenon and to circumvent the terminological habits that had become encrusted in the post-Ballard literature (in violation of Ballard's own conventions, as we have seen), that I (Erdelyi and Becker 1974) chose to introduce the generic term *hypermnesia* (Rapaport 1967; Talland 1968). *Hypermnesia* was used in a purely descriptive, theoreti-

Table 5.2 Recall on three successive tests following a filled interval of 2 minutes ("immediate" group), 11 minutes ("short delay" group) or 20 minutes ("long delay" group)

Condition	Items recalled				
Immediate	Test 1	Test 2	Test 3		
(2 min)	25.6	27.9	30.1		
Short delay		Test 1	Test 2	Test 3	
(11 min)		25.1	27.5	29.8	
Long delay			Test 1	Test 2	Test 3
(20 min)			25.6	28.9	31.3

Source: Roediger and Payne 1982, 69.

cally noncommittal fashion to designate net improvement of memory over time, whether retrieval effort was or was not involved (Erdelyi 1984; Erdelyi and Becker 1974; Erdelyi and Kleinbard 1978).

Consensus rapidly developed, however, that retrieval effort of some sort was essential to hypermnesia. Not only had silent retrieval intervals enhanced recall in the Erdelyi and Becker and the Shapiro and Erdelyi studies, but Roediger and Payne (1982), using a design similar to that of Gray (1940) and Ammons and Irion (1954)—and Ballard (1913, 36)—published findings showing that when covert retrieval effort was blocked through a distracting task, picture hypermnesia failed to develop. Once the distracting task was terminated and subjects were allowed to attempt multiple recalls of the picture list, hypermnesia kicked in. These findings are shown in table 5.2.

It is interesting, as Roediger and Payne note, that no recall decrement is evident after either the short (11 minutes) or long (20 minutes) filled interval, as one might expect from Ebbinghaus. Does this mean that no forgetting occurred? It does not. What this flat function illustrates is the seemingly arcane point made earlier that the Ebbinghaus function is really an *amnesia curve* rather than a *forgetting* curve. It may be safely assumed that subjects both forgot (oblivesced) previously recalled items as well as recovered (reminisced) previously unrecalled items. Evidently, Roediger and Payne's distractor task, the reading of an article from the *American Scientist,* fortuitously lead to a clean balance between reminiscence and oblivescence. Had subjects been recalling words, which are more oblivescence prone than pictures, or had they been administered a distractor task that was more interfering, oblivescence would have exceeded reminiscence over the 20-minute interval and produced a more Ebbinghaus-like (amnesic) function. Indeed, recent studies show that by systematically varying the nature of the interpolated activity between recall trials, both amnesia and hypermnesia can be obtained, depending on the nature of the intertest filler activity (Shaw and Bekerian 1991; Payne, Hembrooke, and Anastasi 1993).

What is clear from these various findings is that *recall time,* whether in the form of test duration (Roediger and Thorpe 1978), amount of silent recall effort (Erdelyi and Becker 1974; Shapiro and Erdelyi 1974), or number of overt recall trials (Erdelyi and Becker 1974; Roediger and Thorpe 1978; Roediger and Payne 1982), critically influences hypermnesia. This influence results from the impact of recall time on the components of hypermnesia—reminiscence and oblivescence—both of which increase with recall time (see below). Pictures produce hypermnesic functions with extra recall effort/time because the *balance* between picture reminiscence and picture oblivescence tends to increase with recall time; words also yield increases of both reminiscence and oblivescence, but the balance between the two tends not to increase over time, or not as reliably as with pictures. Therefore hypermnesia for words fails to occur, or occurs less reliably.

A major difference between the modern and the midcentury approach to hypermnesia (improvement) is that recall time (or effort) is viewed as a critical factor and not as an artifact. Thus hypermnesia is not linked to the mere passage of time but to "psychological time" (Erdelyi 1977). It occurs over time but not as an effect of time.

As already noted (chap. 3), the modern cognitive conception of covert recall effort (formerly, "internal review," "covert practice") is not restricted to mere rehash activities but also includes other memory processes such as active retrieval effort, memory reorganization, and stimulus elaboration and recoding. Further, *overt* recall in agreement with Ballard, is accepted as a legitimate contributor to hypermnesia (even though it is not necessary) as long as it involves bona fide memory effects.

Actually, no theoretical distinction is drawn between covert and overt recall. In practice, however, overt recall effort can have more powerful effects than covert recall over long intervals because overt recall ensures that subjects actually engage in the work of recollection. When the recall effort is covert, the experimenter has no direct way of assessing that the subject is carrying out the task. Indeed, subjects readily confess to spending portions of silent think intervals on subject matters other than the stimulus list. Overt recall may also enhance retention of previously recalled items because the subject remembers, in addition to the original stimulus, the act of producing the response, reading the production (or hearing it, if vocalized), and so forth.

Thus recall effort, whether overt or covert, is treated in the modern literature as a critical, perhaps necessary factor in reminiscence and hypermnesia, at least over time intervals of minutes to a few days. (Ongoing research, described in chapter 8, suggests that the rules may change when the intervals extend over months.) The legitimization of recall effort does not, of course, guarantee that the phenomena of reminiscence and hypermnesia are therefore interesting or important. As already suggested, the interest value or "importance" of a phenomenon is a tricky scientific question. Ultimately the issue is settled empirically by the extent to which the phenomenon proves to have implications for the field. Some of these implications have already been touched on; others will be drawn out in what follows. The concluding chapter (chapter 9) systematically addresses some of the theoretical implications of reminiscence and hypermnesia for the psychology of memory and for cognate fields, especially psychodynamics, psychopathology, and subliminal processes.

At this juncture, the critical "significance" issue is statistical rather than conceptual: how reliable are reminiscence and hypermnesia effects? Apparently very reliable, as long as recall effort is allowed and meaningful pictorial materials are used as stimuli.

In the initial Erdelyi and Becker study (1974), all three independent groups produced hypermnesia for pictures. In the follow-up study (experiment 2), both picture groups yielded hypermnesia. Roediger and Payne (1982) further demonstrated picture hypermnesia in three independent groups with a repeated-tests design. Shapiro and Erdelyi (1974) succeeded in obtaining hypermnesia for pictures with a single-test design. The evidence for hypermnesia—and therefore reminiscence—seems to be overwhelming. Indeed, if there is any question about the data it is whether word lists might not also yield hypermnesia effects.

In one early follow-up on the Erdelyi and Becker study, Yarmey (1976) found picture-word differences in hypermnesia of the sort originally reported. As Yarmey's figure (fig. 5.3) shows, picture recall is highly incremental, even more so than in previous studies, but word recall, whether for concrete or abstract nouns, remains constant over trials. Madigan (1976) also found hypermnesia for pictures in the absence of hypermnesia for words. Other investigators, however (for example, Roediger and Thorpe 1978), have reported hypermnesia with word lists as well. In a review of the burgeoning literature, Payne (1987) found that studies using picture stimuli yielded hypermnesia with virtual unanimity—49 of 51 of the reviewed studies, or 96%, did so—whereas fewer than 50% (56 of 121) of the studies with word lists produced reliable hypermnesias. As will be seen below, how the subject encodes the verbal inputs is a major determinant of whether hypermnesia for word stimuli is or is not ob-

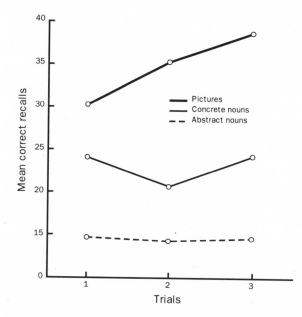

Figure 5.3 Hypermnesia for pictures but not for concrete or abstract words. (Redrawn after Yarmey 1976, 116)

tained, and this factor by itself accounts for a substantial portion of the variability in the word-list data.

Effects Over Long-Term Intervals (Days and Weeks)

The studies considered up to this point have been restricted to a single, one-hour laboratory period. Since the trajectories of the obtained picture hypermnesia functions suggest that further improvement is likely with additional recall effort, a question of theoretical and practical importance is the limit, if any, of picture hypermnesia. Is it possible that, given sufficient time and recall effort, picture recall might approach the vaunted levels of picture recognition memory (Nickerson 1965; Shepard 1967; Standing, Conezio, and Haber 1970)? To probe the question, Erdelyi and Kleinbard (1978) investigated the course of repeated recall over an interval of a week. The first study involved a single subject, the junior author, Jeff Kleinbard. Kleinbard did not know in advance that he would be attempting multiple recall efforts beyond a single laboratory session. I tested him with a list of 40 pictures, in a single laboratory period (of five successive recall tests), on the pretext that he should have the experience of being a subject before testing subjects himself on some yet unspecified hypermnesia experiments. At the conclusion of the five laboratory tests, Kleinbard was not shown the stimulus list but instead was asked to submit to protracted additional testing over the course of a full week's interval. He was to be his own experimenter, testing himself at least three times a day with the forced-recall procedure (for predesignated test intervals of 5 minutes) and to seal his recalls in individual envelopes provided him, to ensure that none of his earlier recalls would be accidentally seen by him. Beyond the formal self-administered tests, Kleinbard was asked to spend as much time as possible thinking and covertly recalling the stimulus list. As a collaborator, Kleinbard could be counted on to operate with high motivation, something of a question with other subjects, given the boring nature of the task (according to subjects).

Figure 5.4 shows Kleinbard's recall curve over the course of a week. It will be readily seen that he achieved a striking amount of hypermnesia, improving from $R_1 = 19$ items to $R_n = 32$ a week later, for a net increase of some 70%. By the last trial, he was recalling 32 of the original 40 stimulus items, or 80% of them. Performance on the last trial, R_n, actually underestimates overall recall of the stimulus items since several of the items were recovered earlier but failed to be carried over to the last trial.

A measure of *cumulative recall,* in which recoveries are cumulated across trials, irrespective of losses (see below), provides a count of total recall up to and including any recall trail, R_i. Figure 5.5 shows Kleinbard's cumulative recall function. Cumulative recall at trial R_n—cum R_n—reached 36, or 90% of the 40 stimulus items. In other words, if the n trials (n = 26) are treated as a "supertrial" consisting of 26 successive subtrials administered over a period of a week, Kleinbard's total recall of stimulus items reached 90%.

The phenomenology of the work of recall may have some bearing on a theoretical accounting of hypermnesia, and so Kleinbard's postexperi-

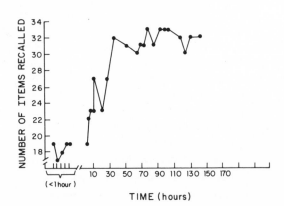

Figure 5.4 Kleinbard's recall level over a week of repeated testing (Erdelyi and Kleinbard 1978, 278). Data points represent recall trials.

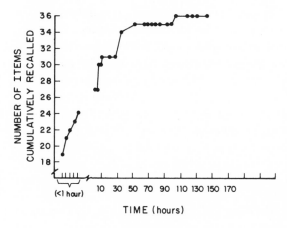

Figure 5.5 Number of stimulus items cumulatively recalled by Kleinbard over successive recall tests (Erdelyi and Kleinbard 1978, 279). Data points represent recall trials over a week of testing.

mental comments on his subjective experiences and strategies are of some interest:

> During the early trials, I began to organize the words into small clusters of two or three items each. Without conscious direction or effort, I evolved a variety of clusters with no one type predominant. Among them were common associations (e.g. tree-snake and key-chain), physical word resemblances (e.g. snake, snail), functional resemblances (e.g. toothbrush, comb), and abstract sets (e.g. appliances: TV, iron, telephone).
>
> I made my hypermnesic recoveries in two distinctly different ways. The first, which occurred relatively early, was via environmental recognitions: e.g., feather—I was returning home from the lab on the first day of the experiment when I saw a feather lying on the ground and suddenly recognized it as one of the picture items; telephone— during the very same trip, I recognized "telephone" as an item upon seeing a pay-phone in a subway station. This recognition had not occurred until 8 hours into the experiment although I had seen numerous telephones earlier in the day; key—particularly interesting is that I recovered this item via an auditory recognition; specifically, I heard the jingle of some keys and recognized "key" as a picture item. This occurred an hour after the lab period.
>
> The second way in which I recovered items was less item-specific but ultimately more productive. By far, the most interesting subjective experience was getting a general "visual feeling" in my mind for a

particular shape such as a length or roundness. I remember seeing a vague, oblong shape in my mind from which I was able to extract such items as gun, broom, and baseball bat; from an inverted cup form—bell, funnel, and bottle (the bottle in the stimulus resembled a bell-jar); from a rectangular box—table and book. Just before many of these recoveries, I often . . . was certain a particular item was on the verge of recovery but which would take its time before suddenly coalescing into an image in consciousness. (Erdelyi and Kleinbard 1978, 279–80)

Since the first study was based on the performance of only a single subject, Erdelyi and Kleinbard (1978, study 2) extended their investigation to a larger sample of six subjects: three subjects who repeatedly attempted to recall 60 pictures and three subjects who attempted to recall 60 word counterparts. Except for an initial and a final set of formal tests in the laboratory, the subjects served as their own experimenters, as had Kleinbard, self-administering forced-recall tests about twice a day for 7-minute intervals. (As before, each recall effort, upon its completion, was sealed in an envelope.)

Figure 5.6 depicts the course of recall for the picture and word groups. On the average, picture recall increased from $R_1 = 26.7$ items in the first few minutes to $R_n = 38.3$ items a week later, for a net gain of some 44% ($p < 0.01$). Although word recall also appears to increase ($R_1 = 25.3$, $R_n = 29.7$), the change was not statistically reliable. Moreover, the stimulus-trial interaction was significant, indicating that the increase in picture recall was greater than the trend in word recall over trials.

Even though word recall failed to improve reliably, it was not inert.

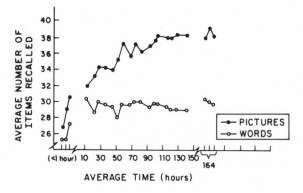

Figure 5.6 The course of recall for picture and word lists over a week's interval of repeated testing (Erdelyi and Kleinbard 1978, 282). Data are for the 3 subjects per group in study 2.

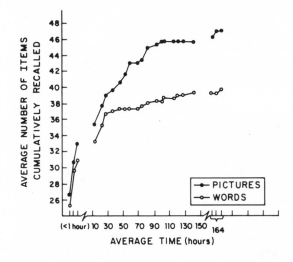

Figure 5.7 Average number of pictures or words cumulatively recalled over the week of testing (Erdelyi and Kleinbard 1978, 283). Data are for the 3 subjects per group in study 2.

This fact is demonstrated in figure 5.7, which presents the course of cumulative recall over trials. Clearly, number of items cumulatively recalled increased for both the picture and the word groups. That is, items continued to be recovered beyond the initial trial R_1. For the word group unlike the picture group, however, the intertest recoveries were roughly offset by interest losses, resulting in a failure of hypermnesia. The superiority of cumulative recall, which does not index forgetting, over regular recall, which does, illustrates Ballard's original point that reminiscence is almost always greater than improvement (hypermnesia), and at least as great.

Since cumulative recall functions such as those of figure 5.7 constitute cumulative counts of item recoveries across trials irrespective of losses, they provide, as discussed below, ideal measures of total reminiscence in multitrial recall. Regular recall functions, such as those of figure 5.6, on the other hand, provide measures of hypermnesia. Thus, as will be seen, cumulative recall functions are linked to reminiscence and regular recall functions to hypermnesia. By this view it is clear—as it was already clear in Ballard's work—that reminiscence is a ubiquitous fact of recall, regardless of the stimulus. Hypermnesia, being a balance phenomenon, is more finicky and appears more reliably with favorable stimuli, such as meaningful pictures.

Some exploratory work has been done on the repeated recall of picture lists for periods of many weeks. The data do not suggest any dramatic increase in recall beyond the 1-week interval employed by Erdelyi and Kleinbard (although research with stories as stimuli, as will be seen in chapter 8, suggests some unexpected very long-term effects). One female

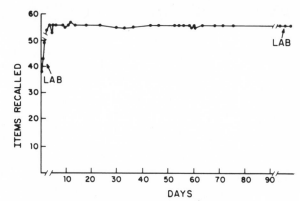

Figure 5.8 The course of recall of 60 pictures over 90 days of repeated testing of subject B.B.B. (Erdelyi 1984, 123)

subject, B.B.B., who repeatedly attempted to recall an original list of 60 pictures for a period of 3 months, settled in, after several days, into an altogether stable level of recall for the remaining period (fig. 5.8).

It might be noted, however, that the subject made her gains rapidly and reached close to perfect recall level (over 90% of the list items). Thus, a ceiling effect might have been masking potential further hypermnesias. Pilot work with two other subjects tested the introduction of free association and other destructuring techniques during later phases of testing (for example, beyond 2 weeks) to determine whether, once a particular recall strategy had produced its maximal effects and had become routinized, a destructuring of frozen retrieval patterns might yield new recoveries. Although some additional recoveries were obtained, no dramatic upsurge in hypermnesia over very long-term intervals materialized. Further work on the course of very long-term repeated recall is indicated. Unfortunately, this type of research is difficult to pursue because of the persistent, long-term demands it places on subjects.

Some work on very long-term hypermnesia for narrative texts is described in chapter 8. Especially intriguing are the vicissitudes of memory for the story "The War of the Ghosts" exhibited by two girls (aged 6 and 9) over the course of several months. This latter work, as will be seen, begins to capture the flavor of some of the clinical data, as well as the Pötzl-Fisher-type primary-process effects described in the previous chapter.

SIX

*Theoretical Issues in the Modern Experimental Literature
on Hypermnesia and Reminiscence*

On the Distinction between Recall and Cumulative Recall
and between Hypermnesia and Reminiscence

Although the distinction between recall and cumulative recall is straight-forward and may already be clear from the preceding chapter, a simple example based on made-up data is provided so as to eliminate any possible ambiguities and to illustrate certain characteristics of recall and cumulative recall functions. Some of these characteristics, as will be seen, are important for a general definition of both hypermnesia and reminiscence, and for efforts at theoretical treatment of the phenomena.

The made-up example of a subject's multitrial recall performance is purposely made simple. The hypothetical subject is a child attempting to recall as many states of the United States as possible over three successive trials. For convenience, the child's hypothetical responses are placed in alphabetical order in each recall trial. Table 6.1 provides these data.

The child produced 10 responses on the first trial, one of them (in brackets) erroneous. Thus his recall score on trial 1 is 9 ($R_1 = 9$). On trial 2 the child also recalled 9 states, for no net gain—and therefore no hypermnesia from R_1 to R_2. Note, however, that the composition of items in the second trial is not the same as those in the first. Three additional states, Hawaii, Michigan, and Texas were recovered (reminiscence) but these three additions to recall level on trial 2 were offset by three losses (oblivescence or forgetting)—Massachusetts, North Carolina, and South Carolina. Thus although no hypermnesia is observed between trial 1 and trial 2, the reminiscence of 3 states was obtained and these 3 recoveries are reflected in the increase of cumulative recall in trial 2, cum R_2, to 12 items. Since *reminiscence* (in Ballard's as well as in the modern sense) refers to recoveries of stimulus items beyond the initial recall effort R_1, reminiscence at trial 2 is given by the total number of stimulus items recalled up to and through trial 2, namely, cum $R_2 = 12$, minus the stimulus items initially recalled, $R_1 = 9$. (Note: always $R_1 = $ cum R_1.)

Table 6.1 Hypothetical recall of states by a child over three successive tests, with computations of recall (R) and cumulative recall (cum R) for the three trials

Trial 1	Trial 2	Trial 3
Alaska	Alaska	Alaska
California	California	California
Florida	Florida	Florida
—	Hawaii	Hawaii
Massachusetts	—	—
—	Michigan	—
[New England]	[New England]	[New England]
New Jersey	New Jersey	New Jersey
New York	New York	New York
North Carolina	—	North Carolina
Ohio	Ohio	Ohio
South Carolina	—	South Carolina
—	Texas	Texas
—	—	Virginia
$R_1 = 9$	$R_2 = 9$	$R_3 = 11$
cum $R_1 = 9$	cum $R_2 = 12$ (R_1 + Hawaii + Michigan + Texas)	cum $R_3 = 13$ (cum R_2 + Virginia)

Thus, for the two initial trials,

$$\text{Rem} = \text{cum } R_2 - R_1 = 3.$$

(Rem = reminiscence.) The reminiscence measure is exactly the same as that of Ballard (1913) and Brown (1923) except that it is here formulated in terms of *cumulative recall* and *recall* scores, a formulation that is convenient when we move from two trials to many trials.

Let us now, actually, proceed to performance on trial 3. On this trial, 11 states are recalled, representing a net improvement of two states over R_1. Thus hypermnesia (Hyp) occurred from R_1 to R_3 (where none did from R_1 to R_2):

$$\text{Hyp} = R_3 - R_1 = 11 - 9 = 2.$$

Note that the corresponding reminiscence from R_1 to R_3 is,

$$\text{Rem} = \text{cum } R_3 - R_1 = 13 - 9 = 4,$$

which simply means that, beyond the items recalled in R_1, the subject additionally recalled 4 new items through trial 3 (Hawaii, Michigan, and Texas in trial 2, and Virginia in trial 3).

From this exercise it is clear that a general definition of hypermnesia in multitrial recall involving n trials is

$$\text{Hyp} = R_n - R_1$$

and the corresponding definition of reminiscence is

$$\text{Rem} = \text{cum } R_n - R_1.$$

These two definitional formulas both clarify and codify the long-standing distinction between reminiscence and hypermnesia (improvement) originally introduced by Ballard:

$$\text{Rem} - \text{Hyp} = (\text{cum } R_n - R_1) - (R_n - R_1) = \text{cum } R_n - R_n.$$

The difference between reminiscence and hypermnesia turns out to be the difference between cumulative recall and recall: cum $R_n - R_n$. What is this difference? Obviously, it is forgetting, specifically forgetting in R_n of previously remembered items. Thus in terms of the example in table 6.1, the difference between cum $R_n = 13$ and $R_n = 11$ is the forgetting of two previously remembered items, Massachusetts (forgotten in trials 2 and 3) and Michigan (forgotten in trial 3).

Since reminiscence (based on cumulative recall) is not masked by forgetting, as is hypermnesia (based on recall), it might be considered a more sensitive indicator of recall improvement than hypermnesia. In some senses it is. Thus reminiscence is readily found when hypermnesia is not, as exemplified in the cumulative recall function for words in figure 5.7: for words as well as pictures, (cum $R_n - R_1$) > 0. This finding, as shown by Ballard (1913), is standard. In the absence of hypermnesia for words, reminiscence is, nevertheless, invariably found. For any stimulus material, reminiscence is ubiquitous. Reminiscence is a bedrock phenomenon of memory, on par with forgetting; hypermnesia is robust but is contingent on a variety of factors.

Nonetheless, reminiscence as a measure of recall improvement has some drawbacks. For one, it does not control for response bias effects: As response productivity increases, so does the reminiscence score. Figure 5.7 suggests that reminiscence for words would have continued to increase, perhaps to a perfect level, with additional time and recall trials. Such increases in "reminiscence" may not, however, reflect memory recovery, but only chance hits resulting from the production of new items in recall. Perhaps the problem could be resolved by including a control base rate group to assess the component of reminiscence due to chance. Unfortunately, some questions turn up in attempting to implement such controls, as will be seen in chapter 7.

Further, there is a conceptual problem: a high reminiscence level need not imply a high recall level. Because forgetting is not reflected in cumulative recall, nil recall at trial n ($R_n = 0$) might still be associated with a high cum R_n because of high recall in early trials. (For example, if $R_1 = 100\%$ but $R_n = 0$, cum $R_n = 100\%$.)

Nonetheless, it must be remembered that reminiscence is the incremental component of hypermnesia and is, in this sense, the more fundamental phenomenon. Also, despite its drawbacks, reminiscence may reveal memory effects missed by hypermnesia—for example, the substantial recovery of word items over successive recall trials. Both phenomena are important, although they may be more or less so in different contexts. More will be said about this below.

The Stimulus and Coding Question

Although a clear picture-word difference in hypermnesia emerged in both studies of Erdelyi and Becker (1974), it cannot be legitimately concluded that only pictures produce hypermnesia. It is possible that pictures are only a subclass of a broader class of effective stimuli or that the pictorial nature of the stimuli expresses the operation of some yet unspecified underlying factor in producing hypermnesia. Evidence for a deeper factor already emerged in the original Erdelyi and Becker experiments. Preliminary analysis of the results, while study 2 was still in progress, revealed that words are not necessarily inert stimuli. Although word lists, *on the average,* failed to produce hypermnesia, there were considerable individual differences, and some subjects produced impressive word hypermnesias, which were offset by other subjects' amnesic functions.

To shed light on the variability of word-recall functions, the remaining subjects in study 2 were queried at the end of the experiment about the coding strategies they had employed at the time of stimulus presentation. Three types of coding strategies were most often mentioned: (1) recoding the words into images, (2) organizing the words conceptually, and (3) silently repeating the words.

A clear relation emerged between coding strategy and repeated-recall performance. Of the three subjects reporting an imagery recoding strategy, all three produced hypermnesia. The other subjects almost uniformly showed amnesia for words or no change in recall level over trials. These informal findings suggested that it was the imaginal coding rather than the nominal stimulus that was responsible for hypermnesia. A straightforward experiment was suggested by these results which was carried out by Erdelyi, Finkelstein, et al. (1976).

The experiment was a direct replication of the picture and word

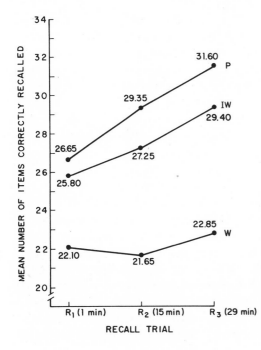

Figure 6.1 Repeated recall performance for a set of pictures (P), words (W), and imaged words (IW). (After Erdelyi et al. 1976, 315)

conditions of study 2 of Erdelyi and Becker, supplemented by a third group. This latter group was also presented the word list but the subjects were instructed beforehand (and this was the only difference between the two word groups) to try to form a vivid pictorial image of what each word stood for, as it was being presented. Figure 6.1 shows the repeated-recall performance of the picture, word, and image-the-words groups.

Visual inspection shows (and statistical analysis confirmed) that the word group that recoded each item into picture images behaved like the picture group rather than the other word group, both in terms of overall recall level and the production of hypermnesia. Thus lists of words can readily produce hypermnesia as long as they are properly encoded by the subject. An internal correlational analysis performed on the uninstructed W group, between magnitude of hypermnesia ($R_3 - R_1$) and coding strategies (as reported by subjects in a postexperimental rating form), tended to replicate the experimental findings: extent of *imagery coding* correlated significantly ($r = 0.76$) with magnitude of hypermnesia, but not with *conceptual organization* ($r = 0.15$) nor with *covert rehearsal* ($r = 0.37$).

A trial-by-trial item analysis (see table 6.2) was also carried out, which

Table 6.2 Item analyses for multitrial recall for the picture (P), word (W), and image word (IW) groups

	Hit-Miss Patterns							
Group	000	001	010	011	100	101	110	111
P	24.2	3.2	0.9	5.0	1.6	1.7	1.7	21.6
IW	26.8	2.6	0.6	4.2	1.8	1.4	1.2	21.2
W	34.2	1.6	0.6	1.4	1.4	1.1	0.8	18.8

Source: Erdelyi et al. 1976, 316.
Note: Average frequencies of hit-miss patterns.

showed that the imagery word group (IW) was more like the picture group (P) than the regular word group (W). Thus more reminiscence— $\Sigma(001) + \Sigma(010) + \Sigma(011)$—was observed in the P and IW groups than in the W group. (P = 3.2 + 0.9 + 5.0 = 9.1; IW = 2.6 + 0.6 + 4.2 = 7.4; and W = 1.6 + 0.6 + 1.4 = 3.6.) Oblivescence from R_1 to R_3—$\Sigma(100) + \Sigma(110)$— did not, however, differ appreciably among the groups (3.2, 3.0, and 2.2 for P, IW, and W, respectively).

The imagery hypothesis was further tested by Erdelyi and Finkelstein (see Erdelyi 1984, 112–13), who replicated the basic Erdelyi, Finkelstein, et al. (1976) image-coding effect with *auditorily presented words* and *oral reports:* subjects orally recalling a set of auditorily presented words failed to produce hypermnesia, whereas another group, identical but for instructions to form a visual image of each item as it was heard, did produce hypermnesia.

Another approach to the imagery-coding hypothesis was pursued by Erdelyi and Finkelstein (1975; see Erdelyi 1984, 113–14). It had been noted by imagery researchers (for example, Bugelski, Kidd, and Segmen 1968; Paivio 1971) that it takes about 1.5 to 2.5 seconds to form an image from a word. If so, imagery-coding instructions such as used successfully by Erdelyi, Finkelstein, et al. (1976) should be ineffective if the word list were presented at a rate too fast for effective imagery coding. In the present study, the 1976 experiment was repeated in every detail except for the rate of stimulus presentation. Instead of the former 5 seconds allowed for each item, words were now presented at a rate of 1 item per second. As figure 6.2 shows, hypermnesia for words was effectively knocked out.

In another experimental tack, Popkin and Small showed that imagery instructions produced hypermnesia for high-imagery words (Hi I) but that the same imagery instructions failed with low-imagery words (Lo I), which presumably are difficult to image, yielding amnesia over repeated recall

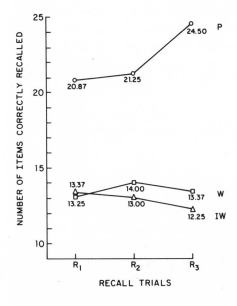

Figure 6.2 Failure of imagery-coding to produce hypermnesia for words when the presentation rate (1 item per second) is too fast for imagery coding to be effected (Erdelyi and Finkelstein, 1975; figure reproduced from Erdelyi 1984, 113)

trials instead. Item analyses of intertrial performance showed that "improved recall of the subjects in Hi I relative to the Lo I subjects occurs because forgetting [10] is less and reminiscence [01] is greater in the Hi I condition" (1979, 379). Taken together, these various lines of evidence seem impressively to converge on the imagery hypothesis. It is not the nominal stimulus but the coding of the stimulus that is crucial for hypermnesia.

This evidence, moreover, dovetails nicely with Ballard's own observations, with the hypnotic hypermnesia literature, and with the clinical impressions of Freud before the turn of the century (Breuer and Freud 1895).

The imagery hypothesis tends to explain, for example, the robust hypermnesias obtained by Ballard with poetry, the imagistic verbal material par excellence. Ballard actually noted "the seeming preponderance of visual imagery" in incremental memory. He writes:

good visualizers were able to see more lines or a more complete scene the second time, e.g.,

J.T. improved from 15 to 21 lines in three days. Imagined she saw the lines in front of her.

J.I. improved from 9 to 10 lines in two days, and from 19 to 21 lines in three days. Pictured the paper with the hectographed lines.

W.R. improved from 13 to 16 lines in two days and from 25 to 26 lines in three days. Imagined the scene, but not the words.

E.G. improved from 10 to 26 lines in two days. Visualized lines.

J.P. improved from 3 to 11 lines in seven days. Pictured the words on the blackboard (the poetry in this case was learnt from the blackboard).

B.G. improved from 9 to 13 lines in seven days. "As I began to write it, I could picture it on the paper before me." (Ballard 1913, 40)

The clinical literature also has tended to link hypermnesia with imagery (Allers and Teler 1924; Breuer and Freud 1895; Holt 1964; Horowitz 1983, 1986; Jung 1935). Seemingly making the same point as Ballard about "good visualizers," Freud writes, "When memories return in the form of pictures our task is in general easier than when they return as thoughts. Hysterical patients, who are as a rule of a 'visual' type, do not make such difficulties for the analyst as those with obsession" (Breuer and Freud 1895, 110).

Freud's interventions in his hypermnesic therapy in *Studies on Hysteria* are typically couched in the terminology of imagery. Repeatedly, Freud speaks not just of memories but of "picture ideas" (315), "memory pictures" (343), and "memory images" (345). When instructing his patients on recovering unconscious memories, he urges them to "bring out pictures and ideas" (193) and assures them, even when they draw a blank initially, that they will ultimately "see" before them "a recollection in the form of a picture" (315). He prods their recall by asking, "Do you see this scene before your eyes?" (153). "Go on looking at the [mental] picture; it will develop and become more specialized. . . . Be patient and just keep looking at the picture" (158). In *The Interpretation of Dreams,* in which Freud makes the claim that "dreams are hypermnesic" (1900, 11–17, 589), a great emphasis is placed on the imagistic-procedural nature of the dream's cognitive format ("plastic word representation," "dramatization").

Finally, as will be detailed in chapter 7, imagistic processes are repeatedly implicated in the hypnotic hypermnesia literature. The classic experiment of White, Fox, and Harris (1940) is prototypical. Using three types of stimulus materials—nonsense syllables, pictures, and poetry—White et al. found significant hypnotic hypermnesias for pictures and poetry, but none for nonsense syllables.

Despite the plethora of converging evidence, there is a problem with the imagery hypothesis. Unquestionably, imagistically coded meaningful stimuli yield hypermnesia. However, just as with pictures, it does not follow that only imagistic materials do so. Just as pictures are subsumed by imagery, so imagery may be subsumed by some still more basic factor. One possibility, explored by Erdelyi, Buschke, and Finkelstein (1977), is that depth of processing (Craik and Lockhart 1972) might be this more fundamental factor. Erdelyi et al. (1977) reasoned that normal word lists were, on the average, accorded "shallow processing," whereas meaningful pictures and imagistically coded words received deep processing.

To probe the issue, a list of very deeply processed stimuli were devised—so deep that no nominal stimuli existed and the to-be-remembered items had to be created from within by the subject. Specifically, "Socratic stimuli" were employed in which the to-be-remembered items were covertly generated by the subject in response to a series of simple riddles (for example, "This longish wooden object is used by baseball players to hit the ball. What is it?"). For comparison purposes, a picture and a word group were tested which received the actual stimulus items (the answers to the riddles) in either pictorial or verbal form. The results of the experiment were that, while word recall failed to increase reliably over five successive trials, recall for both the pictures and the Socratic items were hypermnesic, with the Socratic stimuli significantly exceeding the improvement of the picture group. It might thus be concluded that it is deeply processed stimuli—of which pictures and imagistically coded words are representative—that yield hypermnesia. Unfortunately, the conclusion is problematic because, as Popkin and Small (1979) observed, the Socratic stimuli may have been especially effective not because of processing depth but because of the numerous images generated in the production of the Socratic items. It turns out that it is very difficult, perhaps impossible, to distinguish between imagistic and depth-of-processing accounts of hypermnesia (Erdelyi 1982; Roediger 1982). This can be garnered from the series of experiments reported by Belmore (1981) comparing imagistic versus semantic coding of words on hypermnesia.

In her first experiment, for example, Belmore tested three independent groups: subjects who (1) *repeated* the input words, (2) embedded each word in a made-up *sentence,* or (3) *imaged* each word. The results are summarized in table 6.3.

The repetition group (shallow processing) produced the usual flat multitrial recall pattern. The image recoding and the sentence embedding group, on the other hand, yielded hypermnesia, though the magnitude of the increments were small in both cases. The fact that the image group was not more hypermnesic than the sentence group was construed by Belmore as suggesting "that hypermnesia is equally likely to occur with

Table 6.3 Multitrial recall performance on words as a function of orienting task: repetition, embedding in sentence, and image coding

Orienting Condition	T_1	T_2	T_3
		Repetition	
Number of Words	20.87	20.17	21.04
Cumulative No. Words	20.87	22.78	23.61
$p(0\|1)$	—	.13	.06
$p(1\|0)$	—	.10	.10
		Sentence	
Number of Words	27.30	28.30	29.13
Cumulative No. Words	27.30	29.74	30.87
$p(0\|1)$	—	.05	.03
$p(1\|0)$	—	.19	.14
		Image	
Number of Words	27.43	28.04	28.96
Cumulative No. Words	27.43	29.39	30.65
$p(0\|1)$	—	.05	.04
$p(1\|0)$	—	.16	.17

Source: Belmore 1981, 193.
Note: 0 = forgotten; 1 = recalled

either semantic elaboration or imagery" (1981, 194). The problem here, as in the Erdelyi et al. (1977) study, is that it is impossible to ascertain whether the two effective groups differed in imagery coding. Embedding a word in a sentence may engender more images than the instruction to form an image of the referent of a word. It might be helpful in such experiments to obtain some manipulation checks, such as imagery ratings, to ascertain whether the groups in fact differed on the critical variable.

Similar questions could be raised about Belmore's study 2, in which subjects asked to make semantic judgments ("Is this object a living thing?") produced hypermnesia, whereas another group presumably making imagistic size judgments ("Will this object fit in a grocery cart?") did not. (A third group, receiving orthographic orienting instructions, produced an amnesic trend.) Actually, in a third experiment (experiment 3A), in which *very* abstract words were used, in the vein of Popkin and Small (1979), both an *orthographic* (syllable counting) and a *semantic* orienting task (pleasantness judgments) produced amnesic trends. It is clear that very abstract words might be difficult to image but not immediately evident why they should not be deeply processed. Thus the role of imagery is not effectively excluded by these studies, even though plenty of evidence exists (Belmore 1981, experiments 1 and 2; Erdelyi, Buschke, and Finkelstein 1977; Klein, Loftus, Kihlstrom, and Aseron 1989; Payne and Roediger 1987; Roediger and Thorpe 1978, study 2) that depth-of-processing or elaboration-type instructions will render word lists hypermnesic.

One component of table 6.3 is worth noting since it is often used in multitrial recall analyses instead of the item analyses reported in table 6.2. These are *conditional probability analyses* (for example, Tulving 1967), in which performance on some trial T_j is conditionalized on performance on some other trial, T_i. Belmore conditionalized both recall and forgetting on T_1 performance. In the repetition condition, for example, the probability of forgetting an item in T_2 that had been recalled in T_1—$p(0|1)$—was 0.13. In other words, 0.13 is the probability of oblivescence. In this same trial (and condition), $p(1|0) = 0.10$, giving the probability of reminiscence from T_1 to T_2. Not surprisingly, no hypermnesia is in evidence between T_1 and T_2.

Although further empirical work might clarify the differential bearing of imagery and depth-of-processing on hypermnesia, it is clear that without some theoretical formulation the empirical task becomes an eternal regress. (Even if depth-of-processing is the deeper factor, it may still be subsumed by a yet deeper factor; and so forth.)

We will therefore turn to two theoretical approaches to hypermnesia, neither of which, interestingly, insists on imagery or depth-of-processing as crucial for hypermnesia, though they explain why imagistic or deeply processed items should produce hypermnesia.

The Two-Stage Model of Hypermnesia: The Retrieve-Recognize Framework

A theoretical framework for hypermnesia was proposed by Erdelyi and Becker (1974) based on the classic two-stage, retrieve-recognize model of recall (James 1890; Kintsch 1970) in which the recaller is assumed (1) to retrieve (search, generate, and so on) a succession of candidate items for recall and (2) to make a recognition decision about the aptness of each item. Retrieved items that are recognized are recalled, and those that are not recognized are passed over.

To the extent that with additional recall time more stimulus items are retrieved and that some of these retrieved items are recognized, it follows that recall should increase. This increase in recall will occur whether the additional recall time is provided in the form of extended test periods or a succession of multiple tests (Erdelyi 1977; Roediger and Thorpe 1978). It has already been suggested in the foregoing discussion of cumulative recall that multiple trials may be conceptualized as one supertrial in which recall increases with time (which covaries with trials).

But why hypermnesia? Granted that cumulative recall should increase across trials—the longer we try to remember, the more we remember— why should there be net increments in recall from one trial to the next when each separate trial is of equal duration? Obviously, later trials must benefit from activity in earlier trials. This benefit is the learning that accrues from previous recalls of the stimulus. Each recall is, in effect, a re-presentation of the stimulus. The learning from previous recall leads—as learning invariably does—to faster recall and less forgetting in succeeding trials. Thus, with each successive trial, more of what has been already recalled is retained and what is retained is produced faster, leaving more time in the test trial for additional recall effort—and therefore reminiscence. The extra recall produced by the additional recall time coupled with the better retention of the previously recalled materials should produce net increases in recall in each new trial until no more new material is retrieved, that is, no more reminiscence occurs with extra recall time.

The learning element in hypermnesia is a long-standing theme in theoretical explanations of incremental recall. It corresponds to Brown's (1923) *fixing effects* of earlier trials (see chap. 3) and to the learning effects over which midcentury theorists worried for fear that it rendered the effect an artifact (but which, as shown herein, could not account for hypermnesia without the additional operation of reminiscence). It is also explicitly incorporated in Raaijmakers and Shiffrin's (1981) SAM model of probabilistic memory search under the parameter of "incrementing," and in Payne's (1986) emphasis, in his revision of the level of recall theory of hypermnesia (see below), of increased "item accessibility" as a function of previous retrieval.

Erdelyi and Becker's retrieve-recognize framework explains the picture-word differences in hypermnesia by recourse to the recognition component of the two-stage model. Pictures (and, presumably, imagistically or deeply processed stimuli) are, unlike words, exceptionally recognizable (Nickerson 1965; Shepard 1967; Standing, Conezio, and Haber 1970). In a pilot study with 120 pictures of the sort I used in hypermnesia studies, recognition memory was virtually perfect—subjects garnered 99% hit rates for a 1% false alarm rate (Erdelyi and Stein 1981). Consequently, the retrieved items, when they are pictorial, would almost always be recognized, leading to their successful recall. In line with the model, the items would be better learned with each such success, yielding better retention and faster recall on subsequent trials, leaving more time for new retrievals in succeeding trials.

The situation with words is different. Words are significantly less recognizable than pictures. Because of their poorer recognition, recognition decisions about retrieved word items will be marred by errors (more misses, false alarms, or both) and therefore poorer learning. Also, less overt reminiscence will occur, since retrieval items (covert reminiscence) may not be recognized and, as a result, not produced.

The explanation of the effectiveness of pictures in producing hypermnesia can be generalized to any other stimulus—or memory code—that yields the same effects: high retrievability (covert reminiscence) and high recognizability. Poetry, imagistically or otherwise deeply processed words, items from semantic memory, and so forth should produce hypermnesia to the extent that they produce (1) more and more new item retrievals (covert reminiscence) over time and (2) the retrieved items are recognized and therefore recalled (overtly reminisced). This may be the reason why items from semantic memory (Roediger, Payne, Gillespie, and Lean 1982) or overlearned remote memories like Ballard's Latin nouns (see fig. 1.9) produce hypermnesia. Imagery may be common to all these effective stimuli or memory codes but the basic model does not require imagery. What the retrieve-recognize model requires is material that is both highly retrievable (reminiscent) and recognizable.

Hypermnesia has necessitated modification of traditional probabilistic sampling models of multitrial recall (Estes 1955; Shiffrin 1970) which assumed sampling with replacement of memory items in each new recall trial. Such sampling with replacement leads to intertrial variability (oblivescence and reminiscence) but no net change in trial-to-trial recall levels. This is precisely what is usually obtained with multitrial recall of (unrecoded) word lists. With imagistic or deep stimuli, however, net recall is incremental and therefore requires the introduction of an "incrementing" parameter (Raaijmakers and Shiffrin 1981) to explain the superior yield of each successive sampling of memory. We might note that Raaijmakers and Shiffrin's SAM model, which features 10 parameters, collapses into the two-stage model of hypermnesia, as only 2 of the 10 parameters are used to explain hypermnesia: (1) a *fluctuation* parameter (involving a fluctuation of the recall set from trial to trial which transposes into reminiscence if the fluctuated set contains new correct retrievals) and (2) the parameter corresponding to "fixing" effects or learning, *incrementing.*

Although the retrieve-generate model provides a congenial framework for hypermnesia effects, it suffers from some drawbacks. Its major weakness is that it is rather general, providing a conceptual framework rather than a precise, quantitative theory. Thus the *learning* corollary predicts fixing effects—less forgetting—in subsequent trials, but does not specify how much less forgetting. If the forgetting (oblivescence) trends upon which the reminiscence trends are superimposed are larger than the reminiscence trends, then the recall-recognition model will not yield hypermnesia. Retention is a balance phenomenon; retrieval-recognition only predicts a more positive balance. A more positive balance, however, may be as consistent with less amnesia as with more hypermnesia. Thus without implicitly assuming favorable oblivescence trends (ones lower than the reminiscence trends), the model need not predict hypermnesia. The problem of forgetting, as will be seen, proved critical for the recall-level hypothesis of hypermnesia, to which we will turn presently.

Another ambiguity in the model is the polysemous use of nomenclature to represent both *covert* and *overt* versions of the same process. Terms such as *retrieve, recall, recognition,* and *reminiscence* may all refer to covert (silent) or overt (expressed) events. Although the problem is more terminological than conceptual and context usually indicates which sense of the term is intended, conceptual confusion can nevertheless result, especially if decision processes that intervene between the covert event and its overt manifestation are ignored.

Items which are retrieved or recalled covertly may never be overtly produced because they fail to reach a response decision criterion. This may hold for recognition also, since the subject's criterion for personal conviction may be different from the subject's criterion for public assertion of recognition. Likewise reminiscence: covert retrieval/recall at time 2 of an item not retrieved/recalled at time 1 represents covert reminiscence. Overt reminiscence, however, is based on overt retrieval/recall, which, as noted, is not equivalent to covert retrieval/recall. The issue bears importantly on the operationalization of the retrieve-recognize model.

The recognition component is unproblematic. It is easy to measure and the criterion factor can be readily controlled or partialled out. The retrieval component, however, is vaguer. If one wished to test the retrieve-recognize model, how would "high retrievability" be operationalized? Clearly, high retrievability in the context of the retrieve-recognize model constitutes high reminiscence—but *covert* reminiscence. Overt reminiscence has been given a thoroughly explicit definition (Rem = cum R_n − R_1), but how does one obtain a comparable measure of covert reminiscence, which is the retrieval part of the retrieve-recognize model? The answer is to minimize the intervening criterion factor. If the decision criterion for translating a covertly retrieved item into an overt recall were completely permissive—that is, all candidate items retrieved, irrespective of subjective confidence, are produced as overt recall responses—then overt reminiscence would be equivalent to covert reminiscence. The technique of free association in psychoanalytic therapy has precisely the object of eliminating the criterion filter ("censorship"); free-associative or "uninhibited" recall (Roediger and Payne 1985) provides one technique for estimating "covert reminiscence" (covert retrievability) through overt responding. Similarly, my forced-recall procedure, in which subjects have to produce a large number of what they consider very low criterion responses—mostly viewed as guesses—also yields an overt reminiscence measure (cum $R_n - R_1$) that reasonably estimates the covert reminiscence of interest in the retrieve-recognize model. Thus in order to test the retrieve-recognize model, one wishes to demonstrate that items that are *highly retrievable* (operationalized as high in reminiscence for free-associative or forced recall) and *highly recognizable* once retrieved (operationalized by d' or some homologue) produce more hypermnesia than other items that are less retrievable-recognizable.

Finally, given Kleinbard's subjective reports on his work of recollection (see chap. 5), it must be conceded that *retrieval* is used in a loose sense to refer not only to retrieval from internal memory but to retrieval from the external world—for example, feather, phone, key—which, by dint of being recognized as stimulus items, are correctly recalled overtly.

The highlighting of some of these nuances, especially the identification of retrievability with reminiscence (in low-criterion recall) may facilitate programmatic experimental work to test the retrieve-recognize model of hypermnesia. It would be worth ascertaining whether the stimuli, coding formats, or memory organization schemes that produce hypermnesia (see Davis and Dominowski 1986; Payne and Wenger 1992) are in fact those that are highly reminiscent and recognizable relative to nonhypermnesic materials.

Level of Recall and Hypermnesia

Initial Recall Level (R_1) and Hypermnesia

One characteristic feature of the multitrial recall functions considered in this chapter is that the hypermnesic functions tend to exhibit a higher initial recall level R_1 than the nonhypermnesic functions (figs. 5.1, 6.1, 6.2).

The question naturally arises therefore (Belmore 1981; Erdelyi, Finkelstein, et al. 1976; Erdelyi 1982; Payne 1986) whether hypermnesia is a rich-get-richer phenomenon: the higher R_1 is—for whatever reason—the greater the propensity for recall to increase. Such an accounting could dispense with the difficult problem of attempting to understand the relation between the stimulus, coding, or organization formats and hypermnesia.

The empirical evidence shows, however, that initial recall level R_1 does not predict hypermnesia, that is, $R_n - R_1$. This was first shown by Erdelyi, Finkelstein, et al. (1976), who correlated R_1 with $(R_3 - R_1)$ in each of their three groups, the nonincremental W group, and the hypermnesic IW, and P groups. The respective correlations were $r = 0.09$, 0.05 and -0.43. The negative correlation between R_1 and hypermnesia in the P group, which suggests an inverse relation, may be a ceiling effect (high initial recall has nowhere to go but down).

A number of other lines of evidence argue against initial recall level predicting hypermnesia. In figure 5.1, for example, the two picture groups have virtually the same R_1, but the intervening silent thinking produces significantly more hypermnesia.

Similarly, Madigan (1976) compared multitrial recall for once- and twice-presented picture lists. Although R_1 was higher for the twice-presented list, hypermnesia was equivalent for the two groups. In a second experiment, involving twice-presented words which yielded higher R_1 than the once-presented hypermnesic pictures, no word hypermnesia was obtained.

Yarmey's (1976) comparison of concrete versus abstract nouns (fig. 5.3) further argues against R_1 determining hypermnesia. There was a substantial difference between R_1 for the concrete and abstract nouns, yet neither produced hypermnesia.

Similarly, rapidly presented picture items (see fig. 6.2) which led to lower R_1 than slower stimulus presentations (figs. 5.1 and 6.1), nevertheless produced roughly the same magnitude of hypermnesia. Belmore (1980) also failed to find any relation between recall level and hypermnesia.

The most decisive evidence against R_1 predicting hypermnesia is provided by Payne (1986), who systematically varied levels of recall for pictures and words and found (fig. 6.6) that picture functions with lower R_1 than word functions nevertheless produced greater hypermnesia than the word functions. It would appear, then, and apart from a recent publication by Madigan and O'Hara (1992) it has been the unanimous consensus in the field, that initial level of recall does not predict hypermnesia, except where ceiling or floor effects are operating (Erdelyi 1982; Roediger, Payne, Gillespie, and Lean 1982; Roediger 1982).

In what appears to be a topsy-turvy reading of the literature, Madigan and O'Hara (1992) suggest that, actually, a clear increasing linear relation exists between initial level of recall R_1 and level of reminiscence and hypermnesia. There is, however, far less contradiction here than meets the eye.

First, it should be underscored that, for reasons that will be expanded below, R_1 does indeed predict magnitude of *reminiscence.* This fact, which is a latent tautology, has not been in dispute. What R_1 does not predict is magnitude of *hypermnesia.*

Madigan and O'Hara specifically suggest, however, that hypermnesia is also positively correlated with initial recall level R_1. Yet the figure in which Madigan and O'Hara depict this positive relation (their fig. 5) plots "percentage new items recalled" on test 2 against "percent recalled" on test 1. But since "new items" are reminiscences, it appears that they are only providing another plot of reminiscence (not hypermnesia) increasing with R_1 magnitude. (For a further critical discussion of this work, see Payne and Wenger 1994.) Thus the conclusion continues to hold that R_1 does not predict net increments in recall, that is, hypermnesia.

Level of Cumulative Recall (LOCR) and Hypermnesia

Another version of the level of recall theory of hypermnesia was advanced by Roediger, Payne, Gillespie, and Lean (1982). They proposed that magnitude of hypermnesia was determined by asymptotic level of cumulative recall, cum $R_{n(\infty)}$. The theory is purely descriptive and, like the R_1 notion, cuts the conceptual Gordian knot of the role of stimulus, coding, and organization in hypermnesia: any factor that, for any reason, produces greater asymptotic cumulative recall (which is best estimated by cum R_n) will produce greater hypermnesia.

The background of this theory was Roediger and Thorpe's (1978) exploration of the question whether multiple recall trials produce more total stimulus recoveries (cumulative recall) than a single recall trial lasting as long as the multiple trials combined. Specifically, they compared cumulative recall for three 7-minute tests with total recall in a single 21-minute test. They found that the single test produced the same number of stimulus recoveries as the three shorter tests combined. This $3 \times 7 = 1 \times 21$ effect led them to emphasize the role of recall time on hypermnesia and to consider the possibility that a single recall test that fails to reach the asymptote will allow subsequent tests to add to the original test's recoveries and thus produce hypermnesia.

An important nuance of the level of cumulative recall (LOCR) theory is that the lower the cumulative recall level asymptote, the faster the asymptote is reached; or more generally, that a negative relation exists

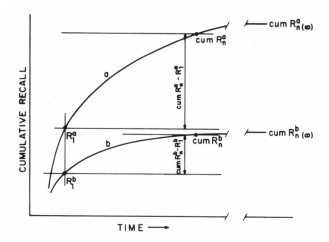

Figure 6.3 Two cumulative recall functions of the form, cum $R_{n(t)}$ = cum $R_{n(\infty)}(1 - e^{-\lambda t})$ with a negative relation between λ and cum $R_{n(\infty)}$ assumed. (After Roediger et al. 1982, 639)

between $R_{n(\infty)}$ and the rate, λ, at which $R_{n(\infty)}$ is approached. This, as will be seen, can explain the failure of word lists to produce hypermnesia when picture lists readily do so. Roediger et al. (1982) assume, based on past empirical work, that cumulative recall curves (fig. 6.3) are reasonably well described by the exponential growth function cum $R_{n(t)}$ = cum $R_{n(\infty)}$ $(1 - e^{-\lambda t})$, where cum $R_{n(t)}$ is the number of items recalled by time t, cum $R_{n(\infty)}$ is the asymptote of the function, e is the base of the natural logarithm, and λ is the rate at which the asymptote is approached, which, as already noted, Roediger et al. assume is negatively correlated with cum $R_{n(\infty)}$.

Figure 6.3 plots two cumulative recall curves of the form stipulated by Roediger et al.'s exponential growth function. The one with the lower asymptotic cumulative recall, as proposed by Roediger et al., asymptotes earlier than the one with higher asymptotic cumulative recall. (It should be noted, however, that the negative relation between λ and cum $R_{n(\infty)}$ is not mathematically obligatory but is, rather, a stipulation based on past experimental work.)

The $3 \times 7 = 1 \times 21$ effect led Roediger et al. to infer that properties of multiple recall functions could be deduced from the cumulative recall function of a single, time-equivalent trial. Thus if the lower curve (which might represent cumulative recall of words over time) is close to asymptote at, say, 7 minutes, it is obvious that no hypermnesia will be obtained, as (virtually) no new items will be recovered in subsequent trials. The higher cumulative recall function (which could be a picture function) has not yet reached asymptote at this time juncture—because of the assumed negative relation between λ and cum $R_{n(\infty)}$—and consequently is open to further item gains in a subsequent trial, and therefore hypermnesia. The LOCR theory underscores the importance of the duration of the initial recall trial, which must not be long enough for the asymptote to be reached if hypermnesia is to be obtained.

The LOCR theory is elegant, simple, and makes clear predictions. Its rationale, moreover, is quite compelling, seeming almost to be logically obligatory, as is suggested by Roediger:

> (a) Hypermnesia—increased recall across repeated tests—is equivalent in terms of the total number of items recalled to performance during a single long test of the same duration. (b) Since hypermnesia is equivalent to cumulative recall, properties of cumulative recall curves are critical for understanding the phenomenon. (c) These cumulative recall curves typically exhibit the property of a negative correlation between the asymptote [of the cumulative recall function cum $R_{n(\infty)}$], and the rate of approaching the asymptote λ. (d) Since the rate of approaching asymptote is greater with lower levels of asymptotic recall, if recall is stopped after a fixed period of time performance will be nearer asymptote in cases of lower than higher recall. Thus further potential gains in recall (hypermnesia) will be greater in cases of higher asymptotic recall. . . . (e) Therefore, hypermnesia (recall growth on repeated tests) will tend to be correlated with [cumulative] recall level [cum $R_{n(\infty)}$]. (Roediger 1982, 662)

Nevertheless, it is not necessarily the case that cum $R_{n(\infty)}$ predicts hypermnesia (Erdelyi 1982). Consider the cumulative recall function (left panel of fig. 6.4) and the corresponding multitrial recall functions (right panel of fig. 6.4) of three subjects tested as pilots for a hypnotic hypermnesia experiment (M.T. Orne 1983, personal communication).

For the subjects tested, it is readily seen that cumulative recall performance (left panel) fails to predict hypermnesia (right panel): the subject with the highest cumulative recall level (A) actually produced the lowest level of hypermnesia ($R_n - R_1 = 1$); the two subjects producing lower but equivalent cumulative recall levels (B and C) achieved quite different magnitudes of hypermnesia ($R_n - R_1 = 12$ and 4, respectively).

David G. Payne (1986), while a doctoral student of Roediger, cinched the issue in a series of programmatic experiments. In the first study, lists of pictures or words were presented once, twice, or three times to vary

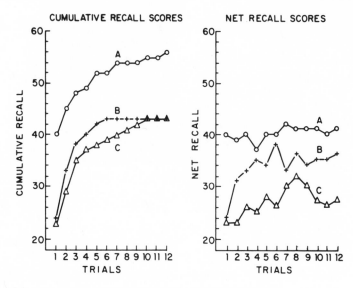

Figure 6.4 Three subjects' cum R and R functions over 12 trials

their level of cumulative recall. As figure 6.5 shows, the list repetition manipulation successfully led to the different levels of cum R_n (the estimate of $R_{n(\infty)}$).

The regular multitrial recall functions (fig. 6.6), however, fail to bear out the LOCR prediction.

In general, pictures produced more hypermnesia than words (which the subjects had been asked to process semantically) and magnitude of hypermnesia was not reliably affected by number of stimulus presentations and therefore cumulative recall level, cum R_n, for either pictures or words. A follow-up study (experiment 1A), which controlled cumulative recall level of picture and word lists through rate of presentation, produced the same pattern of outcomes: pictures produced greater hypermnesia than words and cum R_n failed to predict magnitude of hypermnesia.

Why does the LOCR hypothesis not bear out? One possibility is that the negative relation between λ and cum $R_{n(\infty)}$ (indexed by cum R_n) is not reliable (V. M. Solis-Macias, for example, in an unpublished study, failed to find it [1990, personal communication]). Another critical factor (Erdelyi 1982) is that forgetting, as noted by Roediger et al. (1982, 639), is left out in the LOCR approach. Since hypermnesia is a balance phenomenon—between oblivescence and reminiscence—an analysis omitting the oblivescence component is likely to be limited.

In effect, what the LOCR hypothesis does is to predict level of hy-

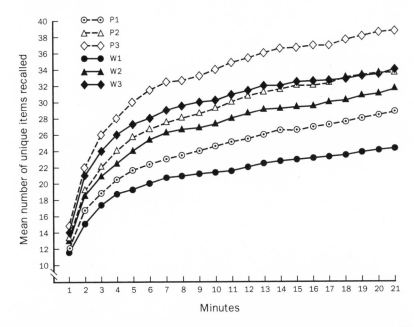

Figure 6.5 Cumulative recall functions for once-, twice-, and thrice-presented picture (P) or word (W) lists (redrawn after Payne 1986, 17). P1, P2, and P3 represent picture lists presented once, twice, or three times, respectively. Similarly, W1, W2, and W3 designate word lists presented once, twice, or three times.

permnesia ($R_n - R_1$) from level of reminiscence (cum $R_n - R_1$), for although it may not be immediately obvious, cum R_n is a perfect correlate—and, therefore, a reliable measure—of reminiscence, cum $R_n - R_1$, given the function assumed by Roediger et al. This can be seen from figure 6.3. For any comparison of the two functions a and b, if

$$\text{cum } R_n^a > \text{cum } R_n^b,$$

then

$$\text{cum } R_n^a - R_1^a > \text{cum } R_n^b - R_1^b,$$

that is,

Reminiscence a > Reminiscence b.

The problem with LOCR, then, is that it reconflates reminiscence and hypermnesia/improvement. This problem is indicated by Roediger's (1982) statement (b) above that "hypermnesia is equivalent to cumulative recall." This is an interesting (but not unusual) phenomenon in psychology of recidivism by a pioneer theorist to a position he has himself

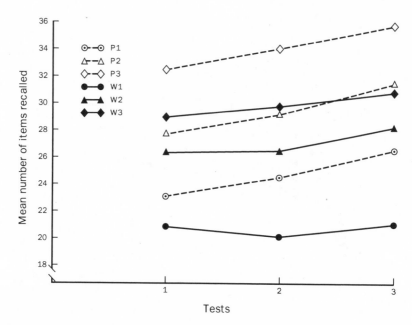

Figure 6.6 Multitrial recall functions for picture and word lists presented once, twice or three times (redrawn after Payne 1986, 19). P1, P2, and P3, and W1, W2, and W3 represent picture or word lists presented once, twice, or three times.

rendered outmoded. It was Roediger and Thorpe (1978), after all, who reintroduced into the field the distinction between reminiscence and hypermnesia (improvement) that Ballard had unsuccessfully attempted to establish.

A concluding comment is in order about R_1 and why it predicts reminiscence but not hypermnesia. With one exception, $R_i \neq$ cum R_i. This exception is the case where $i = 1$. Thus $R_1 =$ cum R_1, the reason being, as table 6.1 already showed, that R_1 "cumulates," that is, includes all items recalled throughout Trial 1. Figure 6.4—and table 6.1—clearly show that $R_1 =$ cum R_1, but that $R_i \neq$ cum R_i, where $i > 1$. In well-behaved cumulative recall functions, and they are usually very well behaved, cum R_1— and, therefore, its equivalent, R_1—predicts cum $R_{n(\infty)}$. Since, as we have seen, cum R_n predicts reminiscence, it follows that its own predictors, cum R_1 (which is equal to R_1) predicts reminiscence. What is not predicted by cum $R_{n(\infty)}$—nor cum R_n, nor cum R_1, nor R_1—is hypermnesia.

A Revised Cumulative Recall Hypothesis: Payne's 2-Factor Theory

What is fascinating about the LOCR hypothesis is that, despite its formal failure, it converged in revision upon the earlier two-stage model of hypermnesia and contributed a crucial refinement to it. The revised LOCR hypothesis of Payne (1986) holds that hypermnesia depends on two factors: "First, the greater the difference between test 1 net recall [R_1] and asymptotic cumulative recall [cum $R_{n(\infty)}$], the more likely it is that hypermnesia will be obtained. Second, hypermnesia also depends on the extent to which retrieving an item increases that item's accessibility" (Payne 1986, 28).

It is evident that the first factor is nothing other than reminiscence: cum $R_n - R_1$. Asymptotic cumulative recall, cum $R_{n(\infty)}$ (estimated by cum R_n), is, as shown above, perfectly correlated with reminiscence. In fact, Payne makes the translation and explicitly posits reminiscence, cum $R_n - R_1$, as the first factor. Thus a critical component of hypermnesia is reminiscence. This reminiscence component turns out to be the "retrievability" component in my original retrieve-recognize framework, for cum R_n is a direct measure of extent of retrievability across trials and also, as has been seen, an indirect measure of reminiscence (since, theoretically, cum R_n is a perfect correlate of cum $R_n - R_1$, that is, reminiscence). Obvious as this retrievability-reminiscence identity may be in retrospect, it was not so until Roediger and his associates' LOCR hypothesis was proposed (and even then not immediately). What LOCR provided was a bridge from the classic retrieve-recognize framework to reminiscence, which, naturally, is a basic component of hypermnesia.

Payne's second factor, increased item accessibility, is basically the learning presumed to result (Erdelyi and Becker 1974) for high-recognizable items. Although Payne does not link this learning component to recognizability, the two models are obviously similar since correctly recognized items are likely to be better learned and therefore to be more accessible on subsequent tests. The convergence of theoretical frameworks, especially given their radically different starting points, is a notable development in the hypermnesia literature.

SEVEN

Special Topics in Hypermnesia

Hypnotic Hypermnesia

The notion that hypnosis can effect the recovery of inaccessible memories is, as Clark Hull put it in his monograph, *Hypnosis and Suggestibility,* "one of the most remarkable" of the alleged powers of hypnosis (1933, 105).

In the Western tradition of hypnosis, the claim of hypermnesia can be traced back to the work of the Marquis Armand de Puységur, Franz Anton Mesmer's most influential follower. Working with a peasant by the name of Victor Race, Puységur produced a paradoxical version of Mesmer's "crisis." Instead of the dramatic, agitated state that Mesmer induced with what he thought was magnetism, Puységur obtained in Race a tranquil, sleeplike trance that Puységur called "artificial somnambulism," and which is known today (after Braid 1843) as hypnotism or hypnosis. Puységur's subject appeared to be asleep but in fact was awake, for he could engage in conversation, and actually exhibited "lucidity," that is, enhanced cognitive functioning (Ellenberger 1970). One aspect of this lucidity was an increased ability to recall past events.

By the turn of the century, the belief that hypnosis had a special power to retrieve lost memories into consciousness had become widespread in clinical psychiatry and figured prominently in the work of the likes of Janet, Breuer, and Freud. We have already encountered this view in chapter 2, in the quote from Janet's (1889) *L'automatisme psychologique:*

> I thought then of putting her into a deep somnambulistic state, capable, as has been seen, of recovering apparently forgotten memories, and I was thus able to recall the exact memory of a scene that she had never been aware of before except in the most incomplete fashion. (Quoted in Bowers and Meichenbaum 1985, 50)

Similarly, the cathartic technique of Josef Breuer (Breuer and Freud 1895) was predicated on the use of hypnosis to recover inaccessible emotional memories for abreaction (Erdelyi 1985). As is well known, Freud broke with the hypnotic tradition after his failure to induce the trance state (whatever that might be) in one of his patients, Miss Lucy R., and proceeding, without hypnosis, with the standard instructions to concentrate and retrieve inaccessible target memories. On the basis of his clinical experience, Freud was to conclude that the "work of recollection" was not enahanced by hypnosis. Surprisingly, Freud's observation was not evaluated experimentally until the 1980s.

Clark Hull (1933), in an effort to bring scientific rigor to notions about hypnosis, drew a mixed conclusion about "hypnotic hypermnesia," as the enhancement of memory through hypnosis had come to be known. He was faced with the problem of reconciling contradictory experimental findings. On the one hand was the impressive experiment of Stalnaker and Riddle (1932) purporting to show that, on the average, subjects under hypnosis could recall 65% more words from poetry learned in the past than in the "wake" state. On the other hand, there were several laboratory studies which failed to produce hypnotic hypermnesia for simple stimuli learned in the laboratory, such as nonsense syllables and lists of digits (Huse 1930; Mitchell 1932; Young 1925). Hull's effort to harmonize the discrepant data led him to the following conclusion:

> The experimental evidence shows rather definitely that recently acquired memory material is recovered no better in hypnosis than in the waking state, which probably indicates that hypnosis does not lower the threshold of recall. There is some striking experimental evidence which, while not absolutely convincing, tends strongly to confirm the clinical observations that hypnosis facilitates the recall of childhood and perhaps other remote memories. (Hull 1933, 127)

The Stimulus and the Test in Hypnotic Hypermnesia

Perhaps because of the unquestioned acceptance in those days of simple laboratory stimuli for the study of learning and memory, Hull did not consider the possibility that it was the nature of the stimulus and not the time of original learning (remote versus recent) that might explain the discrepant data. It remained for White, Fox, and Harris (1940) to demonstrate experimentally that the stimulus was in fact the critical factor. They showed in a simple laboratory study that whereas hypnosis failed to enhance recall of nonsense syllables, it did substantially augment the recall of meaningful visual materials (film segments) and of poetry memorized in the laboratory:

It is immediately apparent . . . that the effect of hypnosis on recall is by no means the same for different types of material. . . . This result annihilates the importance of the time factor [proposed by Hull] and justifies our suspicion that previous investigators by using different types of material created a false dilemma. Hypnotic hypermnesia, it now appears, prevails for meaningful material regardless of the time which has elapsed since learning; but it does not prevail for nonsense. (White, Fox, and Harris 1940, 94–95)

The hypnotic hypermnesia data thus seem nicely to converge with the Ballard tradition and the modern experimental findings on (nonhypnotic) hypermnesia. Knowledge of the stimulus used in laboratory studies brings some order to what might otherwise appear to be a hopelessly contradictory laboratory literature. Nevertheless, even with the stimulus factor taken into account, there remained an unsatisfactory amount of variability among laboratory results to warrant confidence in a reliable hypnotic hypermnesia effect (Smith 1983).

With the recent identification of a second critical factor, the type of memory test employed (Erdelyi, Dinges, et al. 1987; Erdelyi 1988), a remarkable orderliness in the experimental literature emerges. This is shown by figure 7.1, which reveals that when the stimulus factor is crossed

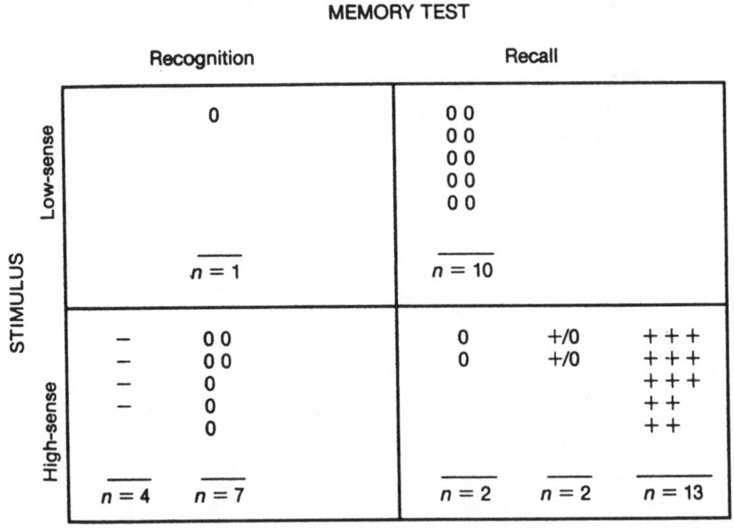

Figure 7.1 Effect of hypnosis on memory as a function of type of stimulus and memory test. Key to outcome symbols: +, positive (enhancement) effect; +/0, positive (enhancement) effect, but not with respect to all control conditions; 0, null outcome or nonsignificant trend; −, negative (decrement) effect. (Erdelyi 1988, 65)

Table 7.1 Documentation of figure 7.1: Outcomes by Stimulus and Test

Outcome	Stimulus and study
	Recognition of low-sense stimuli
0	Inkblots (Young, 1925)
	Recognition of high-sense stimuli
0	Objective, nonleading questions about filmed accident (Putnam, 1979)
−	Leading questions about accident (Putnam, 1979)
− *	Videotape of a theft (Sanders & Simmons, 1983)
0*	Leading questions about filmed crime (Sheehan & Tilden, 1983)
0*	Leading and nonleading questions about filmed crime (Sheehan & Tilden, 1984)
0	Staged assassination (Timm, 1981)
0*	Faces (Wagstaff, 1982)
− *	Slides of objects, people (Wagstaff, Traverse, & Milner, 1982, Experiment 1)
0*	Staged event (Wagstaff et al., 1982, Experiment 2)
0*	Objective, nonleading questions about filmed accident (Zelig & Beidleman, 1981)
−	Leading questions about accident (Zelig & Beidleman, 1981)
	Recall of low-sense stimuli
0	Nonsense syllables (remote) (Barber & Calverley, 1966)
0	Paired-associate words (Das, 1961)
0	Nonsense syllables (Dhanens & Lundy, 1975)
0	Nonsense syllables (Eysenck, 1941)
0	Nonsense syllables; nonsense pictorial figures (Huse, 1930)
0	Three-digit numbers (Mitchell, 1932)
0	Nonsense syllables; innocuous and profane words (Rosenthal, 1944)
0	Word lists (Salzberg & DePiano, 1980)
0	Nonsense syllables (White, Fox, & Harris, 1940)
0	Adjective-noun associates; digits; nonsense syllables; lists of names (Young, 1925)
	Recall of high-sense stimuli
+	Article about a rare chemical (Cooper & London, 1973) (But: Hypnosis enhanced performance only when hypnotic recall followed nonhypnotic recall, and not vice versa)
+	Picture details (Crawford & Allen, 1983)
+	Biographical prose passage (Dhanens & Lundy, 1975) (But: whereas hypnosis with motivational instructions helped those high vs. low in susceptibility [Difference Score = 4.33 vs. 1.89], motivation without hypnosis reversed the pattern [Difference Score = 2.50 vs. 4.22])
+	Meaningful auditory and visual information associated with films inducing low arousal, sexual arousal, and "traumatic" arousal (DePiano & Salzberg, 1981)
+	Emotional events; real-life events (Dorcus, 1960)
+	Pictures (Dywan & Bowers, 1983)

Table 7.1 (*Continued*)

	Recall of high-sense stimuli
+/0	Filmed crime scenarios (Geiselman, Fisher, MacKinnon, & Holland, 1985) (Hypnotic procedure elicited more correct recalls than a standard police interview, but not more than a nonhypnotic guided-memory interview)
+	Pictures (Gheorghiu, 1972)
0	Story (McConkey & Nogrady, 1984)
0	Pictures (Nogrady, McConkey, & Perry, 1985)
+	Poetry; words associated with failure (Rosenthal, 1944)
+	Real-life scene (Sears, 1954)
+	Slide sequence of wallet snatching (Sheehan & Tilden, 1984) (But: Hypnosis increased recall only of peripheral and not of central details)
+	Film material (Stager & Lundy, 1985)
+	Poetry, structured prose (Stalnaker & Riddle, 1932)
+/0	Staged assassination (Timm, 1981) (Hypnotic forensic interview yielded more correct information than free recall, but not more than a regular forensic interview)
+	Travel film segments, poetry (White et al., 1940)

Source: From Erdelyi 1988, 66–67, table 3.1. Copyright 1988 Guilford Press. Reprinted with permission.
Note: Key to Outcome Symbols: +, positive (enhancement) effect; +/0, positive (enhancement) effect, but not with respect to all control conditions; 0, null outcome or nonsignificant trend; −, negative (decrement) effect; *, response bias was controlled or did not vary in the study. These tabulations do not include unpublished studies, PhD dissertations, clinical reports, and publications from Eastern Europe. Also not included in the tabulations are two articles (Sanders and Simmons 1983; Yuille and McEwan 1985) that were difficult to categorize in terms of the dimensions of interest because of the use of mixed lists (high-sense and low-sense materials combined) or mixed tests (recall and recognition combined) or both.

with the test factor, a striking interaction results: hypermnesia is reliably obtained for recall of high-sense (high in meaning) materials but not for any of the other stimulus-test combinations. Thus there is no evidence for recall hypermnesia for low-sense materials nor for recognition hypermnesia for either low-sense or meaningful stimuli (indeed, in the latter case, an amnesic trend is in evidence). Table 7.1 documents figure 7.1.

The overwhelming evidence against hypnotic recognition-hypermnesia failed to be appreciated until recently because of the tendency of hypnosis researchers to use *recall* as a generic term for memory, including recognition memory. In a *recognition* test, the experimenter provides the test items and the subject decides which answer is correct (for example, in a yes/no recognition test, "Did you get a tie for a Christmas gift?" or in a multiple-choice recognition test, "What did you get as a Christmas gift? (a) a car, (b) a tie, (c) a pipe, (d) a lottery ticket). In a *recall* test, the subject himself must produce the required items ("What did you get for Christmas?"). When recognition studies, identified by actual test procedure rather than the label used (correctly or incorrectly) by the investigator, are separated from true recall studies, the previously noisy pattern of results becomes unambiguous.

The recognition data, beyond having implications for the general question of whether recognition hypermnesia exists (see below), also have practical implications, as in forensic settings. It is clear, for example, that hypnosis will not enhance eyewitness memory in a lineup situation (a recognition test) and may, actually, as suggested by figure 7.1, disrupt it slightly.

Is Hypnotic Hypermnesia Anything More than Regular Hypermnesia?

Although the pattern of results becomes clear, the meaning of the results is not. In particular, the positive hypermnesic results for recall of meaningful materials does not clinch the existence of hypnotic hypermnesia. There are two critical methodological problems, each of them potentially fatal.

The most obvious, and surprisingly neglected, issue is whether the hypermnesic results have anything whatsoever to do with hypnosis. Although there is no uniformity among all these studies, the usual design involves an initial recall test R_1, followed by the induction of hypnosis and then the administration, in hypnosis, of a second recall trial R_2. The reliable demonstration of hypermnesia—incremental recall from R_1 to R_2—does not signify that the intervening hypnosis had any active role. Possibly the same level of recall enhancement would have been obtained without hypnosis. This was, as already noted, Freud's conclusion in 1895.

What is needed is a control group that gets repeated testing but no hypnosis. Recent experimental studies that include this control have produced straightforward findings: Significant hypermnesias are obtained, as usual, but *hypnosis contributes nothing to hypermnesia* (Dinges et al. 1992; Nogrady, McConkey, and Perry 1985; Register and Kihlstrom 1987; Whitehouse et al. 1988). Thus what has been conceived of as *hypnotic* hypermnesia is nothing but hypermnesia.

A similar conclusion can be garnered from studies of systematic memory-interviewing techniques (for example, the "cognitive interview") that are supplemented by hypnosis: the addition of hypnosis does not yield additional recall (Geiselman et al. 1985; Mingay 1986; Timm 1981). It would appear that many police departments and intelligence services have been squandering resources on hypnotic interrogation techniques. The fact that enhanced recall is obtained distracts them from the question whether the hypnotic intervention played a role. Probably the same memory enhancement would be obtained with magnets.

Although the conclusion that hypnosis does not add to hypermnesia is by now consensual among researchers, there certainly is no unanimity (Pettinati 1988; Rossi and Cheek 1988). One argument against this negative conclusion about the hypermnesic properties of hypnosis is that laboratory psychologists are once again falling into the stimulus trap. Just as there is a big difference between the effects obtained with nonsense syllables as opposed to "meaningful" materials, so there is, the claim goes, a drastic difference between tame meaningful stimuli and emotionally violent events; it is traumatic memories, not well-behaved memories for poems or pictures that hypnosis helps recover (Rossi and Cheek 1988). One answer to this clinical criticism is that some of the past experiments did use emotional events as stimuli, for example, filmed crime scenarios, a staged assassination, and so forth (see table 7.1). The counterargument is that these are contrived emotional events compared to real, true-life traumas. The one clear exception is the doctoral dissertation of Sloane (1981) with the Los Angeles Police Department, then one of the great centers for the use of hypnosis in criminal investigations. Sloane's subjects were actual victims of violent crimes, such as rapes and shootings. Did hypnosis augment their memory? The experimental findings were that it did not. Unfortunately, Sloane's memory test was made up mostly of recognition items, so the possibility is not completely foreclosed that hypnosis might have augmented *recall* of traumatic memories.

Rossi and Cheek (1988) have also suggested that "nonauthoritarian" Ericksonian hypnosis techniques involving *behavioral* responses to memory queries (for example, raising a finger to say yes, another to say no) succeed in retrieving traumatic memories where recall fails under more standard verbal hypnotic testing. No experimental support, however, has been advanced for this proposal.

The Response Criterion Issue in Hypnotic Hypermnesia

The second problem with the hypnotic recall-hypermnesia results of table 7.1 is that none of the included studies controlled for response criteria. (See chap. 4 for the treatment of the same issue in the recovery of subliminal stimuli, chap. 5 for a solution for recall of memory lists, and chap. 8 and the appendix for a proposed solution of the problem in the recall of narrative materials.) There is little question that hypnosis can increase the subject's response productivity as well as confidence in what is produced. More correct recalls are usually generated under hypnosis—but also more incorrect ones (Dywan and Bowers 1983; Klatzky and Erdelyi 1985; Orne 1979; Orne et al. 1988; Smith 1983; Whitehouse et al. 1988).

When response productivity increases, increases in hits (correct re-calls or recognitions) do not signify increased memory (Klatzky and Erdelyi 1985), just as the accompanying increases in false alarms (false recalls or recognitions, paramnesias, confabulations, and so forth) do not signify diminished or distorted memory (Klatzky and Erdelyi 1985; Sheehan 1988). Without controls over response criteria, it is actually not possible to evaluate memory level. For example, the positive findings in the cell of figure 7.1 involving the recall of high-sense materials are unin-terpretable with respect to true recall level. The overwhelmingly positive pattern could even be consistent with negative trends in recall level, for with false alarms controlled, hit levels (number of correct recalls) could actually be lower under hypnosis.

In an effort to evaluate simultaneously the response criterion issue as well as the role of hypnosis in hypnotic hypermnesia, Dinges et al. (1992) and Whitehouse et al. (1988) evaluated hypermnesia over recall trials with response productivity controlled by means of a forced recall proce-dure (in which subjects are required to produce a constant number of responses in each trial, guessing if necessary). The results showed clearly that with productivity controlled, hypnosis does not produce enhanced recall beyond *nonhypnotic* hypermnesia. Actually, there are hints of a negative trend associated with hypnosis which has already been observed with recognition hypermnesia. In the Dinges experiment, which examined reminiscence as well as hypermnesia effects, a small but statistically reli-able decrement was found in hypnotic reminiscence compared to nonhyp-notic reminiscence (that is, hypnotized subjects produced cumulative re-call functions that grew at a slightly slower pace over multiple recall trials than that of nonhypnotic subjects). The corresponding data of Nogrady et al. (1985), however, showed no reliable difference between hypnotic and nonhypnotic cumulative recall functions.

Conclusion

The negative trend occasionally observed in hypnotic memory may or may not be real (according to Sheehan 1988, it is not). It is underscored here only to show that if the null hypothesis should prove wrong, the effect of hypnosis on memory is likely to be in the opposite direction from the one normally assumed. In any event, no hypnosis-specific diminu-tion should be posited. As I have already proposed (Erdelyi 1988), any cognitive activity that diverts processing resources away from retrieval effort—hypnosis, free association, mental arithmetic—would tend to diminish hypermnesia by reducing new retrievals (reminiscence), enhancing forgetting (oblivescence), or both.

Contrariwise, if hypnosis—or any other intervention—should render a recalcitrant subject more willing to engage in retrieval effort, then hypnosis (or the other intervention) would tend to enhance hypermnesia. This is a nuance worth pondering. It is one thing for the experimenter/clinician to instruct the subject to continue thinking hard and to keep trying to retrieve some memory, and something else for the subject to do it. If belief in hypnosis (or whatever) produces genuine added retrieval effort, then more hypermnesia should result. In this sense, hypnosis could prove hypermnesic. But then so could any other agent—magnets, crystals, a white lab coat, positive transference, an appeal to reason, nagging.

In sum, no hypnosis-specific effect on memory enhancement has been demonstrated. Hypermnesia occurs with or without hypnosis. Hypnosis does not uniquely add to (or subtract from) hypermnesia. Barring some breakthroughs in the future, it may be concluded that hypnotic hypermnesia is nothing more than hypermnesia.

Recognition Hypermnesia

Standard Recognition

Prior to the present chapter, virtually all hypermnesia studies examined, including Ballard's program, employed *recall* or some other type of active reproduction (for example, motor performance, relearning) as indicators of memory. There has been little discussion, and actually very little explicit research done, of hypermnesia in recognition memory, despite its theoretical and applied implications. Indeed Buxton, in the heat of refuting one of the few extant claims of "a rise in certain recognition-retention curves" (English 1942, 505), came close to excluding recognition hypermnesia by definitional fiat ("It seems difficult or impossible ever to say just *how much* reminiscence [hypermnesia] is actually occurring with a . . . recognition test. . . . The definition of reminiscence should probably be based on improvements in terms of a recall criterion" [1942, 503]).

The preceding section on hypnotic hypermnesia unexpectedly provides a trove of experimental data on recognition hypermnesia (fig. 7.1, table 7.1), which, as already noted, were unwittingly collected by a majority of researchers who believed they were investigating recall. The dozen experimental studies reported are fatally unanimous: no hint of recognition hypermnesia exists; if anything, recognition memory declines with repeated testing. These studies, of course, involved hypnosis, and the failure of recognition hypermnesia developing might be ascribed (contrary to the usual expectation) to some interfering effect of hypnosis on memory recovery. If, however, hypnotic hypermnesia is, as concluded in the previous section, nothing but regular hypermnesia, then the studies provide overwhelming evidence against the existence of recognition hypermnesia.

One of the few direct investigations of recognition hypermnesia without hypnosis, that of Payne and Roediger (1987), is completely consistent with the above conclusion: with repeated testing, recognition fails to improve, or declines. An attractive feature of the Payne and Roediger study is that *both* recall and recognition hypermnesia were evaluated for the same stimulus-processing conditions (for example, semantically elaborated or imaginally coded words) and so the failure of recognition hypermnesia cannot be attributed to the investigators' inability to produce hypermnesia effects in their studies. In two separate experiments involving several independent groups, recall-hypermnesia was reliably obtained with the memory materials, but never recognition hypermnesia. Repeated multiple-choice tests (of either the 4AFC [four-alternative forced-choice] or 6AFC variety) produced no performance change over trials; yes/no recognition performance, indexed by d', showed significant decline over trials. In a parallel study of hypermnesia comparing cued-recall with 2AFC recognition, Otani & Hodge (1991) obtained the same outcome: hypermnesia for cued recall but no hypermnesia for recognition memory. Payne and Roediger concluded that "hypermnesia occurs in recall but not in recognition" (145).

Recognition Hypermnesia in Non-Standard Recognition Tests

Payne and Roediger's conclusion aptly describes the recognition-hypermnesia literature that is based on "standard" recognition tests. As will now be suggested, recognition hypermnesia may in fact exist when the recognition test is, in some sense, not standard, as when: (1) the recognition tests employ not the original stimuli but some *transformed* version of the stimuli (for example, paraphrases, parts of the stimuli); (2) at original testing, recognition memory is "absolutely subliminal" (Ionescu and Erdelyi 1992), that is, at chance level; and (3) the retention interval is extremely brief (in the order of 45–90 seconds).

Recognition of transforms or part-forms of the original stimulus set. The typical (that is, standard) recognition test used in the laboratory, whether of a yes/no or multiple-choice variety, involves *re*-presentation of the original stimulus items for recognition. The approach, though convenient, is not as "ecologically valid" as it might be. In real-life recognition we rarely encounter the exact same stimulus a second time; we see the face from a different angle, and perhaps only a part of it; the person may have grown a beard; the theory may have been reworded; the context is vastly different. Despite such transforms, the original stimulus can often be recognized, though some cognitive effort may be needed. Since cognitive effort (retrieval effort, work of recollection, and so forth) is thought to be crucial for hypermnesia, it makes sense to look for recognition hypermnesia where such cognitive effort is required.

The work of English and his associates (English, Welborn, and Killian 1934; English and Edwards 1939) introduces an excellent tactic: the comparison of recognition memory over time for *paraphrases* versus *verbatim* segments of previously administered narrative materials.

With repeated recognition tests (of the yes/no/maybe/I don't remember variety) recognition hypermnesia was variously obtained for paraphrased or summarized stimulus items but not for verbatim test items. The publications feature many experiments, not all of which are fully consistent with each other. Nevertheless, incremental recognition memory was reported for intervals of 24 hours, 8 days, 55 days, and 90 days, leading English and Edwards to conclude that the

> forgetting curve is by no means universal or even typical. . . . The Ebbinghaus-like curve appears to characterize ability to recognize what has been learned by rote [verbatim items] but not the "sense" or substance of material which has been understandingly studied [meanings]. . . . With college students . . . even several months after learning had taken place, no less, but more, of the substance was recognizable. (English and Edwards 1939, 253)

These dramatic findings, unfortunately, are undermined by some potentially deadly artifacts. Buxton (1942), for example, pointed out that the memory materials were about psychology, and since many of the subjects were psychology students, improvement for general "substance" might simply reflect the students' knowing more as their studies progressed. Thus, long-term improvement in performance could reflect learning and not upward-trending memory. Not enough relevant detail is provided by English et al. to evaluate such problems, including possible criterion shifts with repeated testing for gist. Thus this early work can be judged as provocative but not necessarily trustworthy. I am currently pursuing the issue of recognition hypermnesia for paraphrases in my laboratory.

Independent of the work of English et al., Erdelyi and Stein (1981) explored recognition hypermnesia with a similar, though not identical, logic. The idea was to test recognition hypermnesia not with representations of the original stimulus items but with meaningful *parts* of the original stimuli. The stimuli chosen were a large set of cartoons with captions. Pilot work had shown virtually perfect standard recognition memory for the whole cartoons, but subceiling performance on either the pictorial or the verbal (caption) components of the original stimuli. Thus if subjects could, through retrieval effort, recover the inaccessible complement of an unrecognized component (whether picture or caption), then they should recognize the reconstituted whole stimulus and therefore the heretofore unrecognized component.

As a control, a group of subjects were presented with pseudo-cartoons in which the original pictures and captions were scrambled, that is, randomly mismatched, with the expectations that on recognition testing the test items (pictures or captions) would not, despite retrieval effort, yield their semantically unrelated complements. Thus for the test items from the pseudo-cartoons, whether pictures or captions, no recognition hypermnesia was expected.

The control subjects, when tested either on captions or on pictures, in fact failed to improve over three repeated tests (of the yes-no variety, with confidence ratings). The experimental subjects—those originally exposed to semantically coherent, true cartoons—did however produce d' increments from R_1 to R_3 on the picture items, though not on the corresponding verbal captions. The latter failure made sense post-hoc: the picture items tended to suggest the themes of the whole cartoon and therefore helped retrieval effort, but the captions were uninformative as retrieval cues and therefore did not help retrieval. These results and conjectures are also being followed up in my laboratory.

The general idea, then, is that recognition hypermnesia might be obtained with *transforms* (paraphrases, part forms of the original stimuli) since active retrieval effort, leading to the retransformation or reconstitutions of the original stimuli, would produce enhanced recognition. In the case of rote recognition, where the test items are exactly the same as the stimulus items, retrieval processes do not play an active role and so no hypermnesia results. (For discussions of the retrieval component of recognition, see Erdelyi and Stein 1981; Mandler 1980; Rabinowitz and Graesser 1976; Rabinowitz, Mandler, and Barsalou 1977.)

The theory and some of the data are in place but more experimental research is needed before a confident conclusion can be reached about recognition hypermnesia for stimulus transforms.

Recognition hypermnesia over very brief intervals. I know of two experiments on recognition hypermnesia over very short time intervals. The original study by Milner (1968) involved a between-subjects design in which one group was tested immediately and the other 90 seconds after stimulus presentation. The stimulus was an array of 12 faces; the recognition test was an array of 25 faces from which the 12 correct ones had to be chosen. It was found that recognition of faces improved when subjects were tested 90 seconds later as compared to immediately after stimulus presentation. Neurologically involved amnesic patients failed to show such recognition hypermnesia.

The Milner results with normal subjects were followed up by Wallace, Coltheart, and Forster (1970), who found a similar improvement in recognition memory, but at a 45-second interval, both in adults and children. There was also a trend in both the adults' and the children's data for recognition to rise again from a delay interval of 3 minutes, at which recognition was at a low point, to a retention interval of 9 minutes, the longest tested. (The patterns held for a stimulus exposure of 45 seconds but not for the shorter exposure of 15 seconds.)

Of possible relevance to an explanation of these hypermnesic recognition data is Milner's observation that her subjects "appeared to be bewildered by the rapid transition from the first to the second set of photographs" (1968, 201). Perhaps such bewilderment disrupted retrieval in the immediate memory test, subsiding enough after a short interval to allow higher performance in the delay group. Hypermnesic effects resulting from disrupted retrieval at immediate testing are further discussed in the later section of this chapter on arousal and hypermnesia. Of course, the disruption hypothesis is only that; Milner (1968) and Wallace et al. (1970) hew to a consolidation explanation in which traces become more consolidated over time.

Recognition Hypermnesia for Subliminal Lists

In chapter 4 it was shown that no true hypermnesia for subliminal stimuli had been experimentally demonstrated in either recall or recognition. In these early, perceptually oriented studies, a single complex stimulus was flashed tachistoscopically. If, however, as recently proposed by Greenwald (1992), subliminal perception exists but is "dumb," being limited to perhaps a single word or meaning chunk per exposure, then it would be unlikely that enough of a complex stimulus is registered to yield palpable recoveries (Erdelyi 1984). Perhaps a *list* of *simple* subliminal stimuli, with each item presented individually and potentially registered successfully, could accumulate into a recoverable set of inaccessible memories. It was this type of reasoning, as already noted, that led to my shift to memory lists of simple stimuli from the single-flash of a complex stimulus (Erdelyi 1984; Erdelyi and Becker 1974).

In the section following this one, a systematic effort to evaluate *recall* hypermnesia for subliminal lists will be discussed. In the present section on recognition hypermnesia, a recent pair of experiments by Merikle and Reingold (1991), apparently demonstrating recognition hypermnesia for an absolutely subliminal (chance-level) memory list, is reviewed.

Reingold and Merikle's work was only secondarily concerned with the recovery issue; their primary goal was to demonstrate that unconscious stimuli can have palpable indirect effects. Reingold and Merikle used a visual variant of the dichotic listening procedure of Eich (1984): a long list of word pairs were presented for 430 msec per pair. For each word pair exposure, one of the words, indicated by an arrow, was to be called out aloud by the subject. After the subject's response, the next word pair was presented, and so on. After the presentation of all the word pairs, subjects' recognition memory for the words that had been cued (and shadowed) was quite substantial. If, however, subjects were tested for the unattended words, *recognition memory* was at chance level. But when subjects evaluated the extent to which these same words *stood out,* performance was reliably above chance. These results corroborate and extend the striking Kunst-Wilson and Zajonc (1980)—or KWZ— phenomenon (Bonanno and Stillings 1986; Bornstein, Leone, and Galley 1987; Mandler, Nakamura, and Van Zandt 1987; Seamon, Brody, and Kauff 1983a, 1983b; Seamon, Marsh, and Brody 1984). The KWZ phenomenon is the prototypic dissociation effect in subliminal perception (Erdelyi 1986): a *direct* test of stimulus recognition ("Which of the test items were flashed to you earlier?") yields chance performance, or absolute subliminality, yet an *indirect* probe (for example, "Which of the test items do you like best?") results in significantly above-chance choice of the (absolutely subliminal) stimuli that had been flashed. In the Reingold and Merikle studies, the extent to which the *indirect,* contrast judgments indexed unconscious information that the *direct,* conscious effort at recognition failed to contact, the results can be taken as a demonstration of the active operation of unconscious stimuli.

Partly in response to my suggestion (Erdelyi 1986) that in subliminal perception experiments, absolute subliminality cannot be evaluated by testing only immediately after stimulus exposure because of the possibility of hypermnesia, that is, the possibility that initial chance-level performance might become above-chance performance over time, Reingold and

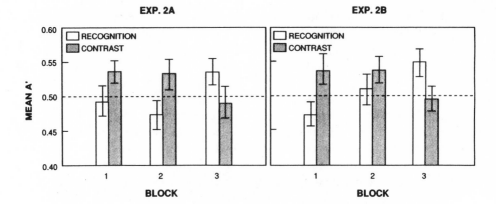

Figure 7.2 Recognition and contrast performance in block 1, block 2, and block 3 in two experiments (2A and 2B), measured by the discriminability index A′, for which 0.50 represents chance performance. (Merikle and Reingold 1991, 230)

Merikle compared recognition memory performance in the first third (block 1), second third (block 2), and third third (block 3) portions of their recognition test. Thus instead of administering multiple recognition tests, these authors tested early, middle, and late performance on a single test. Although overall recognition memory (block 1 + block 2 + block 3) was at chance, recognition performance increased over blocks, reaching significantly above-chance recognition levels by block 3. These results are depicted in the white histograms in the left panel (experiment 2A) of figure 7.2. Curiously, the indirect *contrast* measure, which was above chance level in block 1, dropped to chance level by block 3. The authors undertook a replication of their experiment, producing the results shown in the right panel (experiment 2B) in figure 7.2. Clearly, the previous pattern was reproduced. The two experiments suggest that recognition memory drifted upward from chance to above-chance levels from the earlier phase of testing with time and effort. This unexpected but replicated demonstration of recognition hypermnesia for a subliminal list is made more credible by the failure, in both experiments, of recognition hypermnesia to develop for the supraliminal (that is, shadowed) list of items. Thus, in keeping with the literature, no recognition hypermnesia was observed in the standard recognition situation. Only for the peculiar case where the whole list was strictly subliminal did recognition hypermnesia materialize.

Mandler, Nakamura, and Van Zandt (1987), without looking for recognition hypermnesia, reported a repeated recognition outcome that seems to be consistent with the Merikle and Reingold findings: in an initial recognition test R_1, which produced 46.7% correct 2AFC choices (50% being chance level), an immediately repeated recognition test R_2 produced 52.5% hits. No statistical evaluation of this numerical increase was reported, however.

It is curious in these studies that initial or early-phase recognition seems numerically below chance (this holds for the two Merikle and Reingold studies, the Mandler et al. results, and several of the other studies involving the KWZ effect, including the original KWZ study). Whether some mysterious subchance perception is being produced (Ionescu and Erdelyi 1992; Snodgrass, Shevrin, and Kopka 1993) and whether the resulting recognition hypermnesia is dependent on it—or, at least, absolute subliminality on R_1—is not known at this juncture. Obviously, further research is indicated.

Hypermnesia in Cued Recall

In cued recall the subject is given a cue or clue, usually consisting of a part of the stimulus whole, and asked to generate the remaining part of the stimulus. For example, if the subject is given a list of word pairs such as (1) hot - dog, (2) sloppy - joe, (3) blue - sky, he or she may be tested by being given the first items of the list and asked to supply the second. The latter example is the widely used paired-associates learning procedure. Other variants are possible, as when the subject is presented a list of words and subsequently given the first few letters of each word and asked to recall the whole word (for example, assassin, as ——) or, perhaps, the first few words of the lines of a poem and asked to fill in the rest of the lines.

Can hypermnesia be obtained with cued recall? The answer is clearly yes (Estes 1955; Izawa 1968, 1969, 1989; Payne and Roediger 1987, 1994; Otani and Hodge 1991; Otani and Whiteman 1994; Whitehouse et al. 1988).

Given the positive findings, there is a methodological and a theoretical point worth underscoring.

The cued-recall procedure may have methodological advantages when substantial control over the recall task is desired. Thus the order of recall may be determined, the extent of cuing varied, the responses forced (if forced recall is desired), and complex narrative recall for stories, poems, and even pictures probed systematically.

The theoretical point of interest is that cued-recall, as normally conceived, stands in an intermediate position between free (or forced) recall and recognition. Actually, as Tulving (1985) has cogently argued, recall and recognition may be viewed as the opposite poles of a cued-recall continuum. In regular free (or forced) recall, minimal cues are given (instructions referring to the memory list, the experimental context itself, and so forth) whereas in recognition, an "identity cue" is provided—the memory item itself—and the subject must decide whether he or she recalls it. From this vantage point, the cued-recall hypermnesia question becomes not whether it occurs or not but, rather, how much cuing is necessary for it to occur. It has been already noted that, typically, standard recognition (involving "identity cues") fails to produce hypermnesia, but imperfect cues (for example, nonstandard recognition), which necessitate significant retrieval processes, are more likely to yield hypermnesia.

Thus the previous section on nonstandard recognition, involving transforms, part forms, or otherwise impoverished stimuli, may be conceived of as cued-recall tests in which the cue or clue is not perfect as it is in standard (identity cue) recognition.

Recall Hypermnesia for Subliminal Lists

A programmatic effort to determine whether *recall* hypermnesia for subliminal lists might exist—a recall version of the recognition results discussed above—has been pursued by Ionescu and Erdelyi (1992; Ionescu 1993).

The tactic employed by Ionescu and Erdelyi was to start with a standard list of simple stimuli such as have produced reliable effects in the past (Erdelyi and Becker 1974; Erdelyi and Kleinbard 1978; chap. 5 herein) and progressively shorten item exposure (from the usual 5 seconds per item) until initial list recall R_1 is null, that is, at chance level.

A mixed list of 40 pictures and 40 words were used, with each item flashed, depending on the group, for 5 seconds, 2 seconds, 1 second, 50 milliseconds, or 5 milliseconds. A base-rate control group was presented with sham flashes of 80 blank slides, for 5 milliseconds each, but otherwise treated the same as the experimental group (those actually shown the stimuli).

The left panel of figure 7.3 shows the multitrial pattern for the different exposure groups. As visual inspection suggests, hypermnesia was obtained at all stimulus durations, including the shortest one of 5 msec per item. However, it is readily apparent that even this 5 msec group produced above-chance R_1 ($R_1 = 27.67$ versus the base-rate R_1 of 13.22), and so the list was not "subliminal" in the strict sense adopted.

In order to produce absolute subliminality, as measured in R_1, the stimuli were further degraded at the 5 msec exposure (the lower limit

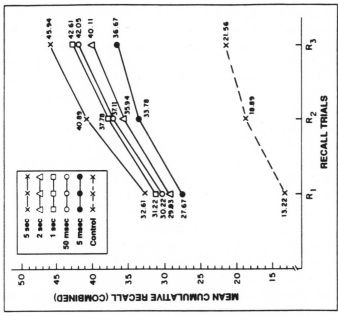

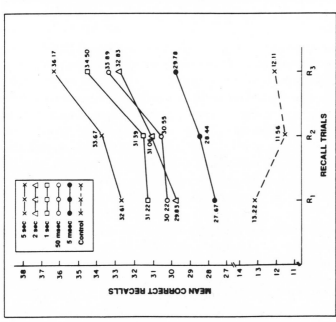

Figure 7.3 Hypermnesia and reminiscence as a function of exposure duration of each item on the stimulus list. *Left panel:* recall performance over three trials by experimental and control subjects in Ionescu's (1993) experiment 2. *Right panel:* corresponding cumulative recall across trials. The recall levels shown are for an 80-item mixed list of 40 pictures and 40 words. (Ionescu and Erdelyi 1992, 158)

of the projection tachistoscope) by positioning neutral-density filters of different strengths in front of the projector lens. A wide sampling of neutral-density filters were used to assure that at least some of the groups would be operating at chance level on R_1.

Eight experimental groups were tested, each at one of the following filter strengths: 0.50, 0.70, 0.90, 1.00, 1.10, 1.20, and 1.40. These strengths are calibrated logarithmically, so light reduction ranged from a factor of 3.16 (antilog of 0.50) to a factor of 25.11 (antilog of 1.40).

The multitrial recall data are presented in figure 7.4 (left panel). Although the least occluded group (the 0.50 filter group) was substantially above chance on R_1 (31.42 versus the base rate's 18.33), no hypermnesia was in evidence; indeed the recall trend was amnesic, though not statistically significant. All the other groups' R_1 performance were not significantly different from chance—the base rate group's R_1—though, surprisingly, numerically lower. It is quite clear from visual inspection (and borne out statistically) that the multitrial recall pattern for these "absolutely subliminal" lists was not hypermnesic. Highly degraded lists, certainly those yielding null (chance-level) initial recall, fail to produce hypermnesia. Were it not for the recognition results reported in the previous section, the simple conclusion would be that stimuli—or lists—that are at or below the chance limen are not recoverable directly.

It is peculiar that multiple recognition tests, which normally fail to produce hypermnesia where recall tests reliably do, should have produced hypermnesia for subliminal inputs. One possibility is that at such degraded levels, not enough information is accessible in *recall* to serve as useful retrieval cues, whereas the *recognition* tests provide more cues, which result in further information retrieval for better performance on subsequent tests. This is a topsy-turvy hypothesis, one positing a role reversal in recall and recognition from supraliminal to subliminal conditions: active retrieval plays little role in standard recognition because of a ceiling effects (the initial recognition test provides all the usable cues, hence no subsequent improvement) whereas in the liminal region, recall is mired in a floor effect (not enough cues are accessible to get the incrementing process in motion). Thus the hypothesis—ad hoc speculation, really—is that what is too much for recognition and effective for recall at supraliminal levels shifts down, respectively, to effective and too little at subliminal levels.

It is important to emphasize, however, that the technique of stimulus "degradation" was different in the successful recognition studies and the unsuccessful recall experiments on subliminal lists: in the Merikle and Reingold experiments the chance-level items were the unattended items

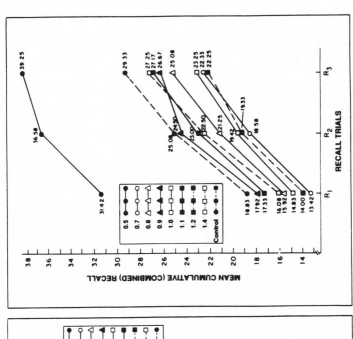

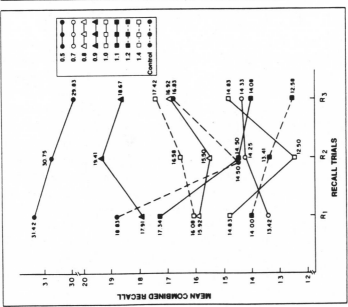

Figure 7.4 Hypermnesia and reminiscence for subliminal lists: *Left panel:* recall performance over three trials for experimental and control subjects in Ionescu's (1993) experiment 3. *Right panel:* corresponding cumulative recall over the three trials. (Ionescu and Erdelyi 1992, 161)

in a list of item pairs; in the Ionescu and Erdelyi studies the items were physically degraded to chance retention through insufficient intensity and exposure. Perhaps the stimuli were not "absolutely subliminal" but altogether unregistered and therefore unrecoverable. Recall hypermnesia could have been obtained with Merikle and Reingold's subliminal stimuli which, presumably, were registered since each stimulus pair in their list was flashed for close to half a second. More research is called for to make a definitive statement.

Before concluding this section, the multitrial cumulative recall patterns (in the right panels of figs. 7.3 and 7.4) should be considered. What these patterns provide are reminiscence functions (Rem = cum R_n − R_1) and therefore address the possibility of reminiscence for subliminal lists. Ionescu and I had considered the possibility that reminiscence might be a more sensitive measure than hypermnesia of the recovery of subliminal stimuli since reminiscence provides a pure index of recovery without being diluted, as is hypermnesia, by losses across trials. Reminiscence turned out, however, to be less sensitive than hypermnesia. In figure 7.3, where hypermnesia was obtained with very brief stimuli (all the way down to 5 msec per item), no reminiscence was obtained beyond chance guessing by the 5 msec group. Although all cumulative recall functions are incremental, the experimental groups' cumulative recall functions are not always much steeper than the base-rate group's, which just guessed from trial to trial. This is particularly so for the 5 msec experimental group. The base-rate control subjects, who saw none of the stimuli and merely produced guesses from trial to trial, cumulated hits at about the same rate as subjects who had actually been exposed to the stimuli for 5 msec and who in fact saw and remembered some of the stimuli (as demonstrated by their above-chance R_1 performance) and produced hypermnesia. Since recoveries due to guessing should, clearly, be factored out of reminiscence functions (in the past no one had bothered to do so, perhaps on the assumption that guessing would yield a trivial rate of new hits), these results raise questions about reminiscence as a sensitive indicator of memory enhancement. (On the other hand, because of the large number of experimental groups, the failure of reminiscence in one of them, the 5 msec group, might be attributed to error variance and should not be overplayed theoretically.)

The left panel of figure 7.4 shows that no hypermnesia was obtained for subliminal lists. The cumulative recall patterns of figure 7.4 (right panel) also show no above-chance reminiscence: cumulative recall for the guesses of the sham-flash group was as steep as the corresponding cumulative recall functions of any of the experimental groups.

Perhaps the most interesting yield of these cumulative recall analyses is a methodological one: cumulative guessing base rates—chance reminiscences—should be estimated and factored out of cumulative recall functions. Such chance-corrected cumulative recall functions provide a purer measure of the memory component of cumulative recall.

Hypermnesia and Arousal

A small but durable literature linking arousal to hypermnesia is reviewed in this section. Although the originally reported effects are dramatic, there are questions about their reliability and generality.

The reference studies are two publications by Kleinsmith and Kaplan (1963, 1964) showing that paired associates of high-arousal stimulus items (as defined by galvanic skin responses, or GSRs) are poorly recalled at short retention intervals but better recalled at longer retention intervals, whereas low-arousal items produce a reverse pattern, with high level of initial retention decreasing over retention interval. Thus associates of high-arousal items are hypermnesic whereas associates of low-arousal items are amnesic.

In the 1963 study, eight words—*rape, vomit, kiss, swim, love, dance, money,* and *exam*—were each paired with a number from 2 to 9 and presented once. Each subject's electrodermal responses to the stimulus words were recorded and the subjects were subsequently tested for the associates of their three highest and their three lowest arousal stimuli. Different groups of subjects were tested at retention intervals of 2 minutes, 20 minutes, 45 minutes, 1 day, and 1 week (fig. 7.5).

Kleinsmith and Kaplan's 1964 study was a modified replication of their earlier work. This time only three retention intervals were tested— 2 minutes, 20 minutes, and 1 week—and guesses were required to stimulus items when subjects felt they could not recall the associated digit (response bias artifacts being thus eliminated). Also, the stimulus items, only six in this study, were zero association value nonsense syllables (*cef, qap, tov, jex, laj, dax*) instead of words. Although it is difficult to grasp how such nonsense syllables could be imbued with differential arousal values that are psychologically meaningful—median splits on each subject's six GSRs operationalized high and low arousal stimuli—the results were about as dramatic as those of the 1963 study (fig. 7.5, bottom panel).

Several successful replications were subsequently reported (Butter 1970; Kaplan and Kaplan 1969; Walker and Tarte 1963). Levonian (1966, 1972) produced the effect with recognition memory for film items. On the other hand, there have been discrepant results as well. Schmitt and

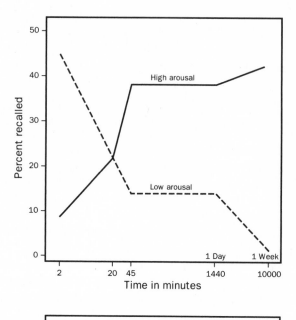

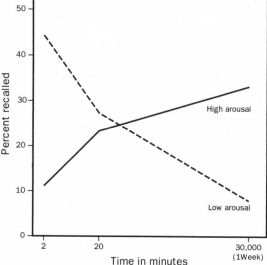

Figure 7.5 Kleinsmith and Kaplan's (1963, 1964) differential recall curves for high- and low-arousal stimulus items. *Top panel:* "differential recall of paired associates as a function of arousal level" (1963, 191). *Bottom panel:* "differential recall of nonsense syllable paired associates as a function of arousal level" (1964, 125).

Forrester (1973), for example, produced a flat-out nonreplication: there was no retention difference between high and low arousal associates either at immediate (2 minutes) recall or at delayed (2 days) recall, and both high- and low-arousal items produced amnesic functions. Similarly, Schönpflug (1966; and in Levonian 1972) found better retention at both

2 and 45 minutes for high-arousal as compared to low-arousal associates. Also, one of the cited "replications," that of Kaplan and Kaplan (1969), could be read the other way, since both high- and low-arousal retention patterns were amnesic from 2 minutes to 2 days except for a small but statistically significant upward bounce at 6 minutes for the high-arousal associates. (Kaplan and Kaplan attributed these discrepancies to greater relaxation among their subjects due to less "ego orientation" toward the task as a result of the study's different instructions.) Further, it seems fairly clear that free recall does not yield the Kleinsmith and Kaplan type of effect (Maltzman, Kantor, and Langdon 1966; M. W. Eysenck 1974).

The theoretical motivation of this family of studies was a "persevarative consolidation" hypothesis, often known as Walker's *action decrement* theory (1958). The action decrement idea holds that memory consolidation takes place after input, during which time the traces being consolidated are relatively inaccessible (action decrement); high-arousal items are better consolidated, ultimately yielding better retention, but are correspondingly more inaccessible during the initial period of more intense and lengthy consolidation. For this reason high-arousal items should show low initial recall but higher later recall and vice versa for low-arousal items. This, of course, was the pattern obtained by Kleinsmith and Kaplan (1963, 1964).

H. J. Eysenck (1967, 1973; Eysenck and Frith 1977) wedded this notion to his neurological theory of introversion-extraversion to predict—and experimentally produce—hypermnesia ("reminiscence") for introverts but amnesia for extraverts. Eysenck's neurological theory posits that introverts are characterized by cortical overarousal, whereas extraverts by underarousal. Consequently, the consolidation process in introverts in contrast to extraverts occurs under high arousal, leading to poorer initial memory but better later memory, that is, hypermnesia. With extraverts the situation is reversed, yielding amnesic retention over time. Figure 7.6 reproduces the results of Howarth and Eysenck (1968), the first direct test of this hypothesis. The recall pattern (for the stimuli and associates of a paired-associates list) are very similar to those of Kleinsmith and Kaplan (1963, 1964). Nevertheless, irrespective of the merits of this neurological theory, the empirical link between hypermnesia and introversion is uncertain. With paired-associates learning, the evidence is mixed (M. W. Eysenck 1976b). With standard multitrial recall, the results are negative: in several unpublished studies, I have failed to obtain differential recall patterns in subjects as a function of test scores on the extraversion or neuroticism scales of the Eysenck Personality Inventory.

Whatever the ultimate empirical status of the arousal-hypermnesia

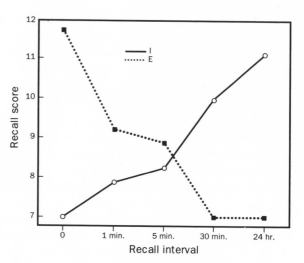

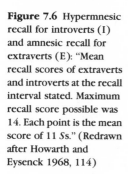

Figure 7.6 Hypermnesic recall for introverts (I) and amnesic recall for extraverts (E): "Mean recall scores of extraverts and introverts at the recall interval stated. Maximum recall score possible was 14. Each point is the mean score of 11 Ss." (Redrawn after Howarth and Eysenck 1968, 114)

connection, the action decrement hypothesis, which originated with research on memory of rats, is not likely to be a satisfactory explanation. As M. W. Eysenck (1976a, 1976b) shows in his detailed reviews, the Kleinsmith-Kaplan-type effect does not materialize with free-recall measures of retention but only with cued-recall involving paired-associates tests, and then only with a between subjects design (in which different subjects are tested only once at different retention intervals). He concludes (on the basis of other considerations as well) that "at present, it is pure conjecture that the critical difference between high- and low-arousal items is in terms of the nature of the consolidatory process to which they give rise" (M. W. Eysenck 1976a, 391).

A more common-sense approach to the possible relation between arousal and hypermnesia arises from the well-known inverted-U function relating performance to arousal (Yerkes and Dodson 1908; Broadhurst 1957). It is not particularly critical whether the relation is symmetrically U-shaped or even squiggle-shaped—or, for that matter, topographically a "catastrophe" phenomenon (Hardy and Parfitt 1991). It is enough to assume the obvious fact that arousal can be too low or too high to support optimal cognitive performance. If, for whatever reason, early testing were associated with excessive arousal (confusion, anxiety, and so on), retrieval processing would be suboptimal, resulting in relatively low retention levels. With diminution of overarousal, retrieval would be more efficient, producing higher retention levels and therefore hypermnesia.

For the pure-memory researcher, such an interference-based hypermnesia effect might verge on the trivial. If a subject is distracted by fear, white noise, or whatever at test 1 but allowed to concentrate on test 2, it is not particularly surprising that performance should prove better on test 2. Yet this very situation characterizes many clinical cases in which hyperarousal (terror, guilt, shame) undermines or even eliminates recall. With the dissipation of the hyperarousal with therapy or, perhaps, just the passage of time, recall can dramatically increase from earlier levels.

The rather obvious notion that overarousal may interfere with processing can account for clinical and laboratory phenomena that are often explained in unnecessarily more complex fashion. As I have suggested in the past (Erdelyi 1985, 1992), putative defense effects such as "perceptual defense" and "repression" may often reflect nothing more than processing disruption ("cognitive masking" [Erdelyi and Appelbaum 1973; Erdelyi and Blumenthal 1973]) due to emotional arousal, resulting in suboptimal processing in coding and retrieval. Individual differences, moreover, such as those observed between "sensitizers" and "repressors" in perception and memory may be explained by individual differences in the extent to which classes of stimuli produce arousal. In effect, personality transduces the stimuli and displaces the inverted-U function on the arousal axis so that a given stimulus is, for different subjects, optimally arousing, inadequate, or overwhelming (Erdelyi 1958; H. J. Eysenck, 1967).

As with several other special topics in this chapter, the hypothesized arousal-hypermnesia connection is experimentally underdeveloped and awaits programmatic treatment.

Long-Term and Very Long-Term Hypermnesia for Complex Narrative Materials

One of the most striking lessons to have emerged from the review of the history of hypermnesia, including the classic hypnotic hypermnesia literature, is the perverse tendency of experimental psychologists to fall into the stimulus trap.

In the service of methodological expediency, experimentalists have reflexively opted for the simplest, most manageable stimuli possible. It was seen in chapter 3 how, despite Ballard's demonstration that nonsense syllables did not yield hypermnesia ("improvement"), where poetry, among other stimuli, did, investigators nevertheless ignored this elementary fact—almost as if they lacked the conceptual schema for grasping it—and typically opted for lists of nonsense syllables, with which, not surprisingly, they had problems replicating the phenomenon reliably.

The methodological impulse toward stimulus simplicity is, of course, salutary, for one can control simple stimuli much better than complex ones. But the guiding principle should not be the use of the simplest stimulus but to use the simplest stimulus that is effective.

Erdelyi and Becker (1974)—see chapter 5—stumbled on an effective stimulus for hypermnesia serendipitously by including pictures in their memory list, for it was with pictures (contrary to their expectation) that hypermnesia kicked in, and not with the words they thought might work in conjunction with intervening free associations. Fortunately, lists of pictures are simple enough to permit the usual objective scoring and controls of mainstream experimental practice, and so hypermnesia was rescued from its now-you-see-it-now-you don't limbo and transformed into something that is not only reliable but methodologically solid.

Still, although they are effective, pictures are not the last word in stimuli. Hoping to learn from history and to avoid blundering into the stimulus trap yet again, I have worried over the past decade about how the phenomenon of upward-trending memory might play out with more complex stimuli. The goal was to move beyond mere lists toward more

real-life stimuli, such as narrative materials, to ascertain not only whether
the phenomenon exists within this more complex stimulus domain but
also whether richer effects or perhaps unforeseen nuances of the phenomenon might reveal themselves in more ecologically valid contexts.

As was detailed in the preceding chapters, Ballard and the successful
hypnotic hypermnesia researchers had already demonstrated the effect
with poetry (Ballard 1913; Stalnaker and Riddle 1932) or pictorial materials, including film segments (White, Fox, and Harris 1940). More recently,
Scrivner and Safer (1988) produced recall improvements for details of a
videotaped violent burglary through repeated testing, with the fourth and
last test being administered after a 48-hour retention interval. The problem with these studies is that response criterion or productivity was not
controlled. In repeated testing designs, subjects typically produce more
responses in later trials than on the first one. Do subjects in these studies
recall more responses because they remember better, or do they recall
more items only because they produce more items? The very same issue, it
might be recalled, arose in the subliminal perception literature, including
Pötzl's dramatic finding of the recovery of subliminal stimuli in dreams
(see chap. 4).

To solve the problem, why not simply use the tried and true (if
overconservative—see appendix) forced-recall procedure? It is not logically impossible to do so, but it is unacceptably artificial in practice. Suppose, for example, that the "stimulus" is a short story such as the much-
investigated "The War of the Ghosts" (Bartlett 1932), which is 334 words
long. How would one implement forced recall? Could one just instruct
subjects to recall as much as they can, but in any case produce 334 words,
guessing if necessary?

I have actually explored variants of this procedure, but subjects, perhaps not surprisingly, treated it as peculiar, if not downright unreasonable.
Maybe for a single recall trial one could coax subjects to produce a set
number of responses (by filling in all 334 blank spaces provided, for example), but this artificial labor of guessing, fitting, and counting would inevitably distort recall on subsequent trials and would undermine the subjects' cooperation. Roediger and his associates (Roediger, Wheeler, and
Rajaram 1993; Roediger, Challis, and Wheeler 1994) have recently shown
that forced recall, relative to free recall, exacerbates memory distortions
(in which guesses are confused with true recollections). Also, Erdelyi,
Finks, and Feigin-Pfau (1989) have demonstrated the existence of a negative "processing bias" in forced recall in which subjects actually resist the
task of retrieval and, while producing more responses, end up producing

poorer recall than free-recall subjects. Thus the forced-recall method has some clear disadvantages and works against the hypermnesia effect (which is powerful enough to overcome the procedure).

My associates and I have developed a criterion control for narrative free recall (it can be used also with plain lists, so it is designated CCFR, for *criterion controlled free recall*) that is completely nonintrusive. It is sketched out below (and, in more detail, in the appendix). Before getting to this more technical section on dealing with the issue of response productivity in narrative recall, however, the question will first be addressed whether, without control for productivity, it might be possible in the first place to obtain incremental recall over time with narrative materials such as "The War of the Ghosts." Bartlett's (1932) own work would suggest not. On the contrary, progressively worse performance with repeated testing over time would be expected (that's what he obtained), not because of Ebbinghaus's "decay" of memory but, presumably, because of the successive working-over of the original memory into a progressively distorted, schema-congruent version of the original memory. (Roediger and Wheeler [1992] and Roediger, Wheeler, and Rajaram [1993] provide a contemporary discussion of the "paradox" of Bartlett effects and hypermnesia co-occurring in memory.)

Amnesia and Hypermnesia for "The War of the Ghosts" Over Periods of Weeks

The first study with "The War of the Ghosts" was conducted by me and my former student Michael Halberstam. Here is the text of the "stimulus":

1 **The War of the Ghosts**

2 One night two young men from Egulac went down to the river to hunt seals,
3 and while they were there it became foggy and calm. Then they heard war-
4 cries, and they thought: "Maybe this is a war-party." They escaped to the
5 shore, and hid behind a log. Now canoes came up, and they heard the noise
6 of paddles, and saw one canoe coming up to them. There were five men in
7 the canoe, and they said:
8   "What do you think? We wish to take you along. We are going up the
9 river to make war on the people."
10   One of the young men said: "I have no arrows."
11   "Arrows are in the canoe," they said.
12   "I will not go along. I might be killed. My relatives do not know where I
13 have gone. But you," he said, turning to the other, "may go with them."
14   So one of the young men went, but the other returned home.
15   And the warriors went on up the river to a town on the other side of
16 Kalama. The people came down to the water, and they began to fight, and

17 many were killed. But presently the young man heard one of the warriors
18 say: "Quick, let us go home: that Indian has been hit." Now he thought: "Oh,
19 they are ghosts." He did not feel sick, but they said he had been shot.
20   So the canoes went back to Egulac and the young man went ashore to
21 his house, and made a fire. And he told everybody and said: "Behold I accom-
22 panied the ghosts, and we went to fight. Many of our fellows were killed,
23 and many of those who attacked us were killed. They said I was hit, and I
24 did not feel sick."
25   He told it all, and then he became quiet. When the sun rose he fell down.
26 Something black came out of his mouth. His face became contorted. The
27 people jumped up and cried.
28   He was dead.

(Bartlett 1932, 65)

Nine subjects, consisting mostly of college students or recent gradu-
ates, but including also a college professor and a nine-and-a-half-year-old
girl, were tested individually. Each subject was given a printed copy of
"The War of the Ghosts" and asked to read it carefully for subsequent
recall. Ten minutes were allowed for the reading, with a few additional
minutes of grace, if required. Then the text was taken away and the subject was asked to recall the story as completely and faithfully as possible
in writing. The written recall (designated as R_{1A}) was removed and the
original story again presented to the subject for a second period of study.
Once the story was again removed—never to be shown again—the subject was asked for a second written recall of the story (R_{1B}). Since the
first recall effort R_{1A} was part of the learning task and was followed by a
re-presentation of the stimulus, the first recall effort after the last presentation of the stimulus, R_{1B}, was treated as the first true recall trial R_1. (Thus
$R_{1B} = R_1$.)

About 10 weeks later the subjects were contacted for further (individual) testing, and three successive recall tests, R_2, R_3, and R_4, were elicited.
Once completed, each new recall effort was removed so that subjects
could never consult their earlier recalls in subsequent recall efforts. On
the completion of R_4, each subject was asked to take a batch of blank
recall protocols and envelopes home and to test himself or herself at least
once a day for the next week and return to the laboratory for a final
period of testing. Each recall produced at home was to be numbered,
dated, and then sealed in an envelope and never inspected on subsequent
recall efforts. Not all subjects were equally diligent at the at-home self-
testing. One of the subjects produced only 5 at-home recalls, so average
recalls for all subjects could be calculated only for the first 5 at-home
recall trials. In the final (third) laboratory meeting, 3 additional recall
tests were administered by the experimenter. Since a different number of

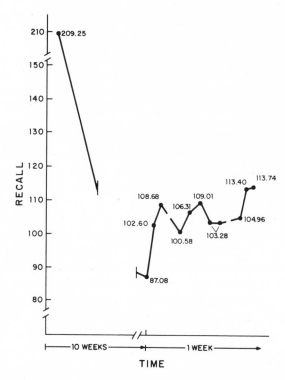

Figure 8.1 Amnesia and hypermnesia for the "War of the Ghosts": Average number of words recalled over some dozen weeks with repeated recall effort in the last week. (Erdelyi 1990, 7)

intervening recall trials had been produced by different subjects in the at-home testing, the last three recall tests in the laboratory are generically designated R_{n-2}, R_{n-1}, and R_n.

There are various ways of scoring the recalls. Fortunately, the same pattern of results was produced by every scoring scheme used, from various subjective-clinical ratings to the most objective, if wooden-headed, procedure of counting the number of words in the original story that appeared in the subjects' recalls. Given the surprisingly high correlation between subjective and word-count scores (typically, $r > 0.90$), the most objective approach, the word-count procedure, was used in the quantitative analyses. Since the story has 334 words, the maximum recall or "hit" score possible by the word-count method is 334. (Past research [Haber and Erdelyi 1967; Rosenberg, Schnurr, and Oxman 1990] had already suggested the effectiveness of word-counts in content analysis of complex materials.) Figure 8.1 shows the subjects' average number of correct words recalled over time and recall trials.

Ebbinghaus made a definite appearance (as did Bartlett, since "omissions" were one of the distortions Bartlett emphasized): over 10 weeks of retrieval neglect, recall level dropped from some 209 correct words to a mere 87.

Yet, Ballard's "improvement" (hypermnesia), and therefore reminiscence, did not fail to materialize either. With systematic recall effort in the last seven days, the subjects improved from 87 words to 114 (a statistically reliable effect). Interestingly, the first 5 take-home recalls failed to produce hypermnesia (100.58 words on the first and 103.28 on the last). Perhaps recall would have improved further with additional days of recall effort in the laboratory.

It may be noted that the significant hypermnesia effect survived an early version of the criterion control to be described below. Also, work in progress by Merryl Feigin-Pfau shows clearly, with larger groups of subjects, that the effect is reliable, though apparently not with any narrative material. She obtained significant hypermnesia effects after several weeks with "The War of the Ghosts" story and a modified version of it, "The Sport of the Ghosts," in which all the violent allusions in the original version were altered, but not in a third and somewhat boring children's tale of roughly equal length, "The Stone on the Road." This latter outcome suggests that narrative complexity as such may be less of a critical factor than interest value.

Amnesia and Hypermnesia for "The War of the Ghosts" over Periods of Months in Two Children, with the Appearance of Freud-Pötzl-Bartlett Effects

As already noted, one of the subjects in the Halberstam study was a nine-and-a-half-year-old child. This girl, named Karina, was included in the study for various reasons: it was of interest how a child might perform in such a long-term repeated testing task, she was available for long-term testing, she appeared to be highly motivated (she was excited to be paid the gaudy, by her standards, hourly honorarium the grown-ups were getting), she had a reputation for a keen memory, and she was highly verbal in spoken and written language. In fact, she produced a slightly higher R_1 score than the average grown-up, and her written recall, except for some creative spelling and punctuation, was not obviously different from that of the other 8 subjects in the study.

What was completely unexpected was her recall performance after some 10 weeks (in her case, 12 weeks). Her above-average R_1 performance collapsed after the 12 week interval to such an extent that even cursory inspection of R_2 protocols showed her to be an outlier. She re-called very little.

Another striking aspect of her postinterval performance, R_2 through R_n, was her censorship from the little that she did recall, of the violent events in the story. Because of this "collapse-of-memory" effect and, also, possible "repression effect," a careful qualitative inspection of her string of recalls was undertaken. A sample of them are presented and discussed here.

Also, to avoid depending on a single subject's data, a second child was tested, Karina's sister, Maya (who was six and a half years old at the time of testing). Maya's recalls (which are published here for the first time) will be examined after Karina's.

Karina's Recall over 3 Months and after an Additional
6-Month Interval

To get a sense of the quality of Karina's immediate recall of "The War of the Ghosts," which was, as already noted, slightly better than the average adult's immediate recall, her R_1 is reproduced, without any changes (including grammatical, spelling, and punctuation errors). All reproduced recalls in this series will have line numbering for ease of reference:

Karina's R_1

1 One day two young men went down to the river to hunt for seals. Suddenly
2 they heard war cries. They heard the sound of paddles splashing in the water.
3 The young men thought this was a war party and hid themselves behind a
4 log. Soon they saw a canoe coming towards them. There was five Indians in
5 the canoe. One of them asked the young men "What do you think",? Will
6 you join us? We are going to war on the people. One of the young men said,
7 "I have no arrows"! The Indian replied "we have arrows in the canoe". Then
8 one of the young men said, "I cannot go for my family does not know where
9 I am; but you can go". Soon they departed one to war and one to his family.
10 The soon arrived at a village further south than Kalama. The villager soon
11 came to the waterfront and started a battle. Many people from both sides
12 died. Soon the young man heard an Indian warrior say, "We better leave that
13 man got hit", So they left for Egulac. The young man then went home and
14 lit a fire and told his story when he was done he sat there to sunrise and
15 then fell down. Something black came out of his mouth. His face was twisted.
16 He was dead (Erdelyi 1990, 23)

Despite Karina's impressive adult-level R_1, numerous Bartlett-type distortions appeared, just as they did in the adults' R_1. For example, her recall begins, "One day," when the actual story starts, "One night"; she continues, "two young men went down," omitting the story's "two young men *from Egulac*"; she writes, "to hunt for seals," intruding the preposition "for," which is not in the story. These types of distortions are ubiquitous in Karina's recall, as they are in the adult subjects'. The possibility that Bartlett effects might not appear when the subject is making a bona fide effort at recalling rather than inventing (Gauld and Stephenson 1967; Roediger, Wheeler, and Rajaram 1993) is unambiguously laid to rest, though, in line with Gauld and Stephenson's suggestion, and consistent with signal detection theory (Green and Swets 1966; Macmillan and Creelman 1991), Halberstam and I found in unpublished analyses that stricter criteria (produced by criterion controls) reduced Bartlett distortions—as well as correct recalls.

As noted already, Karina's R_2 produced about 3 months after R_1, is extremely poor. What little she recalls is riddled with distortions, both Bartlettian and Freudian (Erdelyi 1990, 24):

Karina's R_2 (some 12 weeks after R_1)

1 Two men went fishing. They saw some Soiixx Indians. The were not on the
2 warpath. There were canoes full of Indians. One of the canoes came near
3 the log where they were hiding. It was a very mossy log. The canoe that
4 went by them didn't see them. This all happened out in the woods. The two
5 men were fishing in a lake.

Karina's R_4

1 One day two men went fishing. They went to a lake in the forest. When they
2 were in the middle of fishing some Souixx Indians on the warpath came
3 along. The two men hid from the Indians behind an old mossy log. There
4 were canoes full of Indians. One of these canoes went by the old, mossy log
5 were the two men were hiding. But the Indians did not see the two men.

Karina's R_n

1 One day two men went fishing. While in the middle of fishing some Souixx
2 Indians on the warpath came along. The two frightened men hid behind an
3 old mossy log. One of the canoes went past the log but the Indians didn't
4 see the two men.

In a major effort to unify the Ebbinghaus-Freud-Bartlett traditions, I (Erdelyi 1990, 1993) proposed that Freudian "defense mechanisms" (repression, censorship, negation, denial, displacement, symbolization, undoing, projection, reaction formation, rationalization, and so forth) are standard Bartlettian distortions, but for motive: Bartlettian distortions are motivated by efforts at meaning and coherence whereas the Freudian variety are motivated by efforts at wish fulfillment and defense.

Thus it is noteworthy that in R_2 no reference whatsoever is made to any of the violent events in the story. None of the adults exhibited this propensity toward emotional censorship; if anything, there were occasional exaggerations of the violence, and none of the adults forgot the "something black" that came out of the young man's mouth upon his death. Karina's (presumptive) defensive recall is not all passive. The one allusion to violence is transformed by negation: "The[y] were *not* on the warpath" (emphasis added). In the next recall effort, R_3, this minor aggressive element manages to escape distortion by negation, for now Karina writes, "Some Souixx Indians *on the warpath* came along." Also, the emotion of fear emerges. In R_3 the fear is still only hinted at: "The two men hid. . . ." By R_n, the fear is explicit: "The two frightened men hid behind an old mossy log."

Thus except for what appear to be some minor recoveries of scary details or feelings, little hypermnesia from R_2 to R_n is evident in Karina's recalls. In the adults, by contrast, everyone was hypermnesic. Thus if Karina's multiple recalls were excluded from figure 8.1, an even stronger hypermnesia effect would have been in evidence.

Halberstam and I were particularly perplexed over the degree to which, compared to the adult subjects, Karina's R_2 deteriorated from R_1 after about 3 months. We wondered, by the time the data had been scored (several months later), whether Karina would have any memory left for the story. Would she, if we tested her again, show complete amnesia, in some variant of infantile amnesia?

Since Karina was available, we decided—though we had no original plans to do so—to probe her recall in a last laboratory meeting, which occurred some 6 months after R_n and involved three repeated recall tests in the laboratory, R_{n+1}, R_{n+2}, and R_{n+3}.

Karina's three final recalls are reproduced verbatim (errors and all; Erdelyi 1990, 25):

Karina's R_{n+1} (some 9 months after R_1)

1 There were two men and they went fishing one day. They went to a pond.
2 They caught some fish, then an indian war canoe came and both men hid
3 behind an old rotten moldy log. The indian chief said, "do any of you want
4 to join the trib". Then one man got up and said yes it was, it was his friend.
5 But the other man knew that he had children and a wife and they would be
6 heartbroken if he left them. The other man seemed out of his mind his friend
7 thought. Then he went to his friends home and told them what happened.
8 The wife and children were very heartbroken. Then the friend said, "I'll go
9 join the indian chief and try to get your husband back the friend", said. So

10   the friend went back to pond where he had been fishing recently and found
11   the indian chief still there and joined the tribe. He found his friend and told
12   him and then he decided he would miss his wife so he went with his friend
13   and lived quite happily ever on and erased this from memory.

Karina's R_{n+2}

1   There were two men who went fishing one day at the swamp. Then suddenly
2   an Indian war canoe came down the stream of the swamp. The two men hid
3   behind an old rotting log for they were scared. The chief asked if anyone
4   wanted to join his tribe knowing people were there because they were
5   always there. One of the two men said yes. But the other man persued him
6   out of it saying that he would break his wifes and childrens hearts so the
7   man didn't go. His friend the husbands story and told them never to mention
8   it (the story) to him. So they his family did theat, and the family lived happily
9   ever after and never mentioned it again.
10   The End.

Karina's R_{n+3}

1   One day two peasant farmers went fishing in a swamp. They had caught a
2   couple of fish. Then suddenly an indian war canoe came. The two men hid
3   behind an old rotting moldy log. The chief knowing people were there asked
4   if anyone wanted to join his tribe. One of the men was about to say yes but
5   his friend peursued him not too by telling him how heartbroken his wife
6   and children would be if he joined the tribe. The friend told the family and
7   told them not to mention the incident again to him, so they never did and
8   they lived happily ever after and never mentioned the incident to him scared
9   he might actually leave them and they would all be heartbroken. They all
10   lived *happily* ever after.
11   The End.

We were completely surprised by Karina's performance. We had been expecting no recall or next to no recall. What we got instead was substantial hypermnesia over the half-year interval. Word counts with and without criterion-controls confirm this (figs. 8.2, 8.4), but the more interesting results are captured by the recovered themes and meanings.

Six months after R_n, in Karina's R_{n+1}, the two young men hid, but "the indian chief" in the "war canoe" (line 2) is not fooled (as he is in Karina's R_2 through R_n) and, as in the original story, issues an invitation to the young men. It is true that the emotional aspect is substantially muted: the invitation is not "to make war on the people" but "to join the trib[e]." Yet Karina reflects the ominous undertow of the story—the young men hardly jump for joy at the honor. Just as in the original story— all this is recovered, albeit in distorted, dreamlike form—only one of the young men agrees; the other, worried about his children and wife, "who would be heartbroken if he left them" (lines 5–6), declines. (Note that in the original story the more prudent young man also worries about his "relatives," who serve as his ultimate excuse for not going along.) The remaining portion of R_{n+1} is a veritable Bartlett fest, but with Freudian elements. The very idea of leaving or taking a trip is treated by Freud in *The Interpretation of Dreams* (1900) as a symbol of death. (The prudent young man thought his friend to be "out of his mind" [line 6], and his friend's wife and children were "heartbroken.")

What unfolds is a striking example of "undoing," in this case a positive version of the Orpheus legend: the prudent youth takes it upon himself to find his friend and retrieve him for his loved ones. And he does so, and, in a wish-fulfilling distortion of the ending, they all "lived quite happily ever on" (line 13), with, it might be noted, the help of repression: "and erased this from memory."

Karina's R_{n+2} and R_{n+3} are better defended. R_{n+3} is almost peaceful. There is something reassuring about two stolid "peasant farmers" (compared to "two men"). They even "caught a couple of fish" (lines 1–2), a happy outcome, and one that would lead one to expect them to go home and cook the fish instead of embarking on some deadly adventure. The Indian chief does ask his question, but in R_{n+2} and R_{n+3} the dreaded act of going along with the ghost Indians, which had to be undone in R_{n+1}, is softened into a mere impulse, which the prudent young man successfully dissuades his foolish friend from pursuing. For good measure, the prudent young man instructs the family "not to mention the incident again to him" (line 7) for fear the foolish friend might actually act on the impulse and "leave them" and render them "heartbroken" again. Repress the memory, repress the cues to the memory, Karina seems to be urging through the prudent young man, and to anchor matters, emphatically asserts, in a defensive reversal of the outcome, that they lived *happily* ever after. There is something almost harried about the defensive effort and it is hard to avoid the suspicion that the new version of the conclusion of the story—"The End."—is a plea by Karina to put an end to the exercise. And we ended the experiment at R_{n+3}, more or less happily ever after.

Maya's Recall over 6 Weeks and after an Additional 3-Month Interval

Maya, as already noted, is Karina's sister, and was six-and-a-half years old at the time of testing. Since she was not yet a fluent reader or writer, the story was read to her, and recall efforts were tape recorded and later transcribed. Although such oral reports usually require some editing (even for college professors), the present recordings were transcribed in the raw to avoid any unintended distortion of the data:

Maya's R_1 (after 2 presentations of the story)

1   The War of the Ghosts
2   One night some men going hunting to hunt seals. While they went hunting
3   they heard someone screaming for help. It was the Indians fighting with the
4   young men. One of the Indians was shot. He did not know that he got shot.
5   He told everything to the men. He said the people thought I was shot. Then
6   the man was quiet. He went outside. He tripped over a rock. Something
7   black from his mouth came out. He died. Everybody jumped up and cried.

It is obviously sketchier and more childlike than that of her older sister. Bartlett effects again abound and also some dreamlike Freudian distortions. The story's "war-cries" becomes "someone screaming for help," a distortion which not only reconstructs the original version but seems also to "condense" (Freud's term) the idea of war cries with the notion that someone is in serious trouble (as is the case toward the end of story) and therefore in need of help. In this recall and in some of her subsequent ones, Maya evidences more than her sister the "rationalizations" (Bartlett's *and* Freud's term) that Bartlett's Cambridge University subjects used to render the strange story more rational. Thus, Maya recalls, incorrectly, that "He tripped over a rock" (line 6), which helps to make sense of why "Something black from his mouth came out" (lines 6–7).

Maya's R_2 produced six weeks later, suggests a virtually complete forgetting of the original story:

Maya's R_2 (six weeks after R_1)

1   One night some men were walking. They heard a crowd scream. The men
2   heard them screaming. They rushed and tried to find where the people were
3   screaming. At last, they found them. They were on top of the highest hill.

Is the information irretrievably lost or can some recovery of the material be achieved? Maya's R_3, which immediately followed R_2, shows that indeed much more was available than accessible (Tulving and Pearlstone 1966):

Maya's R_3

1   One night three men were walking. They heard a screech. They tried to find
2   out what it was. It was the Indians calling for help. Then they saw a river
3   nearby. Inside the river was a boat. They all got in the boat. The Indians
4   tricked them because they were enemies. Then they went back home in the
5   boat. Then the boat was starting to crack and the three men were going to

6   drown. Then a man and a other man were nearby and they saw them. And
7   they tried to help them so they could save them and they did.

R_3 is substantially hypermnesic with respect to the immediately preceding
R_2, though the recollections are highly distorted and dreamlike. The
story's "war cries" is recovered, but materializes as a "screech" (line 1).
The two men, in Pötzl-like fashion (Fisher 1956, 1988) are "reduplicated"
as "three men" (line 1). In classic Bartlett fashion, the story's "canoe" is
"familiarized" (Bartlett 1932) into "boat" (line 3). A great deal of the
recall is a condensed mish-mash of the notion that there were two sets
of Indians, the good ones, needing "help" (line 2) and the other, presumably ghost Indians, associated with bad outcomes ("The Indians tricked
them because they were enemies" [lines 3–4]).

Some of the recoveries are straightforward and accurate, for example,
"river" (line 2), "Indians" (line 2), "went back home" (line 4), which is
close to the story's "the other returned home" (story, line 14), though
the context is often—as in dreams—peculiar.

Maya's R_3 is far less emotionally laundered than her sister's. She does
manage to alter the ending to a happy one: "And they tried to help them
so they could save them and they did" (lines 6–7).

Because of her young age, Maya, unlike her sister, was not given
at-home self-tests. Instead, after the completion of the second "laboratory"
session (which actually occurred at her home), comprising R_2, R_3, and R_4,
she was retested by the experimenter Merryl Feigin-Pfau over the next
two days. Thus laboratory 3 tests R_5, R_6, and R_7 were administered the
day after laboratory 2, and laboratory 4 tests R_8, R_9, and R_{10}, a day after
the preceding laboratory 3. Since Maya was not retested again for three
months, her R_n corresponds to R_{10} and her R_{n-1} to R_9:

Maya's R_{n-1} (= R_9)

1   One night three men heard a crowd scream for help. It was the Indians
2   calling for help. They rushed to find out where it was. They saw a boat
3   nearby. They got on the boat and got off it. There were the Indians laughing
4   at once. The whole thing was just a little joke. They got mad because they
5   wanted to save someone. They didn't want it all to be a joke. They went
6   home to go to sleep. They woke up early in the morning to go to work.
7   Their job was to fix things and help people if they had a problem.

Maya's R_n (= R_{10})

1   One night three men heard a crowd scream for help. It was the Indians
2   calling for help. They were trapped from the new hunting dog that came in
3   town this morning. They rushed to find out what it was. They did not hear
4   about the hunting dog. All they wanted to know is what was happening. One

5　man was nearby and the man told him what was happening. The Indians
6　were in trouble because the dog was not supposed to hunt other animals
7　besides rabbits and deers. It was supposed to hunt birds, tigers, and wild
8　bears. The three men wanted to know what was this dog business doing
9　around here and why was it hunting Indians. They all cried. One of the men
10　said, "I guess because the cooks needed more food."

Although these two recalls do not appear to be particularly hypermnesic with respect to R_3 (the word-count scoring, as will be seen below in figs. 8.3 and 8.5, shows them not to be so at all) there were a number of apparent recoveries, though they are highly distorted in a dreamlike way. The end of Maya's R_{n-1} seems to recover, through allusions, the ending of the story in which the final drama is played out in the morning ("When the sun rose he fell down." [story, line 25]). Maya recalls that "they woke up early in the morning" (line 6), and concludes that "their job was to fix things and help people if they had a problem" (line 7), which the young man about to die certainly had. A defensive tendency to make the bad ending a happy one is suggested by Maya's "they wanted to save someone" (lines 4–5). Also there is a joking treatment of the affair (a form of defensive cognition according to Freud [Erdelyi 1985]): "The whole thing was just a little joke" (line 4).

Some direct recoveries are in evidence in R_n, though they are camouflaged in Pötzl-like fashions in incorrect contexts. Thus the story's "*hunt* seals" seems to emerge as "*hunt*ing dog" (line 2) and "*hunt* other animals" (line 6). The story's "they *heard* war-*cries*" seems to emerge as "*heard* a crowd *scream*" (line 1) and "they did not *hear*" (line 3). Toward the end of Maya's R_n there is an almost direct recovery—and for the first time—of the story's, "The people jumped up and cried" (story, lines 26–27): "They all cried" (R_n, line 9). Maya's conclusion, "I guess because the cooks needed more food" (line 10) reintroduces the joking or clowning treatment (which she uses in real life to deal with stressful situations). The "food" may be an allusion to the "mouth" (story, line 26) from which the black something comes out.

Three months, instead of Karina's 6, elapsed before Maya's final three recalls R_{n+1}, R_{n+2}, and R_{n+3} (the final two are reproduced here):

Maya's R_{n+2} (= R_{12}); 3 months after R_n and 4½ months after R_1)

1　One night three men wanted to go on a boat. So they did and they went
2　through the woods to a short cut to the lake. Then they heard something.
3　They tried to see what it was. They looked around. Then two of the men
4　saw Indians coming with lots of feathers and very red skin. And they had
5　very long black, black hair. They had instruments in their hands and they
6　made lots of noise in the forest. The three men did not like the noise and

7 neither did the animals. The Indians were having a great big celebration
8 party because it was the chief's birthday. They stayed all night until three
9 o'clock in the morning. So the men slept far away from the Indians because
10 they were making so much noise that they could hear them at the house.
11 And so they walked a long way. They almost were in the country of New
12 Jersey. They knew there was a big lake in the country so they went to the
13 lake because they knew they could not hear the Indians and they were very
14 happy.

Maya's R_{n+3} (= R_{13})

1 One night three men were walking and they decided to go to the woods.
2 They heard Indians coming and they ducked down because they were shoot-
3 ing things and they did not want to get hurt. So when they ducked down
4 the Indians were not shooting. They were really having a big celebration.
5 But they did not like the white people because their skin was a different
6 color than theirs. Then they went back home to get something to eat. They
7 went back outside to the woods and sat down on a bench to eat. One of the
8 Indians shot an arrow and the arrow got on one of the man's hats but did
9 not get on his head. So the man took the hat off and took out the arrow and
10 put the arrow on a tree. So the man walked back to the bench to finish eating
11 and soon they went back home to throw the napkin away. But the Indians
12 started to make lots of noise and so the three men went someplace quiet.

This material is notably hypermnesic as well as dreamlike. In R_{n+2}
Maya recalls, "Then they heard" (line 2), directly recovering the story's
"Then they heard" (line 3). Momentarily she recovers the fact that there
were "two . . . men" (line 3). The Indians had "instruments" (arrows?)
and had "long black, black hair" (line 5), possibly a displacement of the
"something black" that came out of the youth's mouth. "They made
lots of noise" (lines 5–6) may be a distorted recovery of "they heard
the noise of paddles" (story, lines 5–6) and also the "war-cries." The
"celebration party" mentioned by Maya (R_{n+2}, lines 7–8) suggests a distorted recovery of "war-party" (story, line 4), followed by the Bartlettian
(nondefensive) rationalization, "because it was the chief's birthday" (line
8). The notion that the youth was awake through the night until "the sun
rose" (story, line 25) is suggested by Maya's "They stayed all night until
three o'clock in the morning" (lines 8–9). She recovers the words *noise*
and *house* (Maya's line 10; story lines 5, 21). Maya states, "they walked
a *long* way" (line 11), possibly recovering the story's "I will not go
along." Of course, some of these presumed recoveries may be chance
correspondences but, in the aggregate, they are striking and especially
surprising in that they emerge 3 months after the last recall effort, R_{10}
(= R_n).

The final recall, R_{n+3}, is also hypermnesic and dreamlike. The men "heard Indians coming and they ducked" (line 2) seems to recover the story's "Then they heard war-cries . . . and hid behind a log" (story, lines 3–4, 5). In this final recall, Maya recovers the arrows in the story first by relating, "They were shooting things" (lines 2–3), and then immediately trying to undo (negate, deny) the scary fact by adding, "the Indians were not shooting. They were really having a big celebration" (line 4). The warlike situation immediately resurfaces, however: "But they did not like the white people" (line 5) (note the recovery of the word *people*). Maya relates further that "they went back" (line 6), apparently recovering the story's "so the canoes went back" (line 20). Maya's reference to "something to eat" (line 6) again suggests the "mouth" in the story and the "bench" (line 10), the "log" in the story.

In a rationalization that is as inspired as any of the ones produced by Bartlett's Cambridge students, Maya both recovers and resolves the story's paradoxical "He did not feel sick, but they said he had been shot" (story, line 19). Maya's solution: "One of the Indians shot an arrow and the arrow got on one of the man's hats but did not get to on his head" (lines 7–9). And in a striking use of undoing and displacement, adds: "So the man took the hat off and took out the arrow and put the arrow on a tree" (lines 9–10). Maya's last recall ends with a final recovery: The "men went someplace *quiet*" (line 12). In the story, "he became quiet" (line 25).

If most of these are true recoveries (unfortunately, at this stage of the research we have no adequate base rates and appropriate controls), it is very puzzling that the recoveries of both Maya and Karina occur after the lapse of a prolonged interval (3 and 6 months). The phenomenon does not seem to fit any current theories of memory and points to the need for programmatic research with larger samples of subjects, both experimental and control (that is, subjects not exposed to the original story).

Quantitative Recall Performance of Karina and Maya over Time and Trials

The analysis of Karina's and Maya's recall performance has been qualitative and subjective thus far, with the usual imponderables (for example, is the author seeing things that are not really there?). Does quantitative analysis bear out the upward-trending memory of the two girls? As figures 8.2 and 8.3 make clear, a raw word count shows that both Karina's and Maya's recall in the last laboratory trials (R_{n+1}, R_{n+2}, and R_{n+3}) were hypermnesic relative to R_2 or R_n, after a 3- or 6-month interval.

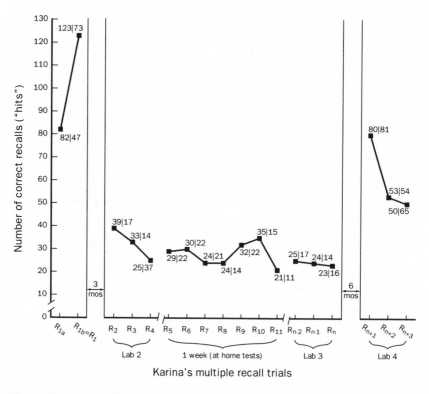

Figure 8.2 Karina's multitrial recall, with the last three, R_{n+1}, R_{n+2}, and R_{n+3}, occurring some 9 months after last exposure to the story, "The War of the Ghosts."

Each data point is represented by two numbers, the first, the number of correct recalls (hits) and the second, the number of false recalls (false alarms). Thus Karina's R_2 is 39|17, meaning she produced 39 correct recalls (words from the story) but also intruded 17 false recalls (words not in the story). The scoring was done by computer in collaboration with Donald Leichter, who has just completed a doctoral dissertation on long-term hypermnesia for self-generated narratives, specifically children's recall of their own responses to TAT (Thematic Apperception Test) cards. In the word-count program employed, the function words, *a, the, and,* were stripped by the computer from both the story and the recalls and so these words did not figure in the word count.

If the false recalls are ignored for the moment (they will be dealt with in the criterion-controlled analysis), Karina's data make sense and fit the foregoing qualitative analysis. The improvement from R_{1A} to R_{1B} is expected from standard learning since Karina got a second exposure to the

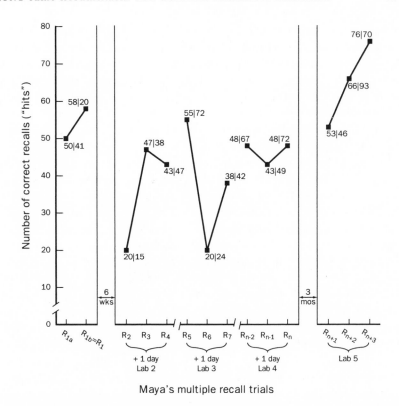

Figure 8.3 Maya's multitrial recall, with the last three, R_{n+1}, R_{n+2}, and R_{n+3}, occurring almost 5 months after last exposure to the story, "The War of the Ghosts."

story between R_{1A} and R_{1B}. The drop from 123 hits to 39 hits, though more drastic than expected or found in the adult subjects' performance, reflects the forgetting that occurred over the three months' retention interval.

No hypermnesia is observed between R_2 and R_n, which, as already noted, was discrepant with the adult subjects' corresponding multitrial performance.

The striking finding is the jump in Karina's recall level by some 250% after the passage of 6 months, from $R_n = 23$ to $R_{n+1} = 80$. As can be readily seen, this half-year delayed recall produced the highest recall level throughout the whole experiment except for the learning phase recall trials immediately following exposure to the story, that is, R_{1A} and R_{1B} (R_1).

Maya's pattern, though more variable, parallels Karina's data, except that Maya does seem to produce hypermnesia over the three successive days of laboratory testing (R_2 to R_n). If, again, false recalls are ignored, Maya's improvement in the three days of laboratory testing is quite dramatic: $R_2 = 20$ to $R_n = 48$ (about 140%). Like Karina, Maya produces her highest recall levels after the passage of a very long retention interval, 3 months in Maya's case. If her very last recall trial, R_{n+3}, is compared to her R_2 of three months before, she is seen to have improved by almost 300% (from 20 to 76 correct recalls).

If the improvements in recall observed in these two girls after the passage of several months of retrieval neglect—but following in both cases an intense series of recall efforts spanning days—is reliable, the phenomenon is alien to the literature of memory for verbal materials, though it does bring to mind the old and mostly forgotten literature (see chap. 3) on "skill" or "motor reminiscence/hypermnesia."

More recently, Bahrick and Hall (1991, 1993) may have produced a cognate effect with "material drawn from a stable knowledge system acquired much earlier" (1993, 206). They produced "robust hypermnesia effects"—in the order of 10% improvements—with a 1-month interval between cued-recall tests for three types of materials, foreign language vocabulary, general knowledge, and names of portraits of famous persons. Herrmann, Buschke, and Gall (1987), using free recall, also reported hypermnesia effects in the order of 10% over a period of 40 days. Squire, Haist, and Shimamura (1989) tested a group of amnesic and normal subjects on public-event information over a period of over two years, with a year separating the first and second test and the second and third test, and found R_1 to R_3 improvement in cued-recall in the order of, again, 10%. Unfortunately, this latter experiment may not truly reflect hypermnesia, since multiple-choice recognition tests were interspersed between the recall trials and the increases may have resulted from the learning of the multiple-choice items and, additionally, from the subjects being exposed to some of the information in the public media over the long interval (Roediger and Wheeler 1993). The previous two studies, however, barring criterion artifacts, do seem to suggest the occurrence of hypermnesia over intervals of a month or more, though not as large as those obtained by Karina and Maya over 6 or 3 months.

If Karina's and Maya's results prove reliable (and, also, not an artifact of laxer response criteria), the outcomes do indicate that the age of the memory (that is, old memories) is not what is important for the effect, as Bharick and Hall (1993) suggest, but that the memories, as Bahrick and Hall also suggest, be "drawn from a stable knowledge system" (206). As these authors argue, highly mastered memories will result in minimal oblivescence ("downward fluctuations") and so the balance between oblivescence and reminiscence ("upward fluctuations") will favor the latter, for a large net gain, that is, hypermnesia. Another possible explanation is dissipation of inhibition (proposed by Pavlov in connection with spontaneous recovery; see chap. 3), or dissipation of fatigue in skill/motor hypermnesia (proposed by Hovland and others; see chap. 3). I have already suggested, in chapter 3, the possibility that "skills," "sensory-motor" phenomena, procedural memories, and maybe even dreams are all aspects of a more general memory system. Perhaps the types of "stable knowledge structures" discussed in this section can be added to the group.

Whatever the conceptualization that is eventually accepted, the basic phenomenon remains: memory—for skills, general knowledge, narrative materials, perhaps traumas—can increase, often dramatically, after the passage of long periods of time, often months and, possibly, years (see chap. 3). Breuer and Freud's (1895) formula, "Hysterics suffer mainly from reminiscences" (see chap. 2 herein) parlays this phenomenon, already observed in the clinic before the turn of the century, into a general theory of psychopathology.

The Problem of Response Criteria in Narrative Recall and a Proposed Solution

The "phenomenon remains"—but only if hypermnesia after very long delays is not artifactual. Hypermnesias of from 100% to 300% were reported for Karina and Maya over intervals of several months, but these were based on correct recall (hit) levels without regard to false recall (false alarm) levels.

Thus Maya correctly recalled 20 words in R_2 and 76 words in R_{n+3} (fig. 8.3) for a net gain of almost 300%. For these same recall trials, however, Maya also produced 15 and 70 false recalls, respectively, an increase of false recall of *more* than 300%. If we had chosen to concentrate on these false recalls instead of the correct recalls, the reverse conclusion would have followed, namely, that recall became worse after several months—and we, along with Ebbinghaus and Bartlett, would not have been surprised.

The problem, obviously, is to know what to make of the hit and false-alarm pairs in tandem (Klatzky and Erdelyi 1985). Is $R_2 = 20|15$ better or worse than $R_{n+3} = 76|70$? If in R_{n+3} Maya had restricted her response productivity so that her false alarm level were 15, what would her corresponding hit level have been? If with this stricter response criterion her hit level had correspondingly declined to 20, the great fuss made over her hypermnesia after the passage of 3 months would have been a huge mistake: in this hypothetical case, her recall would not have changed at all.

If only we could somehow induce subjects to keep false recalls constant (by adjusting their response productivity), then a hit level H, conditionalized on the constant false-alarm level F_c, would provide a compelling index of true recall level. In fact, the criterion control that has been developed has this feature at its core. It pares down recall responses until a fixed false-alarm level F_c is achieved. This conditionalized hit level is designated $H|F_c$.

The paring-down technique and its logic is described in the appendix in some detail. The essential idea, however, can be distilled here. The subject (in the early prototype of the technique) was asked to produce confidence ratings for each recall segment produced. The "segment" could be a sentence, an idea unit, or simply a line of recall. On the assumption that subjects would omit their least confident segments (for example, lines), had they been required to reduce the length of their recall narrative, the least confident segments are dropped in order until the false-alarm number reaches the desired level F_c. Since, of course, each segment (line, and so forth) usually contains both hits and false alarms, the whittling down of segments reduces both the false-alarm number as well as the hit number.

Common sense as well as empirical evidence (see the appendix) suggest that the segments associated with the least confidence will have relatively more false alarms than hits. Thus typically as segments are whittled down, initially more false alarms are deleted than hits.

Once it was shown empirically that the correlation between confidence ratings and false alarms can be quite substantial ($r \geq |0.60|$), an important simplification of the original prototype of the procedure was introduced: the post hoc confidence ratings were dispensed with and their correlate, false alarms per segment, were substituted for the purpose of dropping segments. The segments with the most false alarms were dropped first until the desired false-alarm level F_c was reached. (The appendix elaborates on the procedure and provides an example of its implementation.)

The hit levels for both Karina (fig. 8.4) and Maya (fig. 8.5) are presented when these hit levels are conditionalized on a false-recall level F_c of 10 ($H|(F = 10)$). Since, once chosen, F_c is constant, repetition can be avoided by reporting only the hit value for each criterion-corrected data

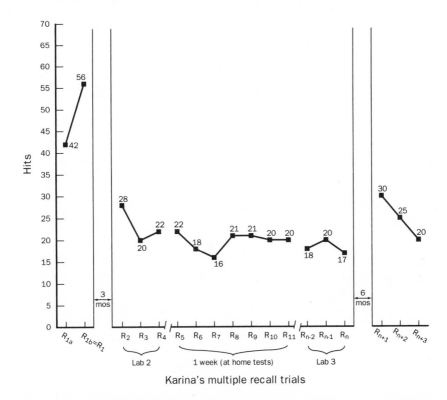

Karina's multiple recall trials

Figure 8.4 Karina's multitrial recall corresponding to figure 8.2 with criterion control such that all hits are conditionalized on a fixed false-alarm level of 10 (H| (F = 10)).

point. Thus Maya's R_2 = 15 is in actuality 15|10; her R_{n+3} = 29 is 29|10; and so on.

Without prejudging the adequacy of the criterion control procedure, it is worth comparing the multitrial pattern of the criterion controlled hits (figs. 8.4 and 8.5) with the pattern obtained with the raw hits (figs. 8.2 and 8.3).

The criterion-controlled multitrial recall pattern of Karina turns out to be essentially the same as the uncontrolled counterpart depicted in figure 8.2. Hit levels (number of correct recalls) are, of course, lower because of the downward adjustment of response production so that F_c = 10, but the basic trends are all sustained. Thus Karina's uncontrolled R_2 of 39|17 becomes a corrected R_2 of 28|10; the uncorrected R_n of 23|16 becomes a corrected R_n of 17|10; and the uncontrolled R_{n+1} = 80|81 of 6 months later becomes the corrected R_{n+1} = 30|10.

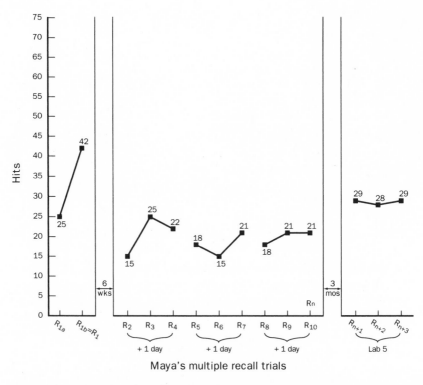

Figure 8.5 Maya's multitrial recall corresponding to figure 8.3 with criterion control such that all hits are conditionalized on a fixed false-alarm level of 10 ($H|$ ($F = 10$)).

The percent improvement, it should be noted, changes because of the change in the actual hit levels. Thus with uncontrolled recall, Karina improves by 248% ($R_n = 23$, $R_{n+1} = 80$) but with the corresponding corrected recalls she improves only 76% ($R_n = 17$, $R_{n+1} = 30$). Statistically inclined readers will be familiar with the problem of change scores (or percent change scores). If the hit scores had been conditionalized on a higher false-recall level, for example, $F_c = 15$, higher adjusted hit levels would have been obtained and higher percent change scores. (Different F_c levels, incidentally, yield remarkably parallel patterns.) As a useful convention, criterion-controlled hit or recall levels will be designated as H' or R' when the context fails to make clear which type of hit or recall level is being considered.

Thus for Maya (fig. 8.3) $R_2 = 20$, $R_n = 48$, and $R_{n+3} = 76$; her criterion-controlled counterparts (fig. 8.5) are $R_2' = 15$, $R_n' \doteq 21$, and $R_{n+3}' = 29$. Again, the pattern of multitrial controlled recall is essentially the same as the raw-score version, though again the percent improvements change. Thus the almost 300% raw-score improvement from $R_2 = 20$ to $R_{n+3} = 76$ becomes a 93% improvement in the adjusted scores ($R_2' = 15$, $R_{n+3}' = 29$).

The criterion control of both Karina's and Maya's multitrial recalls smoothes out the recall functions but preserves the basic findings. Perhaps the one slight difference is to be found in R_{n+1} to R_{n+3} performance, especially in Maya's trials. Thus the last three uncontrolled recalls (fig. 8.3) appear to be incremental but the criterion control flattens them out (fig. 8.5). On the other hand, the criterion control accentuates Maya's learning from R_{1A} to R_{1B}, which the raw scores understate, because it takes into account the substantial drop in false alarms from R_{1A} ($=41$) to R_{1B} ($=20$).

The essential finding, however, is that the criterion-controlled recalls confirm the basic results obtained with the raw recall scores, especially the robust hypermnesia shown in the last laboratory relative to recall trials of 3 or 6 months before.

Two cautions should be voiced in conclusion. First, only two subjects (Karina and Maya) have been systematically tested, and replication of the results with a larger group of subjects will be essential for buttressing the phenomena reported. The second caution is a methodological one, which has already been broached in the discussion of the work of Pötzl and Fisher (chap. 4). No systematic base rates have been collected over the full interval of testing. It would be strange if guessed (made-up) narratives by subjects never exposed to the original story, repeated over intervals of months, should improve over time with respect to the original story that these control subjects never saw. Still, it would be desirable to settle the matter empirically.

Actually, some initial probes have already been undertaken. Several high school students (n = 3) were asked to read Maya's R_2 recall carefully, and then requested to produce an embroidered recall of it ("R_2") that would reproduce it but also expand on it substantially in story themes and details. When the subjects were done, "R_2" was collected and the subjects were asked to produce another embroidered recall ("R_3") of the originally read (Maya's) story, with encouragement to be creative in expanding on the story they had read (Maya's). On the average, these "yoked" control subjects' criterion-controlled "R_2" ($=18$) and "R_3" ($=19$) yielded a net gain of 1 word. (Maya's corresponding R_2 [$=15$] and R_3 [$=25$] produced a net change of 10 words; see fig. 8.5.) Another small group of high school children (n = 4) were yoked to Maya's R_n and given the same instructions as the other yoked subjects. They produced average

"R_n" and "R_{n+1}" values of 13 and 16, for a gain of 3, presumably a meaningless chance fluctuation. As figure 8.5 shows, Maya gained 8 words, from $R_n = 21$ to $R_{n+1} = 29$, even though 3 months separated the two tests.

A large-sample replication of this very long-term study, with the appropriate experimental and control conditions and the ancillary statistical analyses, is indicated.

NINE

Overview and Implications

As we saw in chapter 1, during its hundred-odd years, the scientific study of memory focused on the phenomenon of forgetting. This probably was a legacy of Ebbinghaus's (1885) groundbreaking work, *Memory,* in which, based on his experiments on himself, he reported an inverse logarithmic relationship between retention and time. Common sense also probably contributed to the emphasis on forgetting since we are all too familiar with the depredations that time visits upon memory.

Still, both common sense and Ebbinghaus enshrined an opposite truth, although perhaps more subtly. On the basis of experience rather than experiments, Ebbinghaus noted passingly that fragmentary knowledge, apparently forgotten, does at times return unbidden both in wakeful consciousness as well as in dreams. We are all familiar with such spontaneous recoveries, a fact which necessarily implies that retention is not inexorably downward-bound over time.

The experiment and not experience ruled the scientific psychology of memory of those days and so the subtler counterpoint was mostly lost amidst the bustle of replications of Ebbinghaus-type forgetting curves. Yet ensconced even in the experimental corroborations, the perverse "opposite truth" occasionally beckoned, although diffidently, as we saw in chapter 1. Psychologists, especially those with an applied bent, including no less a figure than Alfred Binet, occasionally took note of the contrary phenomenon, and some even published research on the subject.

In the most applied of psychological settings, the clinic, matters stood otherwise: the phenomenon of upward-trending memory was the dominant motif. The classic work here is Breuer and Freud's (1895) *Studies on Hysteria,* curiously neglected by the scientific mainstream even though it anticipated many of the experimental breakthroughs in memory today. Its theory of neurosis and the psychological therapy it offered were both grounded on the emergence (often indirect) and explicit recovery of unconscious memories. The modern notion of "remembering without

179

awareness" was, as shown in chapter 2, the central premise of this seminal work (its therapeutic goal was the dissolution of the "without").

Ballard over Time

The reference study in experimental psychology that ultimately made the topic of upward-trending memory impossible to ignore was Ballard's (1913) monograph "Oblivescence and Reminiscence," although it took experimentalists some time to confront its findings and implications. Indeed, the field even to this date has failed to assimilate it in meaningful depth and, after decades of distortions and misconceptualizations, this fundamental work on memory continues to be largely ignored or misunderstood.

Reminiscence versus Hypermnesia (Improvement)

It was Ballard who introduced the term *reminiscence* into psychology, adapting it from Plato's fanciful reminiscence theory of learning (learning is really remembering forgotten knowledge from previous reincarnations) to designate the notion of "remembering again of the forgotten without relearning." (Ballard, of course, never espoused or mentioned reincarnation.) The term stuck and is generically familiar to psychologists today although—and here is one of the several peculiarities of experimental psychology's treatment of Ballard—the term as Ballard meant it was distorted to signify another phenomenon. Since the other phenomenon—which is called "hypermnesia" in the modern literature and which Ballard referred to as "improvement"—is more finicky and, unlike the original "reminiscence" of Ballard, readily evanesces if the wrong stimulus or experimental conditions are used (and experimental psychology for several decades did that precisely), doubts developed about the phenomenon mislabeled as "reminiscence." The semantic drift and the resulting conceptual problems are an intriguing illustration of Bartlett effects operating at the level of a research area over several decades.

This strange history is perhaps not quite as stark as hindsight might suggest. Ballard was rather leisurely about making some of his distinctions and often used his terms in misleading contexts, and so the critical distinction between Ballard's two incremental phenomena, "reminiscence" and "improvement," may not be so obvious as it appears now. Indeed, it remained for contemporary researchers (Erdelyi 1984; Roediger and Thorpe 1978; Payne 1986) to recapture the distinction for the field.

What is the distinction? This point has been developed in chapters 1,

5, and 6, with a mock numerical illustration provided in the first pages of chapter 6. Since it is so important and continues to lapse into recidivism, the distinction might be briefly revisited: *reminiscence* refers to recoveries in later trials of initially inaccessible items, whereas *hypermnesia* refers to net improvement of memory level from an earlier trial to a later one. They are not the same. Even if overall recall declines substantially from an earlier recall test to a later test, reminiscence can still occur (and almost inevitably does, as Ballard showed) since the reminiscences (new recoveries) may be swamped by forgetting (oblivescence). Reminiscence is a bedrock phenomenon, probably on par with oblivescence. Every study in Ballard's long series produced it, and I have not seen a single experiment that provides the relevant data where reminiscence failed to materialize. It most certainly is not Buxton's (1943) "now-you-see-it-now-you-don't" chimera. Of course, Buxton was not referring to Ballard's reminiscence anymore (although he was aware of the distinction) but to hypermnesia.

The Stimulus and Coding Format

Is hypermnesia, then, such a delicate flower? Certainly not, although it is not as inevitable as is reminiscence. The problem lies in yet a different misunderstanding—or careless treatment—of Ballard. Ballard showed very clearly (see chap. 1, esp. fig. 1.9) that hypermnesia is obtained with some stimuli (for example, poetry) but not other stimuli (for example, nonsense syllables). Yet somehow researchers tended to overlook this plain fact, and attempted all too frequently to obtain hypermnesia (which they called reminiscence) with the stimuli that had proved ineffective. They were actually replicating Ballard by not getting hypermnesia but construing their failures as failed replications. The story is not quite this simple, but there is a decidedly bewildering aspect to it.

The same issue arose in the more clinical experimental field of hypnotic hypermnesia. To the credit of these more clinically oriented researchers, they hit upon the stimulus factor early and grasped its significance. As we saw in chapter 7, hypnotic hypermnesia (which turns out to be nothing more than hypermnesia) reliably fails to appear with low-sense stimuli (nonsense syllables, lists of unconnected words) but will typically be found in repeated recall of poems, meaningful pictures, or affectively invested words. Perhaps this was a more congenial finding to clinically oriented experimenters than to the standard laboratory scientist. After all, Breuer and Freud in 1895 had already proposed that imagistic materials ("memory pictures," and so forth) characterized the cognition of hysterics

in contrast to word-prone obsessive-compulsives, and that for this reason hysterics were more likely to succeed at the "work of recollection." So different traditions converge in underscoring the role of the stimulus (or coding format) in hypermnesia.

Declarative versus Procedural Memory

Actually, the stimulus—or coding format—factor is more general than this. To Freud (Breuer and Freud), imagery is not so much the opposite of verbal codes but rather an intermediate format in what amounts to a continuum from abstract (for example, verbal) to highly concrete, including, at the extreme, behavior patterns and body language (for example, tics, paralyses, phobias). Today the two polarities would tend to be identified with the "declarative" versus "procedural" knowledge distinction. To Breuer and Freud, "hysterics suffer mainly from reminiscences," that is, from pathogenic retention and recovery of traumatic events in the recondite dialect of body language and behavior scripts. Procedural knowledge, under the guise of "skills" or "sensory-motor" memory had actually been probed for hypermnesia by experimenters even before Ballard (who reviewed some of this work). Positive and often dramatic effects were typically reported. Buxton's (1943) review of "reminiscence," which cast a pall over hypermnesia for some decades, is well known to students of the subject. Universally forgotten, however, is a parallel review, "Reminiscence in the Acquisition of Skill," of a year earlier (Buxton 1942), in which "wide-spread occurrence of reminiscence" (195) was found for "skill-acquisition."

Remembering without Awareness: Skills and Sick Skills

A huge implication lurks in this stimulus-format effect, which, if true, could bridge, perhaps even merge, the hitherto dissociated clinic and laboratory. To the extent that "skills," "sensory-motor" memory, "procedural memory," "conditioned responses" and "spontaneous recovery" (to bring Pavlov into play) are laboratory homologues of clinical phenomena such as hysterical symptoms ("conversion reactions"), maladaptive behaviors (sick skills), and emotional misreactions, it follows that such clinical manifestations may literally be "reminiscences" of past events, emerging in procedural forms but not in declarative knowledge (Erdelyi 1990, 1993). Thus the patient might be remembering in procedural forms what he or she cannot remember declaratively; in short, the patient may be "remembering without awareness." (If true, the conversion metaphor of

Freud may require modification. It might have appeared to Freud that the forgetting, presumably due to repression, of declarative knowledge while procedural knowledge was in evidence indicated a conversion of one form of coding to another when, instead, what may obtain is a differential effect of repression on the two kinds of memory: amnesia in declarative memory and no effect or a contrary effect in procedural memory, hence retention or hypermnesia in the latter.)

One interesting ancillary question (Erdelyi 1990, 1993) is the extent to which dreams contact both declarative and procedural knowledge. If dreams, unlike wakeful thoughts, uniquely tap procedural memory, as would clearly follow from Freud (1900, 1917; Erdelyi 1985), who emphasized that dreams expressed themselves in the language of "plastic-word representation" (imagery) and "dramatization" (behavioral representation of ideas in dream cognition), then dreams may turn out, after all, to be a royal road to the unconscious, that is, to procedural knowledge not accessible to declarative memory.

Reminiscence ≠ Hypermnesia and Oblivescence (Forgetting) ≠ Amnesia

As we have seen, Ballard experimentally codified not one but two memory phenomena, *reminiscence* and *improvement (hypermnesia),* which were unfortunately conflated until recently by scholars in the field. An important implication that perhaps also deserves underscoring is that decremental memory is symmetrical to incremental memory: there are two, not one, decremental memory phenomena, *oblivescence* (forgetting) and (to introduce a new convention) *amnesia.* Amnesia (which need not be tied to pathological memory) is simply the inverse of hypermnesia, and vice versa. When reminiscence exceeds oblivescence, hypermnesia results; when oblivescence is greater than reminiscence, amnesia is the result.

It follows then that Ebbinghaus's "forgetting curve" (as I have occasionally called it in deference to custom, perhaps for the last time), is also a misnomer resulting from the unwitting conflation of oblivescence (forgetting) and amnesia. Although the savings technique of Ebbinghaus does not yield the component analysis that recall does (worth noting is how a particular method may thoroughly mask a major effect; see chap. 1), decremental functions are also balance effects. As is clear from Ballard (fig. 1.9), decremental functions involve steeper forgetting than the actual retention functions because reminiscence mitigates oblivescence. Thus unless reminiscence is partialed out, decremental functions—such as that of Ebbinghaus—are amnesia functions.

It should be clear that Ballard left a fabulous legacy, one that was too rich for psychology to assimilate in short order. Perhaps his most basic contribution, however, which is implied in his title, was that memory is an opponent-process system: it simultaneously tends to decrease (oblivescence) and to increase (reminiscence) over time. Aside from providing a deeper understanding of the nature of memory, the insight has obvious implications for experimental psychology. For example, in most modeling of memory, a decay parameter is built in; rarely is a countervailing growth parameter. The data call for both.

To the extent that retention level is of interest, it is now clear that factors affecting *both* oblivescence and reminiscence need to be considered. Further, it is important to note that indexes of hypermnesia and reminiscence may not always correlate—precisely for this reason they should not be conflated. Thus as we have repeatedly seen through previous chapters, even when no hypermnesia is obtained with some classes of materials, reminiscence is nevertheless operative. What is missed by one index may be captured by the other. If one wished to test experimentally Freud's proposal that "dreams are hypermnesic" (Freud 1900), it may well be worth bearing in mind that, even if the hypothesis failed, it might still be the case that "dreams are reminiscent" relative to wakeful recall (probably this is what Freud really meant). In the chapter 7 section on hypnotic hypermnesia, a brief mention was made of an effort to determine whether in the absence of hypnotic hypermnesia, "hypnotic reminiscence" might nevertheless obtain (Dinges et al. 1992). It is not an implausible scenario. The data, however, failed to bear it out. On the contrary, it suggested that while hypnosis failed to enhance hypermnesia (beyond the hypermnesia level that was obtained without hypnosis), hypnosis actually interfered with reminiscence. The effect was small and might prove unreliable, but again we see the possibility of two indexes, reminiscence and hypermnesia, yielding different memory effects.

Moreover, different measures may be appropriate for different conceptual issues. As noted in chapter 6, reminiscence might be a very misleading index of current level of memory. If, to give a melodramatic example, a subject were to die between trials i and $i + 1$ and the compulsive experimenter insisted on finishing the study, it would be the case that the dead subject's measured reminiscence at trial $i + 1$ would be identical to the still alive subject's reminiscence at trial i. Reminiscence would be the wrong measure; we assume, unlike Plato, that the slate is wiped clean by death, at least insofar as memory is concerned. Note that hypermnesia, if there had been any at trial i, would disappear in $i + 1$; it would be replaced by total amnesia.

Subliminal Processes and Psychodynamics

The Chance Limen and Hypermnesia: Implications for Subliminal
Perception and the Unconscious

If one were interested in overall conscious accessibility, the composite
retention measure hypermnesia/amnesia would presumably be the appropriate index and not a component measure like reminiscence or oblivescence. Let us briefly consider the subliminal perception literature, which
centrally grapples with consciousness—and its absence. The problem of
finding the "limen" dividing conscious from unconscious processes has
been the central methodological conundrum of the field (Holender et al.
1986). In an effort to introduce a maximally strict standard for subliminality, the *chance limen* (or threshold) has been proposed or imple-
mented in recent years (Merikle and Cheesman's [1986] "objective limen"; Erdelyi's [1986] "absolute subliminality"; Kunst-Wilson and Zajonc
1980). This would be the level of performance of a subject never actually
exposed to the stimulus (for example, $d' = 0$). It is so strict that some
scholars have suggested that it might render subliminal effects impossible
(Bowers 1984) or, at the very least, highly unlikely (Macmillan 1986).

Given my experience with hypermnesia, I had a different concern
(Erdelyi 1986): might chance performance at time 1 grow into above-
chance performance at time 2? Merikle and Reingold (1991; see chap. 7
herein) examined some chance-level recognition data that they had already collected to check on this possibility. They divided their test, which
indicated chance-level performance, into thirds, with the idea that if hypermnesia occurred, chance-level performance would rise over time. To
their surprise this happened. They immediately undertook a replication
and once again found chance-level performance growing to above-chance
level. Moreover, as had been suggested by me as a possibility (Erdelyi
1986), their indirect indicator of availability, visual contrast, went the
other way. Thus when the index of consciousness was null, the indirect
indicator was positive. Over time the relation flip-flopped. This certainly
introduces a new perspective on the famous KWZ effect (Kunst-Wilson
and Zajonc 1980), of which Merikle and Reingold's study is an exemplar
(see chap. 7).

Since consciousness grows and fades over time, the limen, however
strict, does not stay constant over time and can move in the direction of
higher and not just lower sensitivity. This finding, as Ionescu and Erdelyi
(1992) have elaborated, has fundamental implications for the notion of
subliminality—and ultimately for the unconscious. It becomes clear that

what has been thought of as methodological problems are often really theoretical questions. There is no set limen over time, no matter how carefully or strictly it is measured; there are only dissociations between different indicators, each of which has different rise-and-fall dynamics. Not only the time of the test but also the time duration of the test determines whether and what kind of dissociation is captured (Erdelyi 1994a; Ionescu and Erdelyi 1992). In other words, there is no instantaneously measurable consciousness, and probably no instantaneous consciousness. Consciousness unfolds over time and yields different measures over time and over different time frames (test lengths). Perhaps this is obvious. It has not, however, been reflected in a century of research on subliminal perception. The insight, moreover, is a ramification of Ballard's work, though we seem to have moved quite a distance from the original. Yet it should be remembered that Ballard, though he avoided clinical and psychodynamic issues, was aware of them and grudgingly admitted that reminiscence (and improvement) implied "subconscious" mentation.

An unanticipated yield of the foregoing research on KWZ effects, in which the indicator of consciousness is at chance when measured initially, is the ghostly phenomenon (it may or may not be real) of "subchance perception" (Ionescu and Erdelyi 1992). If it is the case, as in the Merikle and Reingold studies, that overall chance performance, when broken up into earlier and later phases of testing, moves to above chance over time, does this not imply that early phases of testing yield subchance performance? Ionescu and Erdelyi briefly discuss some of the evidence for this subchance perception effect. It may be a psychological version of cold fusion, but, interestingly, Snodgrass, Shevrin, and Kopka (1993) have published an independent pair of experiments that seem to produce this type of effect, which Van Selst and Merikle (1993) replicated in two studies of their own. Subchance perception, if it could be reliably established, would be a most remarkable and unanticipated empirical find arising, in part, from hypermnesia research.

Repression (= Suppression): Effect on Memory

A final and more obvious implication of Ballard's opponent-process theory of memory to be broached here is its bearing on repression and, more generally, the mechanisms of defense. I have already spelled these out in some detail elsewhere (Erdelyi 1990, 1993). If it is true that retention in any time frame is the balance between reminiscence and oblivescence, is it not likely that we intentionally manipulate factors that affect this balance in a biased fashion so as to maximize accessibility for what we want to be accessible to consciousness and minimize accessibility for that which we wish to avoid?

In short-term situations (in the order of hours, perhaps a few days) *thinking* about the target materials has been shown to maximize hypermnesia (Erdelyi and Becker 1974; Erdelyi and Kleinbard 1978) and *not thinking* (in practice, *else thinking*) to diminish and even eliminate it (for example, Roediger and Payne 1982). Actually, with the typical laboratory stimuli, whether nonsense syllables, lists of words or pictures, or even narratives, not thinking yields amnesia for nonstable memories (Bahrick and Hall 1993; see above, chap. 8). If so, for certain materials at least, not thinking would be an efficient way of achieving amnesia over time, if that is what were desired defensively. This not thinking (I believe) is what Freud meant by repression.

Unfortunately, it has become standard, all the way down to the introductory text level, to distinguish between suppression and repression as, respectively, conscious and unconscious mechanisms of defense. Everyone seems to believe in suppression—the absolutely obvious is difficult to gainsay—but considerable skepticism among experimentalists persists about repression (Holmes 1990; G. Bower 1990) because, ultimately, of the difficulty of demonstrating unconscious defensive not-thinking and the attendant target amnesia in the laboratory.

I have attempted to show (Erdelyi 1990, 1993) that this distinction, between suppression and repression, constitutes another grand Bartlett effect. It is not true, as is universally supposed, that the distinction is inherent in Sigmund Freud's thinking; it seems to have arisen in Anna Freud's reconstructive systematization of her father's work and then perpetuated in the literature. It is an unwarranted distinction that has obstructed the rapprochement of the psychodynamic clinic and the experimental laboratory. Because the absolute demarcation between conscious and unconscious is difficult if not impossible to realize experimentally, as the foregoing discussion on subliminality has suggested, it is not likely that the laboratory will succeed soon in clinching the more complex phenomenon stipulating not only unconsciousness but avoidance and defense in addition. Thought repression often gives the impression of being unconscious; it may well be often. It is hard, however, and perhaps impossible to establish this impression with methodological rigor for the reasons already suggested and, also, for one other: oblivescence. We may forget our defensive not-thinking and in retrospect assume that the process had been unconscious (Holender, 1986).

The point is not that repression cannot be unconscious or that the unconscious is refractory to experimental testing. Rather, the problem is theoretical in that implicit assumptions (for example, the existence of a stationary limen) are foisted upon methodological standards. Thus none of us, probably, would raise doubts about the distinction between childhood and adulthood, nor would we have difficulty in assigning a five-year-old and a fifty-year-old person to the correct category. What we would have problems doing is identifying the precise point in time where the "subadult" or "unadult" crosses into adulthood. The *unconscious* is a useful but pretheoretic term (Erdelyi 1992, 1994a); it is pretheoretic because the assumptions underlying it are not formally spelled out and what seems to subsume it implicitly—for example, that there is a limen of consciousness—is almost surely oversimple and perhaps altogether incorrect. A plausible countervailing model is that *conscious* and *unconscious* constitute not a dichotomy but polarities in a continuum, and a grainy continuum at that, which changes with the method, the time, and the duration of testing. If this were the case, we would not be tempted to lay such an emphasis on an absolute dichotomy between unconscious repression and conscious repression or suppression. If *suppression* is another word for *repression* (which it seems to be for Freud), then it becomes untenable to maintain that suppression is obvious but repression doubtful. (If $x = y$ and x is true, y cannot be false.)

Memory Recovery, False-Memory Syndrome, and Defense

I have tried to show (Erdelyi 1990, 1993) that repression and suppression are essentially the same phenomenon and that in both cases (as extensive textual analysis of Sigmund Freud demonstrates), they amount to some version of intentional not-thinking of target materials. If so, we have identified the mechanism of the undeservedly controversial mechanism of repression. The mechanism, whether it is used for defense or for any other reason, and whether it is deployed consciously or not, is not-thinking (else thinking, cognitive avoidance, selective inattention, inhibition, and so forth). Its consequence, at least with some materials, is amnesia. This is what Ebbinghaus demonstrated in 1885. His retention function may be considered the first experimental study of nondefensive repression (Erdelyi 1990). Note that some recovery from the resulting amnesia is possible (Erdelyi and Halberstam 1987), which is congruent with findings in the clinic, although, as seen in the very long-term functions of Karina and Maya in chapter 8 for "The War of the Ghosts," the recoveries, even when retention is clearly hypermnesic, are a pastiche of true and false recollections. Thus in the contemporary debate concerning "delayed recall" and the "false memory syndrome" (see Banks and Pezdek 1994), both sides are validated. Of course, signal detection theory has already done so decades ago: even if sensitivity goes up, hits are intermingled with false alarms. Partisans in the debate are, in effect, emphasizing one or the other side of the same memory coin.

The mechanism of repression/suppression may not be effective with all stimuli. In cases of traumatic events, patients typically complain of peremptory intrusions of the dreaded event; even their dreams are troubled by unbidden recoveries (Horowitz 1983, 1986). This phenomenon of intrusive imagery (for example, flashbacks) is central to the definition of posttraumatic stress disorder and can be viewed as a failure of the mechanism of repression. About some materials it may not be psychologically possible for us to avoid thinking. Similarly, as suggested above, repression might not succeed in eliminating procedural knowledge, hence the curious phenomenon, which Freud perhaps mistakenly confused for conversion, of amnesia overtaking declarative knowledge without similarly affecting procedural knowledge (in the form of body language, sick skills, and so forth).

Finally, as I have emphasized in my efforts to create a unified framework for the mechanisms of defense involving the traditions of Ebbinghaus, Freud, Ballard, and Bartlett (Erdelyi 1990, 1993), the amnesias in declarative knowledge that repression produces are easily parlayed into the other classic defense mechanisms. To the extent that thought repression (not thinking) produces amnesia over time, that is, a progressively degraded memory of earlier events, the more opportunity exists for Bartlett effects—biased constructions, reconstructions, projections, fillings-in, and so forth—to assert themselves and distort the original memory.

The reconstructive nature of memory has become a virtual truism in experimental psychology and all that needs to be added to generate the classic defense mechanisms is that we distort degraded memories not only according to intellective needs but according to emotional needs as well. To use Bartlett's schema terminology, schemas can be emotional as well as intellective. Defensive distortions such as projection, displacement, and rationalization can be viewed as typical reconstructive distortions occurring in the clinic. They are a subclass of the false-memory syndrome. E. Loftus and her colleagues (Loftus 1979; Loftus and Loftus 1980; Loftus, Schooler, and Wagenaar 1985) have emphasized the distorting effect of postevent information given to subjects. As Roediger and his colleagues (Roediger, Srinivas, and Waddill 1989; Roediger, Wheeler, and Rajaram 1993; Roediger, Challis, and Wheeler 1994) have suggested in their discussion of guessing in forced recall, postevent information need not be external. I now add that guessing is not the only endogenous postevent distorter of memory. Thinking itself may do the trick. By thinking about some target material we tend to enhance hypermnesia; we also, however, tend to generate endogenous postevent information, some of it emotionally biased, resulting in wishful and defensive thinking and memory.

It suddenly seems all so obvious; and, it appears, the laboratory has already produced the experimental foundations for the clinically ubiquitous effects which it has avoided with such suspicion.

Theory of Reminiscence and Hypermnesia

Reminiscence, the levitation engine of incremental memory, is simpler than the composite phenomenon, hypermnesia. Explanatory efforts until recently have been silent on the distinction and have only addressed the general phenomenon of incremental memory.

Perhaps the oldest explanatory framework, which Ballard adopted, was the *consolidation* hypothesis of Müller and Pilzecker (1900), which Hebb (1949) later elaborated in the familiar notion of cell assemblies and which has gained further currency in contemporary work on neural networks and synapse dynamics (Gluck and Rummelhart 1990; Karni et al. 1994; Wilson and McNaughton 1994). Although some type of consolidation process must ultimately underlie reminiscence (and therefore hypermnesia), it is a more ambiguous term than it appears on first blush and, because of its frequent use in hard-science contexts (neuroscience), it has acquired a sort of Pavlovian rigor in which the feeling of rigor is more conditioned response than considered logic. Consolidation is too amorphous a notion to provide a theoretical accounting of reminiscence and hypermnesia. Since the time course of consolidation is not usually spelled out—or, when it is, it cannot provide a general fit to the heterogeneous data—consolidation does not provide a prediction of the time course of incremental memory for different materials and conditions. Thus it fails to provide, at this point, a predictive explanation of stimulus or coding-format differences observed in reminiscence and hypermnesia, or an explanation of why—or if—thinking or not thinking of target materials should alter consolidation or reminiscence or oblivescence, or, indeed, if thinking is itself a form of consolidation. So at best the concept is underdeveloped. Certainly it is not complete.

Another explanation of incremental memory, going back at least to Brown (1923) and reflected in *stimulus sampling* or *probabilistic search* theories of multitrial recall (Estes 1955; Shiffrin 1970) is that a single test does not exhaust the set of available targets and so multiple testing is likely to yield new recoveries. The theory is congenial to much of modern memory work—and to my way of thinking—but, again, outside of computer models (Raaijmakers and Shiffrin's [1980] SAM), there is little prediction of the time course of upward-trending memory, especially as it applies to different stimuli or coding formats. Of course, one can always adjust the parameters to produce a good fit to a particular set of data, but this would not be prediction. Whether it is a good explanative theory or not, probabilistic search models at least describe what happens: with each new test (search), more target items are recovered. Thus as Brown (1923) found, the answer to his own question, "To what extent is memory measured by a single recall?" is, "incompletely."

Various theories of *release from inhibition* (Pavlov, Freud) or other disruptive states (*fatigue, arousal, output interference*) can also supply explanations for reminiscence and hypermnesia (see chaps. 3, 7).

Finally, even developmental hypotheses may be deployed, at least in young children (Piaget and Inhelder 1973): the child may need to mature and develop certain requisite schemas before certain encoded information can be successfully accessed. What we seem to have here is a consolidation theory operating at the level of the organism rather than just the target memory.

Probably none of these hypotheses are entirely wrong and almost surely none of them are sufficient.

The same situation applies to explicit theories of hypermnesia advanced in recent years. It was my assumption at the start of this book that the concluding chapter would be substantially devoted to the resolution of the question of how best to account theoretically for hypermnesia. I have changed my thinking in this regard with the gradual realization that the question misses the mark. *Hypermnesia* is not a single phenomenon but a cover term for a variety of incremental memory effects, including the standard 1-hour effects, the very long-term hypermnesias reported in chapter 8, incubation effects where retrieval effort may be counterproductive (Smith and Vela 1991), the classic phenomena of spontaneous recovery (Pavlov) and sensory-motor and skill hypermnesia, and, also, short- to very short-term effects, including perceptual microgenesis (Werner 1948, 1956).

If hypermnesia is not a single phenomenon, it is not likely to be adequately explained by a single theory. For this reason, technical discussions of some of the contending explanations of hypermnesia—especially my two-stage model (chap. 6), Roediger and his associates' level of cumulative recall hypothesis, and Payne's revision of it into a two-factor model—were undertaken in their local contexts rather than reserved for a final all-purpose theoretical assault.

Perhaps the one caution worth underscoring in this overview is that in any effort at theoretical treatment of hypermnesia, whatever the local context, the propensity to confuse and ultimately conflate hypermnesia with reminiscence is a potential obfuscator. It shipwrecked the field for more than half a century and continues to bedevil it to this day.

If there is one general, overarching insight, it is Ballard's: the dialectical dance between reminiscence and oblivescence determines retention over time, which can be hypermnesic or amnesic. It is a simple, beautiful, and fecund gift to the science of memory.

Appendix

The Technique, Rationale, and Empirical Grounding of Criterion-Controlled Free Recall (CCFR) of Narrative Materials

In this concluding section, the procedure for criterion control of narrative free-recall introduced in chapter 8 is sketched out in more detail. The section is relevant to readers who wish to evaluate the technique and, possibly, make use of it in their own work.

Classic Signal-Detection Theory, ROC Functions, d', P(A), and Conditionalized H%

The essential idea behind the approach derives from a common-sense reading of signal-detection theory's ROC (receiver operating characteristic) functions. Figure A.1 presents two such functions, L and M, in which L depicts an isosensitive function that is lower on the sensitivity (or discriminability) parameter d' than the middle-level function, M.

The sensitivity difference between L and M can be explained by way of the mathematical superstructure of signal detection theory (SDT), but also in quite intuitive terms: for any two isosensitive functions M and L for which M > L in d', it is the case (see fig. A.1) that for any particular false-alarm rate, F%, greater than 0% and less than 100%, the hit rate, H%, of the more sensitive function will necessarily be higher. Thus in the example in figure A.1, for a false-alarm rate of 15%, M yields a hit rate of about 63% while L yields a hit rate of only 33%. For another false-alarm rate, 60%, M yields a hit rate of 95% to L's corresponding hit rate of 80%. If M and L represent the performance of two different subjects, then M is common-sensically more sensitive than L since, for any particular false-alarm

Many individuals played a role in the development, over the past decade and a half, of the criterion-controlled free recall (CCFR) method, which this appendix describes in detail for the first time. The groundwork was laid in a collaborative venture with the Unit for Experimental Psychiatry of the University of Pennsylvania, headed by Martin and Emily Orne and David Dinges. Subsequently, a critical role was played by Michael Halberstam, then an honor student at Brooklyn College, who in collaboration with me developed the first working prototype of the method. Merryl Feigin-Pfau, one of my graduate students, followed up with critical empirical tests of the technique that justified a significant simplification of the procedure. Feigin-Pfau, along with fellow graduate students Marcos Ionescu and Jacqueline Bergstein, conducted successful validation studies of the CCFR which Vermone Wong, an honor student, refined and extended.

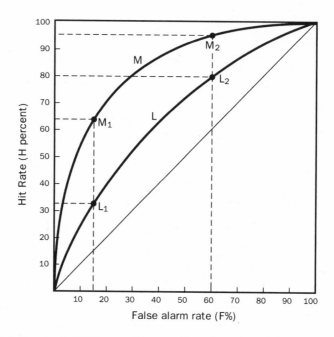

Figure A.1 Hypothetical ROC curves for two subjects, L and M, with low and middle levels of recognition memory (d'). Points on a particular curve represent different criterion placements but the same memory level.

"penalty" within the full range for F% of 0% to 100%, M invariably garners a higher hit rate. Thus if we defined the criterion-controlled hit rate H%' as a hit rate conditionalized on a particular false-alarm rate F%$_c$, that is, H%' = H%|F%$_c$, it would follow that M's H%' > L's H%'. Indeed, if the mathematical assumptions underlying SDT (Green and Swets 1966; Swets 1964) held, H%' would be perfectly correlated with d'. It should be also noted, since it plays a role in what follows, that the proportion of area P(A) under ROC functions, often designated as a nonparametric counterpart of d', would also be perfectly correlated with H%'. (Macmillan and Creelman [1991] show, however, that most so-called nonparametric measures in SDT are actually parametric because of demonstrable implicit mathematical assumptions or homologies that may not be evident on the surface.)

Application of Classic SDT Notions to Recall: From ROC to roc Functions and Conditionalized Hits, H|F$_c$

The proposed criterion-control technique applies the common-sense logic of SDT sketched out above, which is based on recognition measures, to free recall. The central idea is this: rather than forcing a preset number of responses, as in forced-recall (see chap. 8), hits are conditionalized on a preset false-alarm level.

The term *level* instead of *rate* is used advisedly and calls for the interpolation of a technical point at this juncture. In the standard ROC function, which is based on recognition, the subject makes decisions on items in a test set consisting of 50% stimulus items and 50% distractors. It is possible, therefore, to speak of "rates" because one knows the actual number of stimulus and distractor items to which the subject said yes. Thus if a subject says yes to 30 of the 50 stimulus items, his or her hit rate is 60%; if the subject says yes to 10 of the 50 distractors, the false-alarm rate is 20%. In recall, however, we have no way of specifying the number of distractors, and so the notion of rates is inapplicable. (Welford [1989] has recently made the same point.) Thus in free recall, subjects can open-endedly vary their number of false alarms—10, 25, 50, 500—simply by varying their response productivity, and so no prespecified number of distractors can be used to calculate rate. Hence the ROC curves to be considered in free recall—*recall operating characteristic curves*—involve absolute levels, not rates of hits and false alarms. Our recall ROC curves, henceforth designated in lower case as *roc* curves, are defined as $H = f(F)$, that is, number of hits as a function of number of false alarms, rather than the classic recognition ROC function, which is defined as $H\% = f(F\%)$, namely, hit rate as a function of false-alarm rate. These roc curves are the basic isosensitive recall functions in the proposed criterion-controlled free-recall system. The $H|F_c$ index discussed up to now is simply the value of H in the function $H = f(F)$ for $F = F_c$.

Although the roc function is not difficult to generate, as will be demonstrated below, the simplest and most self-evident index of recall sensitivity is the conditionalized H, that is, $H|F_c$. How, in actual practice, can H be conditionalized on a fixed false-alarm level F_c? Suppose a subject produces on one trial 25 hits and 15 false alarms, that is, 25|15, and on another trial, 101 hits and 105 false alarms, that is, 101|105. (These are the actual data of Maya for R_2 and R_{n+2}, without the function words stripped from the recalls, as they were in the computer scoring reported in chapter 8.) Obviously we cannot conditionalize on $F = 105$ since the subject did not produce that many false alarms (or responses, for that matter) in the earlier recall trial. Thus we can only conditionalize down to the lower F, in this case, 15. We can pare down but cannot "pare-up."

Achieving Target False-Alarm Level F_c: Paring Down Narrative Recall Texts

Confidence Ratings of Narrative Segments

Is there a rational way of paring down narrative recall text post hoc to suit our need? For the solution to this question, I turned once again to techniques pioneered in classic SDT, in this case, the use of *confidence ratings* (Egan, Schulman, and Greenberg 1964; Pollack and Decker 1964). In recognition tests using this procedure, the subject is required to rate each of the test items for confidence that the item was part of the original stimulus set (rather than a member of the distractor set). Thus if a 0–3 rating scale is used, a 0 would designate no confidence; 1, low confidence; 2, moderate confidence; and 3, high confidence. The beauty of the approach is that at a later time and at the experimenter's leisure, the ratings can be collapsed to different binary (yes/no) decisions. Thus the experimenter can adopt a strict strategy on behalf of the subject and define only 3 ratings as yes and all the rest as no. Or a laxer criterion can be adopted for the subject in which 2 or 3 responses count as yes and only 0 and 1 as no. The laxer criterion will produce more hits—but also more false alarms. By probing the full range of possible binary cuts, from most permissive to the strictest, the experimenter generates, on a post hoc basis, a set of yes/no responses, which when evaluated against the items rated translate into hits ($Y|$stimulus) and false alarms ($Y|$distractor). From the pairs of H% and F% values thus generated for each binary cut, a standard ROC function can be plotted.

The tactic just described for recognition is applied to recall in the proposed criterion-control technique. After the subject has produced his or her narrative free recall, the experimenter requests that each segment—say, each sentence—be assigned a confidence rating. At a later time, once the false-alarm target F_c is defined (in Maya's example, $F_c = 15$), the experimenter sets out to prune the recall text of low-confidence segments until F_c is achieved. The logic of the procedure is that had the subject been asked to pare down the text, the subject would have cut out the segments of which he or she was least confident. Thus the experimenter would start by cutting 0-rated segments first, then move on to 1-rated segments, and so forth until the pruned recall text reached the target F_c. The number of hits remaining in the adjusted text is H' (that is, $H| (F = 15)$ for this recall text).

Scoring for Hits and False Alarms: Entrail Readings and Word Counts

Two practical issues remained to be resolved. The first is how to score narrative text for hits and false alarms. This problem, worked out by Michael Halberstam and me, has a surprisingly simple solution. We began with a decidedly unwieldy approach: a "clinical" (subjective) content scoring of recall protocols. The original story was segmented into 31 content units, each of which was scored for both hits and false alarms by the rater on a scale of 0 to 4 on the basis of the extent, in his judgment, that the narrative recall accurately rendered the contents of the unit (hit rating) and the extent the recall distorted it (false-alarm rating). The 0–4 ratings for both hits and intrusions for each of the 31 stimulus segments were summed to provide an overall H and F score. Halberstam (the judge) felt uncomfortable with the procedure, which, despite my repeated assurances based on past successes with subjective clinical scoring (for example, Haber and Erdelyi 1967), he felt was unacceptably arbitrary—"like reading chicken entrails," he once complained. We had avoided more objective, "wooden-headed" approaches like word counts because these would mindlessly miss the basic semantic structure, let alone the nuances, of the narrative recall text. Eventually, however, we decided to compare the "entrail readings" with the "wooden-headed" word counts. Perhaps there might be a significant correlation—I had hoped for something in the 0.50 ballpark—which would sufficiently validate the subjective ratings until another judge could blindly rate the same material and permit calculations of interjudge reliability (which I expected to exceed $r =$

0.80). We randomly sampled 10 narrative recall protocols that had been already rated subjectively and carried out a straight word-count scoring of these recalls against "The War of the Ghosts" (see chap. 8). The 334 words in the story were alphabetically ordered in a scoring list that included word repetitions (see table A.1).

A separate copy of this list of 334 words was used for scoring each narrative recall. For each recall text, every word was checked, in order, against the alphabetized stimulus list and if the word was found it was underlined in the recall text to indicate that the recalled word was a hit. (Thus all nonunderlined words are false alarms.) Every time a word correspondence was achieved, the word was crossed out from the stimulus list (or lexicon) so that the subject would not get hits by repeating a word more often than it occurred in the story text. (Thus "Indian" occurs one time in the story and the subject could garner a maximum of one hit by recalling the word *Indian* in his or her recall. If, however, the subject produced *Indian* two times, the first "*Indian*" would be counted a hit and the second one a false-alarm.) In summary, H, the number of hits, was defined as the number of word correspondences between recall text and story text.

We were astonished at the correlations between the subjective scores and the word-count scores: for H, $r = 0.96$ and for F (number of false alarms), $r = 0.92$. Indeed, if an extremely good and an extremely bad made-up recall protocol was added to the 10 recall narratives so as to reduce homogeneity of variance, the correlations approached 0.99. Apparently, the subjective scoring—as done by Halberstam, at least—constituted an implicit word count. We naturally decided to drop the subjective scoring (which has poor face validity among experimentalists—and scorers) in favor of the purely mechanical—indeed, computer scorable—word-count procedure. What would have been an inevitably suspect scoring scheme became the unromantic but completely objective word-correspondence count.

The Circumvention of Confidence Ratings by Actual Per-Segment Hit and False-Alarm Number

The second problem, also tackled collaboratively by Halberstam and me, was the intrusiveness and, even refractoriness, of confidence ratings. How could one sensibly ask a 6-year-old to provide confidence ratings, when even college students often fail to grasp the idea? Moreover, in multitrial recall experiments such as we were conducting, early ratings almost surely influence later recall performance (and, of course, later ratings). Our solution—one of the most satisfying, if also most risky in the project—was to cut the Gordian knot, as it were, and dispense with overt confidence ratings altogether. We reasoned that the subject's actual performance in each recall segment (however defined) would be correlated with the subject's confidence in the segment. Suppose that the segment unit is a line of recall text (which is more convenient and flexible than idea units or sentences, and to which we shifted once word counts replaced clinical scoring), and that one line had 7 correct words and 1 false alarm ($H|F = 7|1$) and another line had 1 correct word and 6 errors ($1|6$). Which line is likely to get the higher confidence

Table A.1 "The War of the Ghosts" alphabetized into its 334 constituent words, with word repetitions included, used for word-count scoring of each of the narrative recalls

Order #	WORD	Order #	WORD	Order #	WORD
42	a	160	but	140	gone
53	a	198	but	235	had
174	a	231	but	216	has
256	a	30	calm	113	have
266	accompanied	57	came	139	have
303	all	184	came	143	he
93	along	317	came	220	he
127	along	69	canoe	226	he
21	and	80	canoe	234	he
29	and	120	canoe	259	he
36	and	56	canoes	300	he
50	and	240	canoes	305	he
59	and	70	coming	312	he
66	and	325	contorted	332	he
81	and	331	cried	33	heard
165	and	35	cries	61	heard
189	and	334	dead	203	heard
194	and	227	did	51	hid
245	and	296	did	252	his
254	and	85	do	320	his
258	and	134	do	322	his
262	and	14	down	218	hit
269	and	185	down	293	hit
280	and	314	down	164	home
294	and	12	egulac	213	home
304	and	244	egulac	253	house
330	and	46	escaped	19	hunt
95	are	261	everybody	112	i
117	are	323	face	123	i
224	are	229	feel	128	i
115	arrows	298	feel	138	i
116	arrows	313	fell	265	i
250	ashore	277	fellows	291	i
285	attacked	193	fight	295	i
242	back	273	fight	78	in
130	be	257	fire	118	in
27	became	76	five	215	indian
306	became	28	foggy	41	is
324	became	11	from	26	it
217	been	5	ghosts	302	it
236	been	225	ghosts	328	jumped
191	began	268	ghosts	181	kalama
52	behind	126	go	131	killed
264	behold	150	go	197	killed
316	black	212	go	279	killed
141	but	96	going	288	killed

Table A.1 (*Continued*)

Order #	WORD	Order #	WORD	Order #	WORD
136	know	162	other	108	the
210	let	178	other	119	the
54	log	276	our	147	the
255	made	318	out	156	the
101	make	65	paddles	161	the
202	man	44	party	166	the
248	man	105	people	171	the
195	many	183	people	177	the
274	many	327	people	182	the
281	many	199	presently	187	the
149	may	209	quick	200	the
39	maybe	307	quiet	206	the
10	men	133	relatives	239	the
77	men	163	returned	246	the
110	men	17	river	267	the
158	men	99	river	309	the
129	might	172	river	326	the
321	mouth	311	rose	73	them
132	my	83	said	152	them
7	night	111	said	31	then
114	no	122	said	25	there
63	noise	144	said	74	there
125	not	233	said	23	they
135	not	263	said	32	they
228	not	290	said	37	they
297	not	67	saw	45	they
55	now	208	say	60	they
219	now	20	seals	82	they
3	of	49	shore	121	they
64	of	237	shot	190	they
107	of	230	sick	223	they
155	of	299	sick	232	they
180	of	179	side	289	they
205	of	153	so	87	think
275	of	238	so	40	this
282	of	315	something	283	those
319	of	310	sun	38	thought
222	oh	91	take	221	thought
103	on	214	that	15	to
169	on	1	the	18	to
176	on	4	the	47	to
6	one	16	the	72	to
68	one	48	the	90	to
106	one	62	the	100	to
154	one	79	the	146	to
204	one	98	the	173	to
148	other	104	the	186	to

Table A.1 (*Continued*)

Order #	WORD	Order #	WORD	Order #	WORD
192	to	102	war	278	were
243	to	167	warriors	287	were
251	to	207	warriors	84	what
272	to	292	was	308	when
260	told	333	was	137	where
301	told	188	water	22	while
175	town	88	we	284	who
145	turning	94	we	124	will
8	two	270	we	89	wish
58	up	13	went	151	with
71	up	159	went	86	you
97	up	168	went	92	you
170	up	241	went	142	you
329	up	249	went	9	young
211	us	271	went	109	young
286	us	24	were	157	young
2	war	75	were	201	young
34	war	196	were	247	young
43	war				

rating? It seemed likely that the better line would (usually) get the higher rating. If so, we could bypass the overt production of confidence ratings and infer them from actual recall performance in each segment. Merryl Feigin-Pfau was later to demonstrate empirically that, indeed, confidence ratings are significantly correlated with recall performance.

Thus recall performance on each line became the basis for pruning recall texts to a desired F_c. There are a number of ways of defining performance per line—for example, H, H − F, H/(H + F), F—but they all amount to the same relative measure as long as the number of words per line is approximately constant, which is easy to arrange with typed texts by setting left and right margins. (The measures mentioned would be perfectly correlated if the number of words per line were actually made constant, which was the case with the computer program used by Don Leichter that generated the data in chapter 8.)

In our laboratory we have usually taken F per line as an inverse indicator of recall quality (and presumed confidence rating). Thus in lines averaging 7 words (we usually allow few words per line), a line with F = 6 would be treated as poorer—and dropped earlier—than one with F = 5. In case of ties, we look at H to decide (for example, 5|3 is treated as superior to 4|3). (If both the H and F are equal, the one closest to the top is usually treated as better—a not altogether arbitrary rule since the first few lines typically are the best; recently we have also given high priority to the last 3 lines to take advantage of both ends of the serial position curve.)

Implementing the CCFR Procedure: Illustration of the Computation of $H|F_c$

The criterion-control procedure is illustrated with Maya's R_2 and R_n in tables A.2 and A.3. (To minimize details, the illustration does not strip the narratives of function words, as was partially done in the computer scoring reported in chapter 8.)

Underlined words indicate correspondences between recall text and stimulus text (hits); ununderlined words are errors (false alarms). First, each line of text is scored for H and F (see columns to the right of the text). For total H and F for the entire recall protocol, the per-line H's and F's are summed. Since the lowest total F was produced in R_2 (F = 15), the paring down targets this F value. Thus $F_c = 15$.

The order of line cuts for R_n is indicated in the rightmost column of table A3. The worst lines, defined by the highest F's per line, are, as explained above, cut first, and the cutting is continued (in this case up to 16 of the 25 lines) until $F_c = 15$. (In actual practice, one often cannot get the exact F_c because the dropping of the last line cuts F below the target F_c and the keeping of the line leaves the F value a trifle higher than F_c. This obviously is a small point. We have taken to dropping a fraction of a line when necessary and prorating F's and H's: a fraction of the F's in the line are cut so that the exact F_c is achieved; a corresponding fraction of the line's H's is then also dropped.)

Empirical Validation of the CCFR

With the basic procedure outlined, empirical validation becomes the critical issue. The first set of studies evaluated the idea that performance does correlate with confidence ratings. In several probes conducted by Merryl Feigin-Pfau and me, we correlated F's per line with confidence ratings per line for a number of subjects. The r's varied substantially across subjects, averaging around a significant but not overly large $r = -0.30$. It was not clear whether the subjects, most of them taken

Table A.2 Maya's R_2

		H	F
1	One night some men were	4	1
2	walking. They heard a crowd	3	2
3	scream. The men heard them	4	1
4	screaming. They rushed and	2	2
5	tried to find where the people	4	2
6	were screaming. At last, they	2	3
7	found them. They were on top	4	2
8	of the highest hill.	2	2
	Total H|F	25|15	
	Adjusted H: H| (F_c = 15)	25|15	

Table A.3 Maya's R_{10} ($R_{10} = R_n$)

		H	F	Order of line cut
1	One night three men heard	4	1	
2	a crowd scream for help. It	2	4	8
3	was the Indians calling for	3	2	
4	help. They were trapped from	2	3	14
5	the new hunting dog that came	4	3	
6	in town this morning. They	4	1	
7	rushed to find out what it	4	2	
8	was. They did not hear about	5	1	
9	the hunting dog. All they	3	2	
10	wanted to know is what was	3	3	15
11	happening. One man was near	2	3	13
12	by and the man told him what	4	3	16
13	was happening. The Indians	1	3	10
14	were in trouble because the	2	3	12
15	dog was not supposed to hunt	2	4	7
16	other animals besides rabbits	1	3	9
17	and deers. It was supposed to	2	4	6
18	hunt birds, tigers, and wild	1	4	4
19	bears. The three men wanted	2	3	11
20	to know what was this dog	1	5	2
21	business doing around here and	2	4	5
22	why was it hunting Indians.	0	5	1
23	They all cried. One of the	5	1	
24	men said, "I guess because the	4	2	
25	cooks needed more food."	0	4	3
	Total H|F	63|73		
	Adjusted H: H| ($F_c = 15$)	36|15		

from the subject pool, always understood the task or if they executed it seriously when they did. In any case, the relation becomes more impressive when F's are aggregated (and averaged) for each confidence level: average F for each confidence rating is substantially correlated with confidence rating (in the order of $r = -0.60$, or better). Thus the average F for high-confidence lines tends to be low, and the average F for low-confidence lines tends to be high. From work that is still in progress, it appears that even higher correlations will be obtained when the notion of confidence is more optimally conveyed to the subject. But even at this juncture, the bypassing of the intrusive confidence ratings seems to be empirically justified.

A more fundamental issue is whether the $H|F_c$ measure is really a criterion-controlled index of free recall. Can we, for example, be sure that Maya's adjusted recall scores are in fact criterion controlled? A very interesting point arises in this connection: the procedure cannot be evaluated, as in recognition memory, by simply comparing the criterion-controlled recalls of two groups of subjects, one given lax and the other strict recall instructions. When we did this, the lax subjects actually performed slightly better than the strict ones. This observation does not, however, undercut the procedure, since the lax subjects spent more time recalling and, as we have seen throughout this book, the more recall time invested in recall, the higher the recall (including forced recall). This finding has important theoretical implications for the concept of criterion in recall, which however goes beyond the scope of this essentially methodological appendix. Obviously, there are criteria and there are criteria. When the criteria apply to processing stop rules (that is, at what point do I stop further retrieval efforts?), criterion changes produce bona fide memory changes. In Erdelyi, Finks, and Feigin-Pfau (1989) this "processing-bias" issue was explored in some detail, and criterion effects producing d'-type effects in recall were dubbed β'.

The type of criterion we wish to control concerns the stop rules for the production of responses, that is, productivity. Thus the type of empirical validation we seek is related to the question of whether a group of subjects instructed to fabricate (guess) a large number of responses beyond those produced by a bona fide experimental group (one actually recalling the story), and who consequently produce more hits and false alarms, will be successfully dealt with by the criterion-control procedure.

Several studies have been carried out by me and my students (Merryl Feigin-Pfau, Marcos Ionescu, Jacqueline Bergstein, and Vermone Wong) and only the most recent one (with Vermone Wong) will be summarized, though all of them proved extremely successful. In this last study two groups of experimental subjects (the low- and high-memory groups) were first exposed to "The War of the Ghosts"—one of them once and the other twice—and then required to produce a narrative recall of the material. It is assumed that the group exposed to the story twice had, on the average, better memory for the story than the group exposed to it only once. The recalls of both experimental groups were then transcribed and 6 blank lines were inserted in the middle and at the end of each recall text. Control subjects who had never been exposed to "The War of the Ghosts" were each yoked to one of the transcribed experimental recalls with interspersed lines. (Each of these recall texts, of course, varied in length.) These yoked subjects were instructed to fabricate story materials in the interspersed lines in such a way that when their interpolated fabrications were typed in, a judge should not be able to distinguish between the original recall narrative and the interweaved fabrications. The task was presented as a verbal game, and (for once) the subjects found it both challenging and fun. The critical point is that they fabricated a large amount of extra material that fit in with the context of the original recall narrative and, consequently, as will be seen, produced many more hits as well as false alarms.

Thus there were four groups in all: two experimental groups (X_1, X_2), the (relatively) high- and low-memory subjects; and two corresponding yoked control groups (Y_1, Y_2). The question was whether the CCFR would "cure" the criterion "disease" without killing the true memory effect (the difference between high- and low-memory experimental subjects).

The average number of hits produced by the high-memory group was 161 (with F = 50); the low-memory group garnered 114 hits (with F = 38). Thus the raw, uncontrolled hit levels are consistent with the expectation that recall in the experimental group exposed to the story twice would be superior to the group that read the story only once. But now let us consider the control subjects yoked to each of these two groups of experimental subjects. The Y_2 subjects (control subjects yoked to X_2 subjects—experimental subjects exposed to the story two times) produced some 196 hits (F = 132); the Y_1 subjects (yoked to X_1 subjects, that is, experimental subjects exposed to the story once) produced 157 hits (F = 117).

Now, we know that the yoked subjects could not have better memory for "The War of the Ghosts" than the experimental subjects since the yoked subjects never saw the story. Still, they substantially exceeded in hit levels the performance of their experimental counterparts because of successful guessing—but at the expense of a binge in false alarms. The acid test of the CCFR procedure is whether it corrects for this excess of hits due to successful fabrications; that is, after the criterion control, the yoked subjects should not be substantially different in hit level from their experimental counterparts. If the CCFR succeeds in this basic goal, it is still crucial that the cure should not be too toxic to the true effects; that is, the criterion control should not destroy the true memory difference between the high- and low-memory experimental subjects. It turns out that the CCFR "medicine" was highly successful on both counts.

Since conditionalized hits $(H|F_c)$, as noted earlier, represent only one point on the isosensitive roc functions, it may be easiest to assess the criterion control's effect by plotting the entire roc functions for the four groups. These roc functions are generated by varying F_c (allowing the former constant, c, to vary). Thus we may select a range of F_c's—in the present exercise, 0, 1, 5, 18, 38, and the average F associated with the raw H level for the low- and high-memory experimental subjects, 38 and 50, respectively—and compute the H levels associated with each of these F levels. This set of H and F pairs allows us to plot the roc function H = f(F). Figure A.2 presents the four roc functions of interest (note that X_1 and X_2 are shorthand, respectively, for experiment groups exposed to the story once and twice; Y_1 and Y_2 are the corresponding two yoked control groups).

The roc plots are very clear; the high- and low-memory experimental subjects produce two different isosensitive functions that distinguish the groups as expected. For any false-alarm level chosen, $H|F_c$ is consistently greater for the high-memory subjects than for the low-memory subjects. Thus the CCFR does not kill true memory effects. What it does do, apparently most effectively, is to eliminate illusory memory differences due to lax response criteria, that is, fabrications: there is no question, despite the substantial H difference between the yoked and experimental subjects that, in fact, the yoked subjects are no different in true recall than their experimental counterparts; they generate the same roc functions. Thus for any F_c chosen, the yoked subjects have the same H as their experimental counterparts.

Alternatives to the $H|F_c$ Index of Criterion-Controlled Free Recall

I will conclude this appendix with a few finer-grained issues. First, SDT experts may be jolted by the positive H levels associated with F = 0. This is neither an

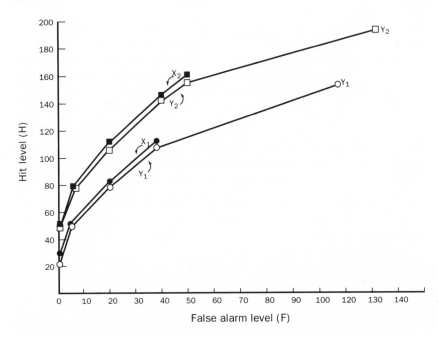

Figure A.2 The roc functions for the low- and high-memory experimental groups (X_1 and X_2) and their two yoked counterparts (Y_1 and Y_2).

error nor a problem. We are not dealing with hit rates but with hit *levels,* and the positive H values simply mean that on the average subjects produced 2 or 3 perfect lines, that is, lines with only hits and no false alarms. Therefore, these lines—and the hits contained in them—did not have to be dropped when the target $F_c = 0$.

Another detail question, which may already have occurred to the reader, is which F_c target one should choose for the $H|F_c$ index. The smooth regularity of the roc functions suggests that it doesn't much matter. It is best to avoid extremely low F_c's (0, 1, maybe 5) because error variances associated with them are high. (Also, high F_c's have to be avoided because not all subjects produce a large number of F's.) Still, a careful researcher might want to probe several F_c targets to insure that the resulting $H|F_c$'s are consistent. Or better still, one could average $H|F_c$'s associated with different F_c's.

More Sophisticated Measures of CCFR: p(a)

This averaging tactic suggests an even more desirable solution: rather than average $H|F_c$'s associated with a handful of F_c's, why not average $H|F_c$'s for all F_c's? This, of course, would be infinitely tedious; the conceptual counterpart would be to take the area under the roc function in question. That is, integrate the roc function within a reasonable range of F, from $F = 0$ to $F = F_n$ and divide by A_{max}, the area that a perfect roc would produce (the area would be that of a rectangle, maximum possible H $\times$ F_n). This measure ($\int_{F=0}^{F=Fn} f(F)\, dF$)/$A_{max}$, is the counterpart of P(A) in classic ROC functions. With computers, each subject's data could be fitted with the appropriate roc function, integrated, and then divided by A_{max}, for an index we may designate as p(a).

Of course, these programs have to be written and most researchers (including myself) might prefer to avoid the complications of curve fitting and integration. A simple solution seems to have turned up. Vermone Wong and I have found that when the H and F levels are transformed to logarithmic scales—when the roc functions are plotted on log-log graph paper—that the curvilinear functions straighten out into linear functions. Thus, if verified, log H = m(log F) + c, where m is the slope of the linear function and c the y-intercept (in this case, the H-intercept). The computation of the area under such a linear function reduces to the computation of the area of a triangle and the area of a rectangle. Thus for parsimonious purists, a fine index of true recall might turn out to be p(a) calculated on logarithms of H and F which we may designate $p_l(a)$.

Because of the impressive regularity of the roc functions, however, these alternative indices of true recall may turn out to be superfluous, and the common-sensical conditionalized hit-level index $H|F_c$, or H', serve as the standard measure of criterion-controlled free recall.

Simplistic Alternatives to $H|F_c$ and p(a): Shortcuts to Dead Ends

This appendix concludes with a consideration of potentially simpler approaches to criterion-controlled free recall—and why they are not likely to be adequate:

1. Why not use H − F as the criterion-controlled free recall? The answer is that hits minus false alarms, unlike $H|F_c$ or p(a), is not constant with productivity for a particular true memory level. If we had forced Maya to confabulate 500 words at the end of any of her stories, we would have H − F scores in the region of −400. This simple subtraction approach obviously does not control hits for different levels of productivity.

2. Why not use some proportion measure, such as H/F or H/(H + F)? The defect here is the same as that described above; these ratios would not remain constant with productivity, as $H|F_c$ does.

3. Why not use standard SDT recognition techniques to evaluate recall level? The answer is that recognition level is often not correlated with recall level, and phenomena such as hypermnesia that are robust with recall are hard or impossible to get with standard recognition (see chap. 7).

4. Why not randomly drop responses until a desired response number is achieved? Again, because the resulting H' would not be constant for different levels of response productivity. This fact can be appreciated from the roc functions, which are not linear. Dropping responses from an initial high number of responses (rightmost region of the roc functions) would result in a smaller loss of hits than dropping responses from an initially low number of responses (leftmost region of the roc functions). Another way of putting the point is that a conservative recall effort is likely to have a relatively high density of hits; an extremely lax recall effort, say one with 500 guessed words thrown in, would be relatively sparse in hits. To subtract randomly some constant number of responses would penalize the richer conservative recall text.

5. *Why not drop lines from the bottom of recall protocols until a desired number of recall responses is reached?* This would not be a bad idea if subjects reserved their poorest responses to the end. Serial position curves suggest that this is not likely, so that dropping lines from the bottom is bound to yield the loss of some of the better recalls. Dropping lines from the middle of the text might be a better idea, but not as good an idea as empirically evaluating the quality of lines and dropping the ones that are actually the poorest or least confident ones, which is what $H|F_c$ does.

It is possible that some other simple procedure will prove adequate. In that case it may replace the $H|F_c$ index. On the other hand, the $H|F_c$ index is simple enough and conceptually compelling.

References

Adams, J. A. 1967. *Human memory*. New York: McGraw-Hill.

Allers, R., and J. Teler. 1924. On the utilization of unnoticed impressions in associations. Trans. J. Wolff, D. Rapaport, and A. H. Annin. *Psychological Issues* 2: 121–50.

American Psychiatric Association. 1980. *Diagnostic and statistical manual of mental disorders*. 3d ed. Washington, D.C.

———. 1994. *Diagnostic and statistical manual of mental disorders*. 4th ed. Washington, D.C.

Ammons, H., and A. L. Irion. 1954. A note on the Ballard reminiscence phenomenon. *Journal of Experimental Psychology* 48:184–86.

Ammons, R. B. 1947a. Acquisition of motor skill I: Quantitative analysis and theoretical formulation. *Psychological Review* 54:263–81.

———. 1947b. Acquisition of motor skill II: Rotary pursuit performance with continuous practice before and after a single test. *Journal of Experimental Psychology* 37:393–411.

Archibald, N. C., and R. D. Tuddenham. 1965. Persistent stress reactions after combat. *Archives of General Psychiatry* 12:475–81.

Baddeley, A. D. 1976. *The psychology of memory*. New York: Basic Books.

Baker, S. R., and D. Boaz. 1983. The partial reformulation of a traumatic memory of a dental phobia during trance: A case study. *International Journal of Clinical and Experimental Hypnosis* 31:14–18.

Bahrick, H. P., and L. K. Hall. 1991. Preventive and corrective maintenance of access to knowledge. *Applied Cognitive Psychology* 5:1–18.

———. 1993. Long intervals between tests can yield hypermnesia: Comments on Wheeler and Roediger. *Psychological Science* 4:206–7.

Ballard, P. B. 1913. Oblivescence and reminiscence. *British Journal of Psychology* 1 (monograph suppl.).

Banks, W. P., and K. Pezdek, eds. 1994–95. The recovered memory/false memory syndrome debate. *Consciousness and Cognition* 3–4.

Barber, T. X., and D. S. Calverley. 1966. Effects on recall of hypnotic induction, motivational suggestions, and suggested regression: A methodological and experimental analysis. *Journal of Abnormal Psychology* 71:169–80.

Bargh, J. A. 1984. Automatic and conscious processing of social information. In *Handbook of social cognition*. Ed. R. S. Wyer and T. K. Srull, 3:1–43. Hillsdale, N.J.: Erlbaum.

Bartlett, F. C. 1932. *Remembering.* Cambridge: Cambridge University Press.

Bartlett, J. C. 1977. Effects of immediate testing on delayed retrieval: Search and recovery operation with four types of cue. *Journal of Experimental Psychology—Human Learning and Memory* 3:719–32.

Bass, E., and L. Davis. 1994. *The courage to heal.* 3d ed. New York: Harper and Row.

Bekerian, D. A., and J. M. Bowers. 1983. Eyewitness testimony: Were we misled? *Journal of Experimental Psychology: Memory, Learning, and Cognition* 9: 139–45.

Belli, R. F. 1989. Influences of misleading postevent information: Misinformation interference and acceptance. *Journal of Experimental Psychology: General* 11:72–85.

Belmore, S. M. 1981. Imagery and semantic elaboration in hypermnesia for words. *Journal of Experimental Psychology: Human Learning and Memory* 7: 191–203.

Benson, D. F., and N. Geschwind. 1967. Shrinking retrograde amnesia. *Journal of Neurology, Neurosurgery and Psychiatry* 30:539–44.

Bernstein, M. 1956. *The search for Bridey Murphy.* New York: Lancer.

Binet, A. 1904. Sommaire des travaux en cours à la société de psychologie de l'enfant. *L'Année psychologique* 10:116–30.

Bjork, R. A. 1975. Retrieval as a memory modifier: An interpretation of negative recency and related phenomena. In *Information processing and cognition.* Ed. R. L. Solso. New York: Wiley.

Boldt, C. 1905. Studium über Merkdefkte. *Monatsschr. für Psychiat. u. Neur.* 17; cited by G. O. McGeoch 1935.

Bonanno, G. A., and N. A. Stillings. 1986. Preference, familiarity, and recognition after repeated brief exposures to random geometric shapes. *American Journal of Psychology* 99:403–15.

Book, W. F. 1910. The role of the teacher in the most expeditious and economic learning. *Journal of Educational Psychology* 1:183–99.

Boreas, T. 1930. Experimental studies of memory, second preliminary communication: The rate of forgetting. *Praktika Akademia Athens* 5:382–96.

Bornstein, R. F., D. R. Leone, and D. J. Galley. 1987. The generalizability of subliminal mere exposure effects: Influence of stimuli perceived without awareness on social behavior. *Journal of Personality and Social Psychology* 53: 1070–79.

Bornstein, R. F., and T. S. Pittman, eds. 1992. *Perception without awareness: Cognitive, clinical, and social perspectives.* New York: Guilford.

Bower, G. 1990. Awareness, the unconscious, and repression: An experimental psychologist's perspective. In *Repression and dissociation: Defense mechanisms and personality styles.* Ed. J. L. Singer, 209–31. Chicago: University of Chicago Press.

Bowers, K. S. 1984. On being unconsciously influenced and informed. In *The unconscious reconsidered.* Ed. K. S. Bowers and D. Meichenbaum, 227–72. New York: Wiley.

Bowers, K. S., and E. R. Hilgard. 1988. Some complexities in understanding memory. In *Hypnosis and memory*. Ed. H. M. Pettinati, 3–18. New York: Guilford.

Bowers, K. S., and D. Meichenbaum, eds. 1984. *The unconscious reconsidered.* New York: Wiley.

Braid, J. 1843. *Neurypnology; or, the rationale of nervous sleep, considered in relation with animal magnetism.* London: Churchill.

Breuer, J., and S. Freud. [1895] 1955. *Studies on hysteria.* In vol. 2 of *The standard edition of the complete psychological works of Sigmund Freud.* Trans. and ed. J. Strachey. London: Hogarth Press.

Broadhurst, P. L. 1957. Emotionality and the Yerkes-Dodson law. *Journal of Experimental Psychology* 54:345–52.

———. 1959. The interaction of task difficulty and motivation: The Yerkes-Dodson Law revived. *Acta Psychologica* 16:321–38.

Brown, R., and D. McNeill. 1966. The "tip of the tongue" phenomenon. *Journal of Verbal Learning and Verbal Behavior* 5:325–37.

Brown, W. 1923. To what extent is memory measured by a single recall? *Journal of Experimental Psychology* 6:377–82.

———. 1924. Effects of interval on recall. *Journal of Experimental Psychology* 7:469–74.

Bruner, J. S. 1964. The course of cognitive growth. *American Psychologist* 19: 1–15.

Bugelski, B. R., E. Kidd, and J. Segmen. 1968. Image as a mediator in one-trial paired associate learning. *Journal of Experimental Psychology* 76:69–73.

Bunch, M. E. 1938. The measurement of reminiscence. *Psychological Review* 45: 525–31.

Bunch, M. E., and W. K. Magsdick. 1933. The retention in rats of an incompletely learned maze solution for short intervals of time. *Journal of Comparative Psychology* 16:385–409.

Butter, M. J. 1970. Differential recall of paired associates as a function of arousal and concreteness-imagery levels. *Journal of Experimental Psychology* 84: 252–56.

Buxton, C. E. 1942. Reminiscence in the acquisition of skill. *Psychological Review* 49:191–96.

———. 1943. The status of research in reminiscence. *Psychological Bulletin* 40: 313–40.

Ceci, S. J., and M. Bruck. 1993. Suggestibility of the child witness: A historical review and synthesis. *Psychological Bulletin* 113:403–39.

Ceci, S. J., M. L. C. Huffman, E. Smith, and E. F. Loftus. 1994. Repeatedly thinking about a non-event: Source misattribution among preschoolers. *Consciousness and Cognition* 3:388–407.

Cermak, L. S. 1982. *Human memory and amnesia.* Hillsdale, N.J.: Erlbaum.

Cleveland, A. A. 1907. The psychology of chess and of learning to play it. *American Journal of Psychology* 18:269–308.

Cofer, C. N. 1967. Does conceptual organization influence the amount retained in immediate free recall? In *Concepts and the structure of memory*. Ed. B. Kleinmuntz, 181–214. New York: Wiley.

Colvin, S. S., and E. J. Myers. 1909. The development of imagination in school children and the relation between ideational types and the retentivity of material appealing to various sense departments. *Psychological Monographs* 11, no. 44:85–126.

Cooper, L. M., and P. London. 1973. Reactivation of memory by hypnosis and suggestion. *International Journal of Clinical and Experimental Hypnosis* 29:312–23.

Craik, F. I. M., and R. S. Lockhart. 1972. Levels of processing: A framework for memory research. *Journal of Verbal Learning and Verbal Behavior* 11: 671–84.

Crawford, H. J., and S. N. Allen. 1983. Enhanced visual memory during hypnosis as mediated by hypnotic responsiveness and cognitive strategies. *Journal of Experimental Psychology—General* 112:662–85.

Crews, F., et al. 1995. *The memory wars: Freud's legacy in dispute.* New York: A New York Review Book.

Crowder, R. G. 1976. *Principles of learning and memory.* Hillsdale, N.J.: Erlbaum.

———. 1989. Modularity and dissociations in memory systems. In *Varieties of memory and consciousness.* Ed. H. L. Roediger and F. I. M. Craik, 271–94. Hillsdale, N.J.: Erlbaum.

Darley, C. F., and B. B. Murdock. 1971. Effects of prior free recall testing on final recall and recognition. *Journal of Experimental Psychology* 91:66–73.

Davis, S. C., and R. L. Dominowski. 1986. Hypermnesia and the organization of recall. *Bulletin of the Psychonomic Society* 24:31–34.

Das, J. P. 1961. Learning and recall under hypnosis and in the wake state: A comparison. *Archives of General Psychiatry* 4:517–21.

DePiano, F. A., and H. C. Salzberg. 1981. Hypnosis as an aid to recall of meaningful information presented under three types of arousal. *International Journal of Clinical and Experimental Hypnosis* 29:383–400.

de Rochas, A. 1896. *Les états profonds de l'hypnose.* 3d ed. Paris: Charmel.

Dhanens, T. P., and R. M. Lundy. 1975. Hypnotic and waking suggestions and recall. *International Journal of Clinical and Experimental Hypnosis* 23: 68–79.

Dinges, D. F., W. G. Whitehouse, E. C. Orne, J. W. Powell, M. T. Orne, and M. H. Erdelyi. 1992. Evaluating hypnotic memory enhancement (hypermnesia and reminiscence) using multiple forced recall. *Journal of Experimental Psychology—Learning, Memory, and Cognition* 18:1139–47.

Dixon, N. F. 1981. *Preconscious processing.* Chichester: Wiley.

Domangue, B. B. 1985. Hypnotic regression and reframing in the treatment of insect phobias. *American Journal of Psychotherapy* 34:206–14.

Donaldson, W. 1971. Output effects in multitrial free recall. *Journal of Verbal Learning and Verbal Behavior* 10:577–85.

Dorcus, R. M. 1960. Recall under hypnosis and amnesic events. *International Journal of Clinical and Experimental Hypnosis* 8:57–60.

Doré, L. R., and E. R. Hilgard. 1937. Spaced practice and the maturation hypothesis. *Journal of Psychology* 4:245–59.

————. 1938. Spaced practice as a test of Snoddy's two processes in mental growth. *Journal of Experimental Psychology* 23:359–74.

Dywan, J., and K. S. Bowers. 1983. The use of hypnosis to enhance recall. *Science* 222:184–85.

Easterbrook, J. A. 1959. The effect of emotion on cue utilization and the organization of behaviour. *Psychological Review* 66:183–201.

Ebbinghaus, H. [1885] 1964. *Memory.* Trans. H. A. Ruger and C. E. Bussenius. New York: Dover.

Egan, J. P., A. I. Schulman, and G. Z. Greenberg. 1964. Operating characteristics determined by binary decisions and by ratings. In *Signal detection and recognition by human observers.* Ed. J. A. Swets, 172–86. New York: Wiley.

Eich, E. 1984. Memory for unattended events: Remembering with and without awareness. *Memory and Cognition* 12:105–11.

Ekstrand, B. R. 1972. To sleep, perchance to dream (about why we forget). In *Human memory: Festschrift for Benton J. Underwood.* Ed. C. P. Duncan, L. Sechrest, and A. W. Melton, 59–82. New York: Appleton-Century-Crofts.

Ellenberger, H. F. 1970. *The discovery of the unconscious.* New York: Basic Books.

English, H. B. 1942. Reminiscence—Reply to Dr. Buxton's critique. *Psychological Review* 49:505–12.

English, H. B., E. L. Welborn, and C. D. Killian. 1934. Studies in substance memorization. *Journal of General Psychology* 11:233–60.

English, H. B., and A. L. Edwards. 1939. Studies in substance learning and retention: XI, The effect of maturity level on verbatim and summary retention. *Journal of General Psychology* 11:233–60.

Erdelyi, M. H. 1958. *Perceptual defense and vigilance.* Unpublished paper, College of Wooster, Wooster, Ohio.

————. 1968. The recovery of unavailable perceptual input. Ph.D. diss., Yale University.

————. 1970. Recovery of unavailable perceptual input. *Cognitive Psychology* 1:99–113.

————. 1972. The role of fantasy in the Poetzl (emergence) phenomenon. *Journal of Personality and Social Psychology* 24:186–90.

————. 1977. *Has Ebbinghaus decayed with time?* Paper presented at the Eighteenth Annual Meeting of the Psychonomic Society, Washington, D.C.

————. 1981. Not now: Comments on Loftus and Loftus. *American Psychologist* 36:527–28.

————. 1982. A note on the level of recall, level of processing, and imagery hypotheses of hypermnesia. *Journal of Verbal Learning and Verbal Behavior* 21:656–61.

————. 1984. The recovery of unconscious (inaccessible) memories: Laboratory studies of hypermnesia. In *The psychology of learning and motivation: Advances in research and theory.* Ed. G. Bower, 95–127. New York: Academic Press.

————. 1985. *Psychoanalysis: Freud's cognitive psychology.* New York: Freeman.

————. 1986. Experimental indeterminacies in the dissociation paradigm of subliminal perception. *The Behavioral and Brain Sciences* 9:30–31.

————. 1988. Hypermnesia: Effect of hypnosis, fantasy, and concentration. In *Hypnosis and memory.* Ed. H. M. Pettinati, 64–94. New York: Guilford.

————. 1990. Repression, reconstruction, and defense: History and integration of the psychoanalytic and experimental frameworks. In *Repression and dissociation: Defense mechanisms and personality styles.* Ed. J. L. Singer, 1–31. Chicago: University of Chicago Press.

————. 1992. Psychodynamics and the unconscious. *American Psychologist* 47: 784–87.

————. 1993. Repression: The mechanism and the defense. In *Handbook of mental control.* Ed. D. M. Wegner and J. W. Pennebaker, 126–48. Englewood Cliffs, N.J.: Prentice-Hall.

————. 1994a. Dissociation, defense, and the unconscious. In *Dissociation: Culture, mind, and body.* Ed. D. Spiegel, 3–20. Washington, D.C.: American Psychiatric Press.

————. 1994b. Hypnotic hypermnesia: The empty set of hypermnesia. *International Journal of Clinical and Experimental Hypnosis* 42:379–90.

————. 1995. Freud and memory: An exchange [with F. Crews]. *The New York Review of Books* 42 (23 Mar.):65–66.

Erdelyi, M. H., and A. Appelbaum. 1973. Cognitive masking: The disruptive effect of an emotional stimulus upon the perception of contiguous neutral items. *Bulletin of the Psychonomic Society* 1:59–61.

Erdelyi, M. H., and D. Blumenthal. 1973. Cognitive masking in rapid sequential processing: The effect of an emotional picture on preceding and succeeding pictures. *Memory and Cognition* 1:201–4.

Erdelyi, M. H., and J. Becker. 1974. Hypermnesia for pictures: Incremental memory for pictures but not words in multiple recall trials. *Cognitive Psychology* 6: 159–71.

Erdelyi, M. H., and S. Finkelstein. 1975. Failure of imagery-recoding instructions to produce hypermnesia for words when rate of input is too rapid for effective recoding. Unpub.

Erdelyi, M. H., S. Finkelstein, N. Herrell, B. Miller, and J. Thomas. 1976. Coding modality vs. input modality in hypermnesia: Is a rose a rose a rose? *Cognition* 4:311–19.

Erdelyi, M. H., H. Buschke, and S. Finkelstein. 1977. Hypermnesia for Socratic stimuli: The growth of recall for an internally generated memory list abstracted from a series of riddles. *Memory and Cognition* 5:283–86.

Erdelyi, M. H., and J. Kleinbard. 1978. Has Ebbinghaus decayed with time? The growth of recall (hypermnesia) over days. *Journal of Experimental Psychology—Human Learning and Memory* 4:275–89.

Erdelyi, M. H., and B. Goldberg. 1979. Let's not sweep repression under the rug: Toward a cognitive psychology of repression. In *Functional disorders of memory.* Ed. J. F. Kihlstrom and F. J. Evans, 355–401. Hillsdale, N.J.: Erlbaum.

Erdelyi, M. H., and J. B. Stein. 1981. Recognition hypermnesia: The growth of recognition hypermnesia (d') over time with repeated testing. *Cognition* 9: 23–33.

Erdelyi, M. H., and M. Halberstam. 1987. Hypermnesia for "The War of the Ghosts": Preliminary report, with observations on a collapse of memory phenomenon and a Freudian Bartlett effect in a child. Department of Psychology, Brooklyn College of the City University of New York. Unpub.

Erdelyi, M. H., D. F. Dinges, M. T. Orne, W. G. Whitehouse, and E. C. Orne. 1987. The stimulus and the test in hypnotic hypermnesia. Unpub.

Erdelyi, M. H., J. Finks, and M. Feigin-Pfau. 1989. The effect of response bias on recall performance, with some observations on processing bias. *Journal of Experimental Psychology* 118:245–54.

Erdelyi, M. H., and J. D Frame. 1995. The case of Dr. John D. Frame's first memory: Historical truth and psychological distortion. *Consciousness and Cognition* 4:95–99.

Eriksen, C. W. 1958. Unconscious processes. In *Nebraska symposium on motivation.* Ed. M. R. Jones. Lincoln: University of Nebraska Press.

———. 1960. Discrimination and learning without awareness: A methodological survey and evaluation. *Psychological Review* 67:279–300.

Estes, W. K. 1955. Statistical theory of spontaneous recovery and regression. *Psychological Review* 62:145–54.

Eysenck, H. J. 1941. An experimental study of the improvement of mental and physical functions in the hypnotic state. *British Journal of Medical Psychology* 18:304–16.

———. 1957. *The dynamics of anxiety and hysteria.* London: Routledge and Kegan Paul.

———. 1965. A three-factor theory of reminiscence. *British Journal of Psychology* 56:163–81.

———. 1967. *The biological basis of personality.* Springfield, Ill.: Charles C Thomas.

———. 1973. Personality, learning, and "anxiety." In *Handbook of abnormal psychology.* 2d ed. Ed. Eysenck. London: Pitman.

Eysenck, H. J., and C. D. Frith. 1977. *Reminiscence, motivation, and personality.* New York: Plenum Press.

Eysenck, M. W. 1974. Extraversion, arousal, and retrieval from semantic memory. *Journal of Personality* 42:319–31.

———. 1976a. Arousal, learning, and memory. *Psychological Bulletin* 83: 389–404.

———. 1976b. Extraversion, verbal learning, and memory. *Psychological Bulletin* 83:75–90.

Fisher, C. 1954. Dreams and perception. *Journal of the American Psychoanalytic Association* 3:380–445.

———. 1956. Dreams, images, and perception: A study of unconscious-preconscious relationships. *Journal of the American Psychoanalytic Association* 4:5–48.

———. 1960a. Subliminal and supraliminal influences on dreams. *American Journal of Psychiatry* 116:1009–17.

————. 1960b. Introduction. In *Preconscious stimulation in dreams, associations, and images.* Trans. and ed. J. Wolff, D. Rapaport, and S. H. Annin, 1–40. *Psychological Issues* 2, no. 3, monograph 7.

————. 1988. Further observations on the Pötzl phenomenon: The effects of subliminal visual stimulation on dreams, images, and hallucinations. *Psychoanalysis and Contemporary Thought* 11:3–56.

Fisher, C., and I. H. Paul. 1959. The effect of subliminal stimulation on images and dreams: A validation study. *Journal of the American Psychoanalytic Association* 7:35–83.

Frankel, F. H., and C. W. Perry, eds. 1994. Hypnosis and delayed recall. *International Journal of Clinical and Experimental Hypnosis* 42.

Freud, S. [1900] 1958. *The interpretation of dreams.* In vols. 4–5 of *The standard edition of the complete psychological works of Sigmund Freud.* Trans. and ed. J. Strachey. London: Hogarth Press.

————. [1912] 1958. A note on the unconscious in psychoanalysis. In vol. 12 of *The standard edition of the complete psychological works of Sigmund Freud.* Trans. and ed. J. Strachey. London: Hogarth Press.

————. [1914] 1958. Remembering, repeating, and working-through: Further recommendations in the technique of psychoanalysis, II. Trans. J. Riviere and J. Strachey. In vol. 12 of *The standard edition of the complete psychological works of Sigmund Freud.* Trans. and ed. Strachey. London: Hogarth Press.

————. [1915] 1957. The unconscious. Trans. C. M. Baines and J. Strachey. In vol. 14 of *The standard edition of the complete psychological works of Sigmund Freud.* Ed. Strachey. London: Hogarth Press.

————. [1917] 1963. *A general introduction to psychoanalysis.* Trans. J. Riviere. New York: Liveright.

————. [1917] 1961–63. *Introductory lectures on psychoanalysis.* In vols. 15 and 16 of *The standard edition of the complete psychological works of Sigmund Freud.* Ed. Strachey. London: Hogarth Press.

Gates, A. I. 1917. Recitation as a factor in memorizing. *Archives of Psychology* 6, no. 40:1–104.

Gauld, A., and G. M. Stephenson. 1967. Some experiments relating to Bartlett's theory of remembering. *British Journal of Psychology* 58:39–49.

Geiselman, R. E., R. P. Fisher, D. P. MacKinnon, and H. L. Holland. 1985. Eyewitness memory enhancement in the police interview: Cognitive retrieval mnemonics versus hypnosis. *Journal of Applied Psychology* 70:401–12.

Gentry, J. R. 1940. Immediate effects of interpolated rest periods on learning performance. *Contributions to Education,* no. 799. New York: Columbia University Press.

Gheorghiu, V. 1972. Experimentelle unter suchungen zur hypnotischen hypermnesie [Experimental investigation of hypnotic hypermnesia]. In *Hypnose und psychosomatische medizin.* Ed. D. Langen, 42–46. Stuttgart: Hippokrates Verlag.

Giddan, N. S. 1967. Recovery through images of briefly flashed stimuli. *Journal of Personality* 35:1–19.

Gillette, A. E. 1935–36. Learning and retention: A comparison of three experimental procedures. *Archives of Psychology* 28, no. 198:56.

Gluck, M. A., and D. Rummelhart, eds. 1990. *Neuroscience and connectionist theory.* Hillsdale, N.J.: Erlbaum.

Goggin, J. 1966. Retroactive and proactive inhibition in the short-term retention of paired associates. *Journal of Verbal Learning and Verbal Behavior* 5: 526–35.

Goldiamond, I. 1958. Indicators of perception: I. Subliminal perception, subception, unconscious perception: An analysis in terms of psychophysical indicator methodology. *Psychological Bulletin, 55,* 373–411.

Gordon, G. H. 1990. Awareness, the unconscious, and repression: An experimental psychologist's perspective. In *Repression and dissociation: Defense mechanisms and personality styles.* Ed. J. L. Singer, 209–31. Chicago: University of Chicago Press.

Gordon, K. 1925. Class results with spaced and unspaced memorizing. *Journal of Experimental Psychology* 8:337–43.

Gorer, G. 1965. *Death, grief, and mourners in contemporary Britain.* New York: Doubleday.

Graf, P., L. R. Squire, and G. Mandler. 1984. The information that amnesic patients do not forget. *Journal of Experimental Psychology: Learning, Memory and Cognition* 10:164–78.

Gray, S. 1940. The influence of methodology upon the measurement of reminiscence. *Journal of Experimental Psychology* 27:37–44.

Green, D. M., and J. A. Swets. 1966. *Signal detection theory and psychophysics.* New York: Wiley.

Greenwald, A. G. 1992. New Look 3: Unconscious cognition reclaimed. *American Psychologist* 47:766–79.

Grinker, R. R., and J. P. Spiegel. 1945. *Men under stress.* New York: McGraw-Hill.

Grünbaum, A. 1984. *The foundations of psychoanalysis: A philosophical critique.* Berkeley: University of California Press.

———. 1986. Is Freud's theory well-founded? *Behavioral and Brain Sciences* 1986:266–84.

Guillet, C. 1917. A study of the memory of young women. *Journal of Educational Psychology* 8:65–84.

Haber, R. N., and M. H. Erdelyi. 1967. Emergence and recovery of initially unavailable perceptual material. *Journal of Verbal Learning and Verbal Behavior* 6:618–28.

Hardy, L., and G. Parfitt. 1991. A catastrophe model of anxiety and performance. *British Journal of Psychology* 82:167–78.

Harvey, M. R., and J. L. Herman. 1994. Amnesia, partial amnesia, and delayed recall among adult survivors of childhood trauma. *Consciousness and Cognition* 3: 295–306.

Hebb, D. O. 1949. *The organization of behavior.* New York: Wiley.

Henderson, E. N. 1903. A study for connected trains of thought. *Psychological Monographs* 5, no. 23:1–94.

Herman, J. L. 1992. *Trauma and recovery.* New York: Basic Books.

Herrman, D. J., H. Buschke, and M. B. Gall. 1987. Improving retrieval. *Applied Cognitive Psychology* 1:27–33.

Hilgard, E. R. 1962. What becomes of the input from the stimulus? In *Behavior and awareness.* Ed. C. W. Eriksen, 46–72. Durham, N.C.: Duke University Press.

Hogan, R. M., and W. Kintsch. 1971. Differential effects of study and test trials on long-term recognition and recall. *Journal of Verbal Learning and Verbal Behavior* 10:562–67.

Holender, D. 1986. Semantic activation without conscious identification in dichotic listening, parafoveal vision, and visual masking: A survey and appraisal. *Behavioral and Brain Sciences* 9:1–66.

Holmes, D. S. 1972. Repression or interference? A further investigation. *Journal of Personality and Social Psychology* 22:163–70.

———. 1974. Investigations of repression: Differential recall of material experimentally or naturally associated with ego threat. *Psychological Bulletin* 81: 632–53.

———. 1990. The evidence for repression: An examination of sixty years of research. In *Repression and dissociation: Defense mechanisms and personality styles.* Ed. J. L. Singer, 85–102. Chicago: University of Chicago Press.

Holt, R. R. 1964. Imagery: The return of the ostracized. *American Psychologist* 62:497–503.

Horowitz, M. J. 1983. *Image formation and psychotherapy.* London: Jason Aronson.

———. 1986. *Stress response syndromes.* 2d ed. London: Jason Aronson.

———. 1988. *Psychodynamics and cognition.* Chicago: University of Chicago Press.

Hovland, C. I. 1938a. Experimental studies in rote-learning theory I: Reminiscence following learning by massed and distributed practice. *Journal of Experimental Psychology* 22:201–24.

———. 1938b. Experimental studies in rote-learning theory II: Reminiscence with varying speeds of syllable presentation. *Journal of Experimental Psychology* 22:338–53.

———. 1939a. Experimental studies in rote-learning theory IV: Comparison of reminiscence in serial and paired-associate learning. *Journal of Experimental Psychology* 24:466–84.

———. 1939b. Experimental studies in rote-learning theory V: Comparison of distribution of practice in serial and paired-associate learning. *Journal of Experimental Psychology* 25:622–33.

———. 1951. Human learning and retention. In *Handbook of experimental psychology.* Ed. S. S. Stevens, 613–89. New York: Wiley.

Howarth, E., and H. J. Eysenck. 1968. Extraversion, arousal, and paired-associate recall. *Journal of Experimental Research in Personality* 3:114–16.

Huguenin, C. 1914. Reviviscence paradoxale. *Archieves de psychologie* 14: 379–83.

Hull, C. L. 1933. *Hypnosis and suggestibility: An experimental approach.* New York: Appleton-Century-Crofts.

———. 1935. The conflicting psychologies of learning—a way out. *Psychological Review* 42:491–516.

Huse, B. 1930. Does the hypnotic trance favor the recall of faint memories? *Journal of Experimental Psychology* 13:519–29.

Ionescu, M. 1993. Hypermnesia for subliminal stimuli. Ph.D. diss., City University of New York.

Ionescu, M. D., and M. H. Erdelyi. 1992. The direct recovery of subliminal stimuli. In *Perception without awareness.* Ed. R. F. Bornstein and T. S. Pittman, 143–69. New York: Guilford.

Izawa, C. Z. 1968. Effects of reinforcement, neutral and test trials upon paired-associate acquisition and retention. *Psychological Reports* 23:947–59.

———. 1969. Comparison of reinforcement and test trials in paired-associate learning. *Journal of Experimental Psychology* 81:600–603.

———. 1989. *Current issues in cognitive processes: The Tulane Floweree symposium on cognition.* Hillsdale, N.J.: Erlbaum.

Jacoby, L. L., and D. Witherspoon. 1982. Remembering without awareness. *Canadian Journal of Psychology* 32:300–324.

James, W. [1890] 1950. *The principles of psychology.* New York: Dover.

Janet, P. 1889. *L'automatisme psychologique.* Paris: Alcan.

Jenkins, J. J., and K. M. Dallenbach. 1924. Oblivescence during sleep and waking. *American Journal of Psychology* 35:605–12.

Johnson, H., and C. W. Eriksen. 1961. Preconscious perception: A reexamination of the Pötzl phenomenon. *Journal of Abnormal and Social Psychology* 62:497–503.

Jung, C. G. [1935] 1968. *Analytical psychology: Its theory and practice.* New York: Random House.

Kaplan, R., and S. Kaplan. 1969. The arousal-retention interval interaction revisited: The effects of some procedural changes. *Psychonomic Science* 15:84–85.

Karni, A., D. Tanne, B. S. Rubenstein, J. J. M. Askenasy, and D. Sagi. 1994. Dependence on REM sleep of overnight improvement of a perceptual skill. *Science* 265:679–82.

Keppel, G., and B. J. Underwood. 1967. Reminiscence in the short-term retention of paired-associate lists. *Journal of Verbal Learning and Verbal Behavior* 6:375–82.

Kihlstrom, J. F. 1987. The cognitive unconscious. *Science* 237:1445–52.

Kimble, G. A. 1949. An experimental test of a two-factor theory of inhibition. *Journal of Experimental Psychology* 39:15–23.

———. 1961. *Hilgard and Marquis' conditioning and learning.* New York: Appleton-Century-Crofts.

King, I., and T. B. Homan. 1918. Logical memory and school grades. *Journal of Educational Psychology* 9:262–69.

Kintsch, W. 1970. Models for free recall and recognition. In *Models of human memory.* Ed. D. A. Norman, 331–73. New York: Academic Press.

Klatzky, R. L., and M. H. Erdelyi. 1985. The response criterion problem in tests of hypnosis and memory. *International Journal of Clinical and Experimental Hypnosis* 33:246–57.

Klein, S. B., J. Loftus, J. F. Kihlstrom, and R. Aseron. 1989. Effects of item specific and relational information on hypermnesic recall. *Journal of Experimental Psychology—Learning, Memory, and Cognition* 15:1192–97.

Kleinsmith, L. J., and S. Kaplan. 1963. Paired-associate learning as a function of arousal and interpolated interval. *Journal of Experimental Psychology* 65: 190–93.

———. 1964. Interaction of arousal and recall interval in nonsense syllable paired-associate learning. *Journal of Experimental Psychology* 67:124–26.

Kline, M. V. 1958. The dynamics of hypnotically induced anti-social behavior. *Journal of Psychology* 45:239–45.

Kling, J. W. 1971. Learning: Introductory survey. In *Woodworth and Schlosberg's experimental psychology.* 3d ed. Ed. J. W. Kling and A. Riggs, 551–613. New York: Holt.

Kolb, L. C. 1988. Recovery of memory and repressed fantasy in combat-induced post-traumatic stress disorder of Vietnam Veterans. In *Hypnosis and memory.* Ed. H. M. Pettinati, 265–74. New York: Guilford.

Kunst-Wilson, W. R., and R. B. Zajonc. 1980. Affective discrimination of stimuli that cannot be recognized. *Science* 207:557–58.

Lamb, C. S. 1985. Hypnotically-induced deconditioning: Reconstruction of memories in the treatment of phobias. *American Journal of Clinical Hypnosis* 28: 56–62.

Laurence, J. R., and C. Perry. 1984. Mental processing outside of awareness: The contributions of Freud and Janet. In *The unconscious reconsidered.* Ed. K. S. Bowers and D. Meichenbaum, 9–48. New York: Wiley.

Lepley, W. M. 1932. A theory of serial learning and forgetting based upon conditioned reflex principle. *Psychological Review* 39:279–88.

Levonian, E. 1966. Attention and consolidation as factors in retention. *Psychonomic Science* 6:275–76.

———. 1972. Retention over time in relation to arousal during learning: An explanation of discrepant results. *Acta Psychologica* 36:290–321.

Lobsien, M. 1906. Aussage und Wirklichkeit bei Schulkindern. *Beitrage zur Psychologie der Aussage* [after 1906: *Zeitschrift für angewandte Psychologie und psycholische Sammelforschung*] 1:26–89.

Loftus, E. F. 1979. *Eyewitness testimony.* Cambridge, Mass.: Harvard University Press.

———. 1993. The reality of repressed memories. *American Psychologist* 48: 518–37.

———. 1994. The repressed memory controversy. *American Psychologist* 49: 443–45.

Loftus, E. F., D. G. Miller, and H. J. Burns. 1978. Semantic integration of verbal information into a visual memory. *Journal of Experimental Psychology—Human Learning and Memory* 13:585–89.

Loftus, E. F., and G. R. Loftus. 1980. On the permanence of stored information in the human brain. *American Psychologist* 35:409–20.

Loftus, E. F., J. W. Schooler, and W. A. Wagenaar. 1985. The fate of memory: Comment on McCloskey and Zaragoza. *Journal of Experimental Psychology—General* 114:375–80.

Loftus, E. F., and H. G. Hoffman. 1989. Misinformation and memory: The creation of new memories. *Journal of Experimental Psychology—General* 118: 100–104.

Loftus, E., and K. Ketcham. 1994. *The myth of repressed memory.* New York: St. Martin's Press.

Luborsky, L., H. Sackeim, and P. Christoph. 1979. The state conducive to momentary forgetting. In *Functional disorders of memory.* Ed. J. Kihlstrom and F. Evans, 325–53. Hillsdale, N.J.: Erlbaum.

Luh, C. W. 1922. The conditions of retention. *Psychological Monographs* 31.

Macmillan, N. A., and C. D. Creelman. 1991. *Detection theory: A user's guide.* Cambridge: Cambridge University Press.

Madigan, S. 1976. Reminiscence and item recovery in free recall. *Memory & Cognition* 4:233–236.

Madigan, S., and R. O'Hara. 1992. Initial recall, reminiscence, and hypermnesia. *Journal of Experimental Psychology—Learning, Memory, and Cognition* 18:421–425.

Mahl, G. F., A. Rothenberg, J. M. R. Delgado, and H. Hamlin. 1964. *Psychosomatic Medicine* 26:337–68.

Malamud, W. 1934. Dream analysis: Its application in therapy and research in mental disease. *Archives of Neurology and Psychiatry* 31:356–72.

Malamud, W., and F. E. Linder. 1931. Dreams and their relationship to recent impressions. *Archives of Neurology and Psychiatry* 25:1081–99.

Maltzman, I., W. Kantor, and B. Langdon. 1966. Immediate and delayed retention, arousal, and the orienting and defensive reflexes. *Psychonomic Science* 6: 445–46.

Mandler, G. 1980. Recognizing: The judgment of previous occurrence. *Psychological Review* 87:252–71.

Mandler, G., Y. Nakamura, and B. J. S. Van Zandt. 1987. Nonspecific effects of exposure on stimuli that cannot be recognized. *Journal of Experimental Psychology—Learning, Memory, and Cognition* 13:646–48.

Marcel, A. J. 1983a. Conscious and unconscious perception: Experiments on visual masking and word recognition. *Cognitive Psychology* 15:197–237.

———. 1983b. Conscious and unconscious perception: An approach to the relation between phenomenal experience and cognitive processes. *Cognitive Psychology* 15:238–300.

Markowitsch, H. J. 1983. Transient global amnesia. *Neuroscience and Biobehavioral Review* 7:35–43.

McClelland, D. C. 1942. Studies in serial verbal discrimination learning I: Reminiscence with two speeds of pair presentation. *Journal of Experimental Psychology* 31:44–56.

McCloskey, M., and M. Zaragoza. 1985. Misleading postevent information and memory for events: Arguments and evidence against memory impairment hypothesis. *Journal of Experimental Psychology—General* 114:3–18.

McConkey, K. M., and H. Nogrady. 1984. Hypnosis, hypnotizability, and story recall. *Australian Journal of Clinical and Experimental Hypnosis* 12: 93–98.

McDaniel, M. A., and M. E. J. Masson. 1985. Altering memory representations through retrieval. *Journal of Experimental Psychology—Learning, Memory, and Cognition* 11:371–85.

McGeoch, G. O. 1935. The conditions of reminiscence. *American Journal of Psychology* 47:65–89.

McGeoch, J. A. 1932. Forgetting and the law of disuse. *Psychological Review* 39: 352–70.

———. 1942. *The psychology of human learning*. New York: Longmans, Green.

McGeoch, J. A., F. McKinney, and H. N. Peters. 1937. Studies in retroactive inhibition IX: Retroactive inhibition, reproductive inhibition and reminiscence. *Journal of Experimental Psychology* 20:131–43.

Melton, A. W. 1963. Implications of short-term memory for a general theory of memory. *Journal of Verbal Learning and Verbal Behavior* 2:1–21.

Melton, A. W., and J. M. Irwin. 1940. The influence of degree of interpolated learning on retroactive inhibition and the overt transfer of specific responses. *American Journal of Psychology* 53:157–73.

Melton, A. W., and G. R. Stone. 1942. The retention of serial lists of adjectives over short time-intervals with varying rates of presentation. *Journal of Experimental Psychology* 30:295–310.

Merikle, P. M., and J. Cheesman. 1986. Consciousness is a subjective state. *Behavioral and Brain Sciences* 9:4.

Merikle, P. M., and E. M. Reingold. 1991. Comparing direct (explicit) and indirect (implicit) measures to study unconscious memory. *Journal of Experimental Psychology—Learning, Memory, and Cognition* 17:224–33.

Miller, A. 1986. Brief reconstructive hypnotherapy for anxiety reactions: Three case reports. *American Journal of Clinical Hypnosis* 21:134–47.

Miller, R. R., and A. D. Springer. 1973. Amnesia, consolidation, and retrieval. *Psychological Review* 80:69–79.

Miller, R. R., and N. A. Marlin. 1979. Amnesia following electroconvulsive shock. In *Functional disorders of memory*. Ed. J. F. Kihlstrom and F. J. Evans, 143–78. Hillsdale, N.J.: Erlbaum.

———. 1984. The physiology and semantics of consolidation. In *Memory consolidation: Psychobiology of cognition*. Ed. H. Weingartner and E. S. Parkers, 85–110. Hillsdale, N.J.: Erlbaum.

Milner, B. 1968. Visual recognition and recall after right temporal-lobe excision in man. *Neuropsychologia* 6:191–209.

Minami, H., and K. M. Dallenbach. 1946. The effect of activity upon learning and retention in the cockroach. *American Journal of Psychology* 59:1–58.

Mingay, D. J. 1986. Hypnosis and memory for incidentally learned scenes. *British Journal of Experimental and Clinical Hypnosis* 3:173–83.

Mitchell, M. B. 1932. Retroactive inhibition and hypnosis. *Journal of General Psychology* 7:343–59.

Müller, G. E., and A. Pilzecker. 1900. Experimentelle beitrage zur Lehre von Gedachtnis. *Zeitschrift für Psychologie und Physiologie der Sinnesorgane* 2 (suppl. 1):1–288.

Myers, G. G. 1913. A study of incidental memory. *Archives of Psychology* 4, no. 26:1–108.

———. 1914. Recall in relation to retention. *Journal of Educational Psychology* 5:119–30.

———. 1917. Confusion in recall. *Journal of Educational Psychology* 8:166–75.

Neisser, U. 1967. *Cognitive psychology.* New York: Appleton-Century-Crofts.

———. 1981. John Dean's memory. *Cognition* 9:1–22.

Neisser, U., and N. Harsch. 1992. Phantom flashbulbs: False recollection of hearing the news about *Challenger.* In *Affect and accuracy of recall.* Ed. E. Winograd and U. Neisser, 9–31. Cambridge: Cambridge University Press.

Nelson, T. O. 1978. Detecting small amounts of information in memory: Savings for nonrecognized items. *Journal of Experimental Psychology—Human Learning and Memory* 4:453–68.

———. 1985. Ebbinghaus's contribution to the measurement of retention: Savings during relearning. *Journal of Experimental Psychology—Learning, Memory, and Cognition* 11:472–79.

Nelson, T. O., and C. M. MacLeod. 1974. Fluctuations in recall across successive test trials. *Memory and Cognition* 2:687–90.

Nemiah, J. C. 1984. The unconscious in psychopathology. In *The unconscious reconsidered.* Ed. K. S. Bowers and D. Meichenbaum, 49–87. New York: Wiley.

Nickerson, R. S. 1965. Short-term memory for complex meaningful configurations: A demonstration of capacity. *Canadian Journal of Psychology* 19:155–60.

Nicolai, F. 1921. Experimentelle Untersuchungen über das Halften von Gesichtseindrucken und dessen zeitlichen Verlauf. *Archiv für die Gesamte Psychologie* 42:132–49.

Nogrady, H., K. M. McConkey, and C. Perry. 1985. Enhancing visual memory: Trying hypnosis, trying imagination, and trying again. *Journal of Abnormal Psychology* 94:195–204.

Norsworthy, N. 1912. Acquisition as related to retention. *Journal of Educational Psychology* 3:214–18.

Ofshe, R., and E. Watters. 1994. *Making monsters: False memories, psychotherapy, and sexual hysteria.* New York: Charles Scribner's Sons.

Orne, M. T. 1979. The use and misuse of hypnosis in court. *International Journal of Clinical and Experimental Hypnosis* 27:311–41.

Orne, M. T., W. G. Whitehouse, D. F. Dinges, and E. C. Orne. 1988. Reconstructing memory through hypnosis: Forensic and clinical implications. In *Hypnosis and memory.* Ed. H. M. Pettinati, 21–63. New York: Guilford.

Otani, H., and M. H. Hodge. 1991. Does hypermnesia occur in recognition and cued recall? *American Journal of Psychology* 104:101–16.

Otani, H., and H. L. Whitman. 1994. Cued recall hypermnesia is not an artifact of response bias. *American Journal of Psychology* 107:401–21.

Paivio, A. 1971. *Imagery and verbal processes.* New York: Holt, Rinehart, and Winston.

Paris, S. G. 1978. Memory organization during children's repeated recall. *Developmental Psychology* 14:99–106.

Parkin, A. J. 1987. *Memory and amnesia: An introduction.* Oxford: Blackwell.

Pavlov, I. 1927. *Conditioned reflexes: An investigation of the physiological activity of the cerebral cortex.* London: Oxford University Press.

Payne, D. G. 1986. Hypermnesia for pictures and words: Testing the recall level hypothesis. *Journal of Experimental Psychology—Learning, Memory, and Cognition* 12:16–29.

———. 1987. Hypermnesia and reminiscence in recall: A historical and empirical review. *Psychological Bulletin* 101:5–27.

Payne, D. G., and H. L. Roediger. 1987. Hypermnesia occurs in recall but not in recognition. *American Journal of Psychology* 101:145–65.

Payne, D. G., H. A. Hembrooke, and J. S. Anastasi. 1993. Hypermnesia in free recall and cued recall. *Memory and Cognition* 21:48–62.

Payne, D. G., and M. J. Wenger. 1992. Repeated recall of pictures, words, and riddles: Increasing subjective organization is not sufficient for producing hypermnesia. *Bulletin of the Psychonomic Society* 30:407–10.

———. 1994. Initial recall, reminiscence, and hypermnesia: Comment on Madigan and O'Hara (1992). *Journal of Experimental Psychology—Learning, Memory, and Cognition* 20:229–35.

Payne, D. G., J. S. Anastasi, J. M. Blackwell, and M. J. Wenger. 1994. Selective disruption of hypermnesia for pictures and words. *Memory and Cognition* 22:542–51.

Penfield, W. 1951. Memory mechanisms. *Transactions of the American Neurological Association* 76:15–31.

———. 1959. The interpretive cortex. *Science* 129:1719–25.

Penfield, W., and P. Perot. 1963. The brain's record of auditory and visual experience. *Brain* 86:595–696.

Perry, C. W., J.-R. Laurence, J. D'Eon, and B. Tallant. 1988. Hypnotic age regression techniques in the elicitation of memories: Applied uses and abuses. In *Hypnosis and memory.* Ed. H. M. Pettinati, 128–54. New York: Guilford.

Peterson, L. R. 1966. Reminiscence in short-term retention. *Journal of Experimental Psychology* 71:115–18.

Peterson, L. R., and M. J. Peterson. 1962. Minimal paired-associate learning. *Journal of Experimental Psychology* 63:521–27.

Pettinati, H. M., ed. 1988. *Hypnosis and memory.* New York: Guilford.

Piaget, J., and B. Inhelder. 1973. *Memory and intelligence.* Trans. A. J. Pomerans. London: Routledge and V. Paul.

Pollack, I., and L. R. Decker. 1964. Confidence ratings, message reception, and the operating characteristic. In *Signal detection and recognition by human observers.* Ed. J. A. Swets, 592–608. New York: Wiley.

Pomeroy, D. S. 1941. Retention of a motor act as a function of interpolated activity. Master's thesis, State University of Iowa.

Popkin, S. J., and M. Y. Small. 1979. Hypermnesia and the role of imagery. *Bulletin of the Psychonomic Society* 13:378–80.

Pötzl, O. 1917. The relationship between experimentally induced dream images and indirect vision. Trans. and ed. J. Wolff, D. Rapaport, and S. H. Annin. *Psychological Issues* 2, no. 3 (monograph 7):41–120.

Putnam, W. H. 1979. Hypnosis and distortions in eyewitness memory. *International Journal of Clinical and Experimental Hypnosis* 27:437–48.

Pyle, W. H., and J. C. Snyder. 1911. The most economical unit for committing to memory. *Journal of Educational Psychology* 2:133–42.

Raaijmakers, J. G. W., and R. M. Shiffrin. 1980. SAM: A theory of probabilistic search of associative memory. In vol. 14 of *The psychology of learning and motivation: Advances in research and theory.* Ed. G. H. Bower. New York: Academic Press.

Rabinowitz, J. C., A. C. Graesser II, 1976. Word recognition as a function of retrieval processes. *Bulletin of the Psychonomic Society* 7:75–77.

Rabinowitz, J. C., G. Mandler, and L. W. Barsalou. 1979. Generation-recognition as an auxiliary retrieval strategy. *Journal of Verbal Learning and Verbal Behavior* 18:57–72.

Raffel, G. 1934. The effect of recall on forgetting. *Journal of Experimental Psychology* 17:828–38.

Rapaport, D. 1967. *Emotions and memory.* New York: International Universities Press.

Redlich, E. C., L. J. Ravitz, and G. H. Dession. 1951. Narcoanalysis and truth. *American Journal of Psychiatry* 107:586–93.

Regard, M., and T. Landis. 1984. Transient global amnesia: Neuropsychological dysfunctions during attacks and recovery of two "pure" cases. *Journal of Neurology, Neurosurgery and Psychiatry* 47:668–72.

Register, P. A., and J. F. Kihlstrom. 1987. Hypnotic effects on hypermnesia. *International Journal of Clinical and Experimental Hypnosis* 35:155–70.

Reingold, E. M. 1990. Using indirect and direct measures to study unconscious processes. Ph.D. diss., University of Waterloo, Ontario.

Reingold, E. M., and P. M. Merikle. 1988. Using direct and indirect measures to study perception and awareness. *Perception and Psychophysics* 44:563–75.

Roediger, H. L. 1982. Hypermnesia: The importance of recall time and asymptotic level of recall. *Journal of Verbal Learning and Verbal Behavior* 21:662–65.

Roediger, H. L., and D. G. Payne. 1982. Hypermnesia: The role of repeated testing. *Journal of Experimental Psychology—Learning, Memory, and Cognition* 8: 66–72.

———. 1985. Recall criterion does not affect recall level or hypermnesia: A puzzle for generate/recognize theories. *Memory and Cognition* 13:1–7.

Roediger, H. L., D. G. Payne, G. L. Gillespie, and D. S. Lean. 1982. Hypermnesia as determined by level of recall. *Journal of Verbal Learning and Verbal Behavior* 21:635–55.

Roediger, H. L., and F. I. M. Craik. 1989. *Varieties of memory and consciousness: Essays in Honour of Endel Tulving.* Hillsdale, N.J.: Erlbaum.

Roediger, H. L., and L. A. Thorpe. 1978. The role of recall time in producing hypermnesia. *Memory and Cognition* 6:296–305.

Roediger, H. L., and B. H. Challis. 1989. Hypermnesia: Improvement in recall with repeated testing. In *Current issues in cognitive processes: The Tulane Floweree symposium on cognition.* Ed. C. Z. Izawa. Hillsdale, N.J.: Erlbaum.

Roediger, H. L., K. Srinivas, and P. Waddill. 1989. How much does guessing influence recall? Comments on Erdelyi, Finks, and Feigin-Pfau. *Journal of Experimental Psychology—General* 118:255–57.

Roediger, H. L., and M. M. A. Wheeler. 1993. Hypermnesia in episodic and semantic memory: Response to Bahrick and Hall. *Psychological Science* 4:207–8.

Roediger, H. L., M. M. A. Wheeler, and S. Rajaram. 1993. Remembering, knowing, and reconstructing the past. In vol. 30 of *The psychology of learning and motivation: Advances in research and theory.* Ed. D. L. Medin, 97–134. New York: Academic Press.

Roediger, H. L., B. H. Challis, and M. M. A. Wheeler. Effects of confabulation on later recall. In preparation.

Rosenberg, S. D., P. P. Schnurr, and T. E. Oxman. 1990. Content analysis: A comparison of manual and computerized systems. *Journal of Personality Assessment* 54:289–310.

Rosenthal, B. G. 1944. Hypnotic recall of material learned under anxiety- and non-anxiety producing conditions. *Journal of Experimental Psychology* 34: 369–89.

Rosner, S. R. 1970. The effects of presentation and recall trials on organization in multitrial free recall. *Journal of Verbal Learning and Verbal Behavior* 9: 69–74.

Rossi, E. L., and D. B. Cheek. 1988. *Mind-body therapy: Methods of ideodynamic healing in hypnosis.* New York: Norton.

Rubenstein, R., and R. Newman. 1954. The living out of "future" experiences under hypnosis. *Science* 119:472–73.

Russell, W. R., and P. W. Nathan. 1946. Traumatic amnesia. *Brain* 69:280–300.

Sanders, G. S., and W. L. Simmons. 1983. Use of hypnosis to enhance eyewitness accuracy: Does it work? *Journal of Applied Psychology* 68:70–77.

Salzberg, H. C., and F. A. DePiano. 1980. Hypnotizability and task motivating instructions: A further look at how they affect performance. *International Journal of Clinical and Experimental Hypnosis* 28:261–71.

Schachter, D. L. 1987. Implicit memory: History and current status. *Journal of Experimental Psychology—Learning, Memory, and Cognition* 13:501–18.

Scheirer, C. J., and J. F. Voss. 1967. Reminiscence in short-term memory. *Journal of Experimental Psychology* 80:262–70.

Schmitt, J. C., and W. E. Forrester. 1973. Effects of stimulus concreteness-imagery and arousal on immediate and delayed recall. *Bulletin of the Psychonomic Society* 2:25–26.

Schönpflug, W. 1966. Paarlernen, Behaltensdauer und Aktivierung. *Psychologische Forschung* 29:132–48.

Scrivner, E., and M. A. Safer. 1988. Eyewitnesses show hypermnesia for details about a violent event. *Journal of Applied Psychology* 73:371–77.

Seamon, J. G., N. Brody, and D. M. Kauff. 1983a. Affective discrimination of stimuli that are not recognized: Effect of delay between study and test. *Bulletin of the Psychonomic Society* 21:187–89.

————. 1983b. Affective discrimination of stimuli that are not recognized: Effects of shadowing, masking, and cerebral laterality. *Journal of Experimental Psychology—Learning, Memory, and Cognition* 3:544–55.

Seamon, J. G., R. L. Marsh, and N. Brody. 1984. Critical importance of exposure duration for affective discrimination of stimuli that are not recognized. *Journal of Experimental Psychology—Learning, Memory, and Cognition* 10: 465–69.

Sears, A. B. 1954. A comparison of hypnotic and waking recall. *Journal of Clinical and Experimental Hypnosis* 2:296–304.

Shapiro, S. R., and M. H. Erdelyi. 1974. Hypermnesia for pictures but not words. *Journal of Experimental Psychology* 103:1218–19.

Shaw, G. A., and D. A. Bekerian. 1991. Hypermnesia for high-imagery words: the effects of interpolated tasks. *Memory and Cognition* 19:87–94.

Sheehan, P. W. 1988. Confidence, memory, and hypnosis. In *Hypnosis and memory*. Ed. H. M. Pettinati, 95–127. New York: Guilford.

Sheehan, P. W., and J. Tilden. 1983. Effects of suggestibility and hypnosis on accurate retrieval from memory. *Journal of Experimental Psychology—Learning, Memory, and Cognition* 9:283–93.

————. 1984. Real and simulated occurrences of memory distortions in hypnosis. *Journal of Abnormal Psychology* 93:47–57.

Shepard, R. N. 1967. Recognition memory for words, sentences, and pictures. *Journal of Verbal Learning and Verbal Behavior* 6:156–163.

Shevrin, H., and L. Luborsky. 1958. The measurement of preconscious perception in dreams and images: An investigation of the Pötzl phenomenon. *Journal of Abnormal and Social Psychology* 58:285–94.

Shevrin, H., and S. Dickman. 1980. The psychological unconscious: A necessary assumption for all psychological theory? *American Psychologist* 35:421–34.

Shiffrin, R. M. 1970. Memory search. In *Models of human memory*. Ed. D. A. Norman. New York: Academic Press.

Shipley, W. C. 1939. The effect of a short rest pause on retention in rote series of different lengths. *Journal of General Psychology* 21:99–117.

Sloane, M. C. 1981. A comparison of hypnosis vs. waking state and visual vs. non-visual recall instructions for witness/victim memory retrieval in actual crimes. Ph.D. diss., Florida State University. (*Dissertation Abstracts International.* 1981. Univ. Microfilms 81-25,873.)

Smith, M. C. 1983. Hypnotic memory enhancement of witnesses: Does it work? *Psychological Bulletin* 94:387–407.

Smith, S., and E. Vela. 1991. Incubated reminiscence effects. *Memory and Cognition* 19:168–76.

Snoddy, G. 1935. Evidence for two opposed processes in mental growth. Lancaster, Pa.: Science Press.

Snodgrass, M., H. Shevrin, and M. Kopka. 1993. The mediation of intentional judgments by unconscious perceptions: The influences of task strategy, task preference, word meaning, and motivation. *Consciousness and Cognition* 2: 169–93.

Spence, D. P. 1982. *Narrative truth and historical truth.* New York: Norton.

Spiegel, H., and D. Spiegel. 1978. *Trance and treatment: Clinical uses of hypnosis.* New York: Basic Books.

Spitzer, H. F. 1939. Studies in retention. *Journal of Educational Psychology* 30: 641–57.

Squire, L. 1986. Mechanisms of memory. *Science* 232:1612–19.

Squire, L. R., and J. J. Cohen. 1982. Remote memory, retrograde amnesia, and the neuropsychology of memory. In *Human memory and amnesia.* Ed. L. S. Cermak. Hillsdale, N.J.: Erlbaum.

Squire, L. R., F. Haist, and A. P. Shimamura. 1989. The neurology of memory: Quantitative assessment of retrograde amnesia in two groups of amnesic patients. *Journal of Neuroscience* 9:828–39.

Stager, G. L., and R. M. Lundy. 1985. Hypnosis and the learning and recall of visually presented material. *International Journal of Clinical and Experimental Hypnosis* 33:27–39.

Stalnaker, J. M., and E. E. Riddle. 1932. The effect of hypnosis on long-delayed recall. *Journal of General Psychology* 6:429–40.

Standing, L., J. Conezio, and R. N. Haber. 1970. Perception and memory for pictures: Single-trial learning of 2500 visual stimuli. *Psychonomic Science* 19: 73–74.

Stelmach, G. E. 1968. Reminiscence and consolidation in a gross motor task. *Perceptual and Motor Skills* 27:1075–78.

Stratton, G. M. 1919. Retroactive hypermnesia and other emotional effects on memory. *Psychological Review* 26:474–86.

Strong, E. K. 1913. The effect of time-interval upon recognition memory. *Psychological Review* 20:339–72.

Swets, J. A., ed. 1964. *Signal detection and recognition in human observers.* New York: Wiley.

Swets, J. A., W. P. Tanner, and T. G. Birdsall. 1961. Decision processes for perception. *Psychological Review* 68:301–40.

Swift, E. J. 1903. Studies in the psychology and physiology of learning. *American Journal of Psychology* 14:201–51.

Talland, G. A. 1968. *Disorders of memory and thinking.* Baltimore: Penguin.

Terr, L. C. 1985a. Children traumatized in small groups. In *Post-traumatic stress disorder in children.* Ed. S. Eth and R. S. Pynoos. Washington, D.C.: American Psychiatric Association.

———. 1985b. Remembered images and trauma. *Psychoanalytic Study of the Child* 40:493–533.

———. 1988. What happens to early memories of trauma? A study of twenty children under age five at the time of documented traumatic events. *Journal of the American Academy of Child and Adolescent Psychiatry* 27:96–104.

———. 1994. *Unchained memories.* New York: Basic Books.

Timm, H. W. 1981. The effect of forensic hypnosis techniques on eyewitness recall and recognition. *Journal of Police Science and Administration* 9:188–94.

Thompson, C. P., and C. Barnett. 1985. Review, recitation, and memory monitoring. *Journal of Educational Psychology* 77:533–38.

Travis, R. C. 1936. The effect of the length of the rest period on motor learning. *Journal of Psychology* 3:189–94.

Tulving, E. 1967. The effects of presentation and recall of material in free-recall learning. *Journal of Verbal Learning and Verbal Behavior* 6:175–84.

———. 1983. *Elements of episodic memory.* New York: Oxford University Press.

———. 1987. Multiple memory systems and consciousness. *Human Neurobiology* 6:6–80.

———. 1989. Remembering and knowing the past. *American Scientist* 77:361–67.

Tulving, E., and Z. Pearlstone. 1967. Availability versus accessibility of information in memory for words. *Journal of Verbal Learning and Verbal Behavior* 6:175–84.

Tulving, E., and D. M. Thomson. 1973. Encoding specificity and retrieval processes in episodic memory. *Psychological Review* 80:352–73.

Tulving, E., D. L. Schachter, and H. A. Stark. 1982. Priming effects in word-fragment completion are independent of recognition memory. *Journal of Experimental Psychology—Learning, Memory, and Cognition* 8:336–43.

Tversky, B., and M. Tuchin. 1989. A reconciliation of the evidence on eyewitness testimony: Comments on McCloskey and Zaragoza. *Journal of Experimental Psychology—General* 118:86–91.

Underwood, B. J. 1961. Ten years of massed practice on distributed practice. *Psychological Review* 68:229–47.

———. 1966. *Experimental psychology.* 2d ed. New York: Appleton-Century-Crofts.

Van Ormer, E. B. 1932. Sleep and retention. *Psychological Bulletin* 30:415–39.

Van Selst, M., and P. M. Merikle. 1993. Perception below the objective threshold? *Consciousness and Cognition* 2:194–203.

Wagstaff, G. F. 1982. Hypnosis and recognition of a face. *Perceptual and Motor Skills* 55:816–18.

Wagstaff, G., J. Traverse, and S. Milner. 1982. Hypnosis and eyewitness memory—two experimental analogues. *IRCS Medical Science: Psychology and Psychiatry* 10:894–95.

Walker, E. L. 1958. Action decrement and its relation to learning. *Psychological Review* 65:129–42.

Walker, E. L., and R. D. Tarte. 1963. Memory storage as a function of arousal and time with homogeneous and heterogeneous lists. *Journal of Verbal Learning and Verbal Behavior* 2:113–19.

Wallace, G., N. Coltheart, and K. I. Forster. 1970. Recognition memory for faces. *Psychonomic Science* 18:335–36.

Ward, L. B. 1937. Reminiscence and rote learning. *Psychological Monographs* 49.

Weiskrantz, L. 1986. *Blindsight.* New York: Oxford University Press.

Welford, A. T. 1989. Recall, recognition and serial learning: A signal-detection measurement. *Perceptual and Motor Skills* 69:415–18.

Werner, H. 1948. *Comparative psychology of mental development.* New York: International Universities Press.

———. 1956. Microgenesis and aphasia. *Journal of Abnormal and Social Psychology* 52:347–53.

Wheeler, M. A., and H. L. Roediger. 1992. Disparate effects of repeated testing: Reconciling Ballard's 1913 and Bartlett's 1932 results. *Psychological Science* 3:240–45.

White, R. W., G. F. Fox, and W. W. Harris. 1940. Hypnotic hypermnesia for recently learned material. *Journal of Abnormal Psychology* 35:88–103.

Whitehouse, W. G., D. F. Dinges, E. C. Orne, and M. T. Orne. 1988. Hypnotic hypermnesia: Enhanced memory accessibility or report bias? *Journal of Abnormal Psychology* 97:289–95.

Whitley, P. L., and J. A. McGeoch. 1928. The curve of retention for poetry. *Journal of Educational Psychology* 19:471–79.

Williams, O. 1926. A study of the phenomenon of reminiscence. *Journal of Experimental Psychology* 9:368–87.

Wilson, M. A., and B. L. McNaughton. 1994. Reactivation of hippocampal ensemble memories during sleep. *Science* 265:676–79.

Winch, W. H. 1914. Children's perceptions. *Educational Psychology Monographs,* no. 12:1–245.

———. 1924. Should poems be learnt by school children as "wholes" or in "parts"? *British Journal of Psychology* 15:64–79.

Woodworth, R. S. 1938. *Experimental psychology.* New York: Holt, Rinehart and Winston.

Woodworth, R. S., and H. Schlosberg. 1954. *Experimental Psychology.* 2d ed. New York: Holt.

Wright, L. 1994. *Remembering Satan.* New York: Knopf.

Yarmey, A. D. 1976. Hypermnesia for pictures but not for concrete or abstract words. *Bulletin of the Psychonomic Society* 8:115–17.

Yerkes, R. M., and J. D. Dodson. 1908. The relation of strength of stimulus to rapidity of habit formation. *Journal of Comparative and Neurological Psychology* 18:459–82.

Young, P. C. 1925. An experimental study of mental and physical functions in the normal and hypnotic states. *American Journal of Psychology* 36:214–32.

Yuille, J. C., and N. H. McEwan. 1985. Use of hypnosis as an aid to eyewitness memory. *Journal of Applied Psychology* 70:389–400.

Zaragoza, M. S., and M. McCloskey. 1989. Misleading post-event information and the memory impairment hypothesis: Comments on Belli and a reply to Tversky and Tuchin. *Journal of Experimental Psychology—General* 118:92–99.

Zelig, M., and W. B. Beidelman. 1981. The investigative use of hypnosis: A word of caution. *International Journal of Clinical and Experimental Hypnosis* 29:401–12.

Name Index

Kihlstrom, J. F., 72, 115, 133, 219–20, 225
Killian, C. D., 138, 213
Kimble, G. A., 61, 65–66, 219
King, I., 11, 219
Kintsch, W., 92, 115, 218–19
Klatzky, R. L., 135, 173, 219
Klein, S. B., 115, 220
Kleinbard, J., 14, 65, 93, 96, 99–103, 119, 144, 187, 214
Kleinsmith, L. J., 149–52, 220
Kline, M. V., 36, 220
Kling, J. W., 60, 65, 220
Kopka, M., 143, 186, 227
Kolb, L. C., 42, 220
Kunst-Wilson, W. R., 141, 185–86, 220

Lamb, C. S., 31, 220
Landis, T., 43, 225
Langdon, B., 151, 221
Laurence, J.-R., 31, 220, 224
Lean, D. S., 117, 120–21, 225
Leichter, D., 170, 200
Leone, D. R., 72, 141, 210
Lepley, W. M., 66, 220
Levonian, E., 149–50, 220
Linder, F. E., 75–76, 221
Lobsien, M., 11, 220
Lockhart, R. S., 113, 212
Loftus, E. F., 7, 36, 40, 189, 211, 220–21
Loftus, G. R., 7, 40, 189, 220
Loftus, J., 115, 220
London, P., 131, 212
Luborsky, L., 79–80, 89, 221, 227
Luh, C. W., 4–5, 45, 221
Lundy, R. M., 131–32, 212, 228

MacKinnon, D. P., 132, 216
MacLeod, C. M., 18, 92, 223
Macmillan, N. A., 161, 185, 194, 221
Madigan, S., 98, 120–21, 221
Magsdick, W. K., 52, 64, 70, 211
Mahl, G. F., 40–41, 221
Malamud, W., 75–76, 221
Maltzman, I., 151, 221

Mandler, G., 25, 139, 141–43, 217, 221, 225
Marcel, A. J., 72, 221
Marie, 25–29, 36–37, 40
Markowitsch, H. J., 143, 221
Marlin, N. A., 43, 222
Marsh, R. L., 141, 227
Masson, M. E. J., 55, 221
Maya, 160, 164–69, 171–78, 188, 195–96, 201–2
McClelland, D. C., 46, 221
McClosky, M., 7, 221, 230
McConkey, K. M., 132–33, 221, 223
McDaniel, M. A., 55, 61, 221
McEwan, N. H., 132, 230
McGeoch, G. O., 11, 13, 20, 50, 52, 60, 62–63, 222
McGeoch, J. A., 5–7, 46, 48, 54, 222, 230
McKinney, F., 48, 222
McNaughton, B. L., 190, 230
McNeill, D., 89, 211
Meichenbaum, D., 75, 128, 211
Melton, A. W., 7, 51, 54 , 222
Merikle, P. M., 80, 141–43, 146, 148, 185–86, 222, 225
Mesmer, F. A., 128
Miller, A., 31, 222
Miller, B., 214
Miller, D. G., 7, 220
Miller, R. R., 43, 222
Milner, B., 140, 222
Milner, S., 131, 229
Minami, H., 8–9, 222
Mingay, D. J., 133, 222
Mitchell, M. B., 129, 131, 222
M.M., 39
Müller, G. E., 43, 190, 222
Murdock, B. B., 55, 92, 212
Myers, E. J., 11, 212
Myers, G. G., 11, 223

Nakamura, Y., 141–42, 221
Nathan, P. W., 43
Neisser, U., 36–38, 40, 223
Nelson, T. O., 1, 18, 92, 223
Nemiah, J. C., 28, 33–35, 38, 223

Subject Index

01, 10, and 11. *See* recall, partitioning components of

abreaction. *See* catharsis
age, 13–14, 19. *See also* hypermnesia: in children
amnesia, 42–43, 96, 156–78, 183–84, 188
   distinguished from forgetting, 96, 183–84
anxiety. *See* arousal
arousal, 71, 149–53, 191
awareness, 4–5, 32, 73, 140–48, 182–83, 186–88
   biased, 186–87
   remembering without, 25–29, 179–80, 182–83

Ballard-William design, 54
base rates, 79, 83, 177–78. *See also* guessing; yoked subjects
bias. *See* distortions
brain trauma, 42–43

catharsis, 31–32, 35, 91, 128–29
CCFR. *See* criterion-controlled free recall
chance limen, 144–49, 185–86
child abuse, xi–xii, 25–30, 33–39
clinical data, xiv–xvii, 24–43
   compared to laboratory data, 24–25
component analysis. *See* recall, partitioning components of
concentration-pressure technique, xvii, 32, 91–92. *See also* thinking

conditionalized hits. *See* criterion-controlled hits
confabulation. *See* false memories
confidence ratings. *See* signal detection theory, and confidence ratings
consciousness. *See* awareness
consolidation, 151–52, 190
criterion-controlled free recall (CCFR), 156, 173–78, 193–207
   empirical validation, 201–5
   rationale and technique of, 173–78, 193–201
criterion-controlled hits, 174–78, 194–207
cued recall, 143–44
cumulative recall, 100–101, 103, 105–8, 121–27

d'. *See* signal detection theory, sensitivity/discriminability
defense, 70–71, 153–69, 188–90
   and guessing, 189–90
   and thinking, 189–90
   and false-memory syndrome, 188–90
   and opponent-process conception of memory, 186–87
   and post-event information, 189–90. *See also* distortions, defensive; repression
depth of processing. *See* stimulus, and coding
depression, 71
dissociation, 30, 75
   paradigm of the unconscious, 80–81

recall
  and coding format. *See* stimulus, and
    coding
  conditional, 114–15
  cued, 90, 143–44
  cumulative, 100–101, 103, 105–8,
    121–27
  electrical, 39–41
  free and forced, 85, 91–92, 155–56
  multitrial, 92–93, 105–10, 113–15,
    117–27
  narrative. *See* narratives
  partitioning components of, 16–18,
    19–23, 29, 110
  relative, 12
  time, 97–98, 121–27
  and truth sera, 41–42.
  See also recognition
recognition, 3, 5, 130–33
  hypnotic, 130–33
  distinguished from recall, 130–33
  memory, 99, 130–33
  and the stimulus, 130–33.
  See also recall
reconstructive memory, 37
  therapy, 27–28, 30–31
recovery, 72–88
  paradigm of the unconscious, 81.
  See also hypermnesia; reminiscence;
    spontaneous recovery
reminiscence, 11–23, 105–8
  and the criterion problem, 23
  and cumulative recall, 105–7,
    121–27
  definition of, 14–18, 105–8
  distinguished from hypermnesia/im-
    provement, 14–18, 105–8,
    121–27, 180–81, 183–84
  confusion of, with hypermnesia/im-
    provement, 11–23, 50–52,
    121–27, 192
  and hypnosis, 130–33, 184
  motor or sensory-motor, 65–71,
    172
  predicted by R_i and cum R_i, 119–27
  redefinition of, 50–52
  simple versus compound, 64–65

symptoms as, 25–36, 182, 190–92
  theory of, 190–92
repression, xi–xii, 30, 160–64,
    186–88. *See also* defense; distor-
    tions, defensive
response bias/criterion. *See* signal de-
    tection theory, response crite-
    rion/bias
retention, 1–10
  and dreaming. *See* sleep, and
    dreaming
  interval, 45, 95–98, 99–104
  during sleep. *See* sleep, and
    dreaming
  over time, 1–10
  and interference, 5–9.
  See also memory; recall; recognition
retrieval, 43
  effort, 65, 93–98, 191
  time, 93–98, 121–26
retrieve-recognize model of hypermn-
    esia. *See* two-stage model of hy-
    permnesia
review, 62–65. *See also* practice
ROC, roc functions, 86–88, 193–95,
    205–6

savings, 1–2, 4–5, 17–18
scoring, 83, 158, 169–70, 174,
    196–97
  free associations, 83
  reliability of, 83, 158, 197
  narratives, 158, 170, 195–207
  word counts, 158, 170, 196–97
sensitivity. *See* signal detection theory,
    and sensitivity/discriminability
serial position, 18, 66–67
signal detection theory
  β. *See* response criterion/bias
  conditionalized hits. *See* criterion-
    controlled hits
  confidence ratings, 174, 195–202
  criterion-controlled hits ($H|F_c$ or
    H'), 174–78, 194–207
  d'. *See* criterion-controlled hits; sen-
    sitivity/discriminability
  false alarms (F), 83–85, 173–78,